Ro

Roy David is one of Britain's most experienced racing writers. His previous books include *The Shergar Mystery* and the bestseller *Lester Piggott: Downfall of a Legend* which was short-listed for the William Hill Sports Book of the Year Award. Born in Liverpool, he is married to a university lecturer, has two stepdaughters, and lives in the Warwickshire countryside.

ROY DAVID

Robert Sangster

TYCOON OF THE TURF

Mandarin

PHOTOGRAPH CREDITS

1. Press Association, 2. Press Association,
3. Gerry Cranham, 4. Gerry Cranham,
5. Gerry Cranham, 6. Gerry Cranham,
7. Gerry Cranham, 8. Gerry Cranham,
9. Liverpool Daily Post/Frank Loughlin,
10. Gerry Cranham, 11. Gerry Cranham,
12. Gerry Cranham, 13. Gerry Cranham,
14. Gerry Cranham

A Mandarin Paperback
ROBERT SANGSTER

First published in Great Britain 1991
by William Heinemann Ltd
This edition published 1992
by Mandarin Paperbacks
Michelin House, 81 Fulham Road, London SW3 6RB

Mandarin is an imprint of Reed Consumer Books Ltd

Copyright © Roy David 1991
The author has asserted his moral rights

A CIP catalogue record for this title
is available from the British Library
ISBN 0 7493 0695 5

Printed and bound in Great Britain by
BPCC Hazells Ltd

Member of BPCC Ltd

Contents

Acknowledgements

The author wishes to make it clear that the cooperation of Robert Sangster was not sought in the preparation of this book; it is, therefore, an unauthorised biography.

He would, however, like to offer his warm thanks to the following people for their valuable help, advice, and kindness:

AUSTRALIA: Colin and David Hayes, Ron, Ray and Peter Hutchinson, *The Melbourne Age*, Ivor and Yvette David, Robert Atkins, John Messara, Les Carlyon, Bob Gunning, John Hawkes, Liz Jeffrey, John Greensill, Andrew Peacock, Cathay Pacific.

HONG KONG: Jonathan Everest.

USA: Dan Farley, The Keeneland Association, Gainesway Farm, Kim Herbert, Charlie Rose, *The Blood-Horse*.

GREAT BRITAIN: Tricia David (the breadwinner), Tony Farragher, Graham Bell, Michael Sissons, *Liverpool Daily Post*, Margot Richardson, and my editor, Tom Weldon.

And the same gratitude goes to all the many others throughout the world who helped me, but who preferred that I did not mention their names.

ONE

High-Rollers

The white Ford of the Fayette County Sheriff cruises almost silently, as if with indolence, between the solid rows of cars parked diagonally in the short tree-lined lanes fronting Kentucky's Keeneland Racecourse. The early-evening sun is still strong enough to bounce shards of piercing brilliance off the V-8's brightwork as the driver, raising his hand to acknowledge the waves from a uniformed huddle of 'car jock' valets, points the bonnet in the direction of the building with the domed redwood roof, hits the accelerator a little, and turns left, beyond what is the Keeneland Sales Pavilion, heading for the comparative peace of the place they call the horse barn area.

Outside the Pavilion more cars arrive to disgorge their occupants, for a few seconds, into the thick sultry heat of a temperature still in the nineties before the *groupes d'élégance* disappear behind the glass doors of the front entrance to the comfort of air conditioning while their vehicles are whisked away by the men in green and gold.

The serious players here for this sales session are those in lightweight jacket and tie, their wives, daughters or lovers dressed to the nines as if they are at the opera, jewellery abounding. The Keeneland Sales catalogues are carried in customised leather wallets that hide either a pristine copy (non-player) or a well-thumbed one that is a testament to hours of sweat, toil and trouble in researching pedigree after blue-blooded pedigree in this two-day sale of yearlings, the most important in the world of thoroughbred breeding, young horses which are untried, unbacked and which could be anything – or nothing. In contrast, on this July evening of 1983, hundreds

1

more people are here simply to stand and watch, ignoring the pleas to stay away which have been constantly broadcast on television and on local radio over the last day and a half. These are the intrigued 'townsfolk' from Lexington and surrounding areas who have driven the five miles or so to the Versailles Road (pronounced Versales) because they'll be damned if they're going to miss one of the best pieces of pure theatre around. Tonight's 7.30 start is set to be a real humdinger of a show, a gladiatorial epic with the mighty dollar the only instrument of victory.

It is the night of the megabuck, the ego and the power that both bring with them. Racehorse king Robert Sangster is in the ring with the Arabian prince.

Word has soon spread that in yesterday's afternoon and evening session, money has been thrown at these horses like rose petals at an Eastern wedding – more than $74 million in fact for the 153 lots on offer, which works out at nearly half a million dollars a yearling (give or take a tankful of gas for the private jet currently standing in line at the Blue Grass Airport opposite the racecourse and sales complex). The more informed know that Sangster is up against the ropes to repel the onslaught and the might of the Arab oil money which, like the black stuff itself, has seeped inexorably into horseracing and breeding over the past few years. Now the Maktoum brothers of Dubai are threatening the position that Sangster has made his own through having revolutionised the whole business on an international scale of immense proportions over the past half-dozen years.

Tonight, though, Sangster, the former Army boxing champion, has taken the gloves off. In his words, it is time for some streetfighting, some canny, perhaps brutal tricks like they pull off on the streets of that tough city Liverpool where the football-pools firm Vernons – named after his father – founded the family fortune which has enabled the only son to indulge in his passion for horses on a business level never before known in the history of the sport.

Sheikh Mohammed Bin Rashid Al-Maktoum, Defence Minister of Dubai, that small speck of a state no bigger than a city at the north-west tip of the United Arab Emirates in the Persian Gulf, is more earnest than his two elder brothers, who are also players here, and tonight he is seated in the main auditorium of the sales complex – almost a half-theatre in the round – looking smart but pensive in a dark-blue, almost black, pinstripe suit, white shirt and red tie. He listens and watches the proceedings intently, surrounded by his team of advisers, top men in the bloodstock field and, like the Sangster camp, about to play the ensuing proceedings with a deadly seriousness. Yesterday the Sheikh's purchasing power was seen within the time it would take one of the townsfolk to slip along to one of the bars for a cold beer and a ryebread sandwich and head back along the crowded top corridor to press up against the glass once again and simply marvel, or gasp in astonishment, to learn the Sheikh has just bought three yearlings for almost $7.5 million.

It was Sangster, however, who rang the bell yesterday with a winning $4.25 million bid for a son, naturally, of Northern Dancer, the world's most influential stallion with a well-worn road to success from outside his stable door and whose progeny reflect that glory in the prices they command. Sangster's costly purchase has equalled the world record he set here the previous year which, itself, had beaten by $750,000 the world record he set the year before that. Those world records are the manifestation of the Sangster intent to stay top of the tree.

But tonight the buzz is that new heights will be scaled, for there is another son of Northern Dancer here to be sold to the highest bidder, a big bay yearling colt who for the last five days back in the barn area has been admired, patted, walked, trotted and presented to the assembled array of horsemen and women with all the pride its owners have amassed over the past fifteen months as they have watched the young horse blossom into a possible star. Certainly on looks (conformation) and pedigree – the only two attributes on which fortunes are risked – there is no disputing the presence of the animal. He has his sire's short powerful neck and muscular front quarters, four white socks and a commanding stance that has caused most experts to make him their nap of the sale. This fellow will not go cheap. He could be, well, anything, perhaps the next Epsom Derby winner, which, to repeat the Sangster successes of the past, would put the colt and his pedigree into the stratosphere as a future stallion, worth say $30 million, maybe 40, possibly more. He could be the one horse Sangster needs every two years or so to keep the whole show ticking over, the financial ace in his full house of 1,000 other thoroughbreds around the world. The bidding, therefore, will be hot, fast and ruthless.

The Sangster camp is, as usual, out of sight of the rubberneck townsfolk pressed up behind the glass screen of the top inner corridor watching the privileged 300 people sitting before them in the turf-green velour seats of the auditorium. Sangster and Vincent O'Brien, that wizard of an Irish trainer whose lively crystal-blue eyes see in horses what mere mortals cannot, are ensconced 'out back' in the holding area, the place backstage to where horses are led from the barns to wait their turn in a line of up to a dozen others before entering the small half-circle, privet-ringed 'stage' of the front sales arena. There, slightly elevated and to one side, is the three-man auctioneer's rostrum, and, opposite this, the electronic numbers board to keep track of the bidding. Here, in this backstage rehearsal room, it is hot, crowded, noisy; the air has that cloying sweetness of horses. People are oblivious to the proceedings; young men stand around in jeans and cowboy boots, a drink in their hand, chatting up girls with long legs in mini-skirts or skintight trousers as if in a nightclub. Someone's fat Aunt Martha in a hideous pink trouser suit with unfashionable bell bottoms is here with the kids, feeding them cold hotdogs from what looks like a brown-paper refugee parcel. There are several foxy ladies around, too, sniffing out the thick wallets while men in loud checked suits shout to each other in rounded, lazy Southern drawls, adding to the excited chatter that is getting louder by the minute.

4

These people are here, as the Irish would say, for the crack, creating their own event within the event. They crowd on to the horses' walkway with an irreverence suggesting that the half-ton of thoroughbred worth maybe a million dollars or two breathing over their shoulders is something of a minor distraction to their thing – sweating horses, perspiring men and the women getting slightly warm. Soon, though, they will all take notice.

A sign near to where Sangster stands says, 'No bidders beyond this point,' which is there so that the bid-spotters in the rear half of the auctioneer's box, which itself is separated from the front half by a row of windows, can see who is playing and pass on the bids to the front. For the past three sessions of this sale, Sheikh Mohammed and his advisers have remained, mostly, in their seats out front, one or another of the bloodstock agents in the camp doing the bidding for a particular horse, often in no more dramatic a style than as a series of nods and winks to a blind horse, a scratch of the chin or, at its most flamboyant, perhaps a raised finger. But for this colt coming up, lot number 308, Sheikh Mohammed and his team leave their seats and in a preconceived move to unnerve the Sangster camp, move out back to the holding area and place themselves, strategically, just out of sight of the opposition, but near enough to let Sangster know from where the heavy money will be coming. Although they are out of direct eyesight of each other, the tousle-haired Joss Collins of the British Bloodstock Agency, who has already bought several lots for Sangster including that $4.25 million world-record equaliser, has already spotted the Sheikh's party pushing through the crowds. He knows he is up against the Sheikh's main man, the bespectacled Dick Warden, who looks the retired colonel he is in his tropics suit. Sheikh Mohammed stands beside him, the bearded features set serious, his deep-brown eyes impassive. Near by is Robert Acton, manager of one of the Sheikh's Newmarket studs, Dalham Hall, smart in dark blazer and white shirt, his golden wavy locks brushed back off his ears.

It is now just past 11 p.m., a time when the whole show, normally, is winding down, when the townsfolk have seen enough of this curious spectacle, and, indeed, when some of the players themselves have moved on so that the auditorium has an uneven, bedraggled look, the rows of seats gaping in a toothless grin. But, now, there is not a seat to be bought or bartered. An air of expectancy settles over the whole building followed by an almost hallowed hush as lot 308 is led into the ring, his white-gloved black handler, resplendent in the Keeneland gold-buttoned green blazer, gripping the yearling's headcollar firmly but with a kindly patience which signals to the wide-eyed colt that, yes, this is a different experience for you, but you are safe with me. The colt's muscles ripple in the light of the powerful overhead spots playing up those white socks. He puts his ears back, looking at the audience, and gives a short, shrill whinny – while a thousand pair of human eyes gaze back.

Announcer Tom Hammond up on the auctioneer's rostrum launches into a spiel about the colt that is not educational to the serious players; they know off by heart, from the hours and hours of exhaustive study of the catalogue carried out weeks before this event, what Hammond tells the audience in his sharp, professional drawl: 'A son of the great sire Northern Dancer . . . from a dam who has produced no less than seven winners including the champion US sprinter, My Juliet, the recent US Stakes winner, Bold Julie, and the British Pattern-placed Lee-Phard's Special [Lyphard's Special, winner of seven races, also placed in Ascot's Royal Lodge and Doncaster's William Hill Futurity as a two-year-old]. . . this is a fine-looking young horse.'

With a wave of his hand, Hammond passes over to auctioneer Scott Caldwell from California, son of Keeneland's number-one caller, the silver-haired Tom Caldwell, a man who has taught Scott and his other auctioneer son Chris all the intricacies and sharp-witted skills he has learned himself as a cattle auctioneer back in Oregon – that speedy incessant tobacco-auction sing-song roll, the words barely perceptible and punctuated only by a slight pause for breath and the emphasis on another bid that registers on the illuminated 'scoreboard'. Scott Caldwell's voice booms out over the microphone. In seconds, incredibly, there is a bid for one million. Then a ringing shout 'Yeah!' from one of the many bid spotters who are watching, eyes like hawks, the various players in their allotted pitches. 'Two million.' A spotter slaps his hands, shouts again, half-wheeling to the rostrum. 'Three million!' exclaims Caldwell. 'What about four?' The crowds love it, horsemen and townsfolk alike. This is unbelievable stuff, unheard of. Jesus H, the bidding's going up a million bucks a shot.

Out back, it is the Sheikh's man, Dick Warden, cutting out the early running. Inside the Pavilion his main protagonist is Wayne Lukas, former US high school basketball team coach and destined to become America's most successful trainer, a man who has filmstar looks and a stableful of patrons to go with the Hollywood-based operation – glitz, glam and very wealthy. Sangster, O'Brien and Joss Collins decide to wait their turn to enter the fray, so they remain motionless as Lukas responds to the Sheikh's money. Sangster's world-record $4.25 million is brushed aside, bringing gasps from the audience while out back someone hollers in delight. Now the Sangster camp decide it is time to test the water, flex their muscles, and Joss Collins confidently joins in so that, soon, the bidding takes on a smooth, steady pattern, rising in $100,000 stages. Over five million, on up to six million, then beyond six. Sangster suddenly decides to test the Sheikh's resolve and Collins throws in a $50,000 'short ball'. But Warden, as if with a will of iron, bounces back with another $100,000.

By now many of the reporters on duty for the world's racing press have battled their way out of the tiny cramped pressbox and, with hard-news colleagues – even the business-section staff of America's most important papers are here – are frantically pushing their way through the crowds to get backstage and witness the action between these two superpowers. This is remarkable copy, headline news. Seven million dollars – for one horse! This creature with the white blaze down his head, an untried horse who nobody can tell will even win spit. Surely it's all madness? But still the bidding goes on, both sides have locked horns, neither budging an inch. The Sheikh's stud man, Robert Acton, is now standing within earshot of the Sangster camp and, although leaving the bidding to Warden, gives the Sangster group a smile and tells them: 'We're going to get this horse – you know that, don't you.' But Sangster is not going to fall for any bluff. He's in the mood to stare anyone out. If the Sheikh and his lot are looking for a fight then they've found one. He's seen all this before, here at the sales and in the boxing ring, knows the opponent can psyche out the man before the bell is sounded. So he pushes on, perhaps insulted, the ego at full stretch, and Collins bids another $100,000, which sends the scoreboard to $7.3 million. But Warden stands firm and twists the knife – signalling a $200,000 double increment bid to $7.5 million.

Now this duel is to the death. It is not simply a bid between two parties for a commodity. There are many other permutations of power swirling below the surface. This is a rip tide of horseracing politics; of authority, influence, ascendancy, control. The vantage ground Sangster possesses must not be surrendered, the years of graft, his clearing of a pathway through this perplexing jungle of precarious commerce to a new, lofty position, will be guarded with a fierce passion and determination.

So Joss Collins is allowed to strike another blow, matching the Sheikh's bid with a $200,000 nod from Sangster. Each camp is trying to outfox the other in a game of high-stakes poker where the nerve is being tested like never before. The scoreboard figure soars to over $8.5 million and the often-hushed spectators crackle into life on a high buzz. The Panama-hatted Vincent O'Brien briefly takes over from Collins and bowls another $50,000 bouncer against Warden at $8.8 million, causing the Colonel to throw a long backward glance to where the Sheikh is standing. But Sheikh Mohammed does not flinch, nor do his eyes even register Warden's enquiry. His stance, as he stares intently at the next yearling due in the ring, says that the money does not matter. As if to endorse the Sheikh's calm, measured resolution, Robert Acton once more addresses the Sangster camp: 'You know you won't get this horse,' he says almost impishly, 'why not quit now?'

But neither Sangster nor O'Brien is ready to pull up stumps. This is their ball game. Christ, they practically wrote the current rule book. As the bidding goes over the $9 million mark, the crowd roars as though a high-wire artist has just carried out a death-defying somersault. At $9.3 million, O'Brien again pitches in short with a $50,000 bid to see if the Sheikh's gas is running out. Warden, however, is still on full tank and there is, it seems, no stopping him. He counter-attacks, taking the figure to $9.6 million. O'Brien, his face, like that of Sangster, drained with the thrill of this white-knuckle ride, leans forward and, in what he hopes will prove the knockout blow, tells Collins to up the ante by $400,000. As the Sangster bid is accepted, the crowd goes wild, hollering, whooping and shrieking in delight. 'Ten million dollars,' Scott Caldwell announces firmly as the scoreboard runs out of digits to record the mammoth play.

Now the onus, once more, is back with the Sheikh. People are everywhere, on this incredible charge from the opium of the dollar, craning their necks, pushing, jostling to see more of the action. Stewards try to maintain a semblance of order but it is impossible. Warden fires back immediately with another $200,000 to $10.2 million. Sangster can hardly believe it. In the lull that follows, Phonsie O'Brien, Vincent's brother, is approached by Will Farish, one of America's foremost bloodstock breeders, and the two men briefly exchange whispered words. Phonsie returns to the Sangster group, white-faced and almost breathless, shocked at the heights to which the stakes have risen. They gather round him and listen, his voice barely audible above the din, as he urges sanity, control. Events are now completely out of order, this thing is a runaway with no one at the wheel. It's just . . . well . . . madness.

Scott Caldwell calls for another bid while everyone holds their breath. But there is no gesture from Sangster. The steam has evaporated. Caldwell waits until the last possible moment then, abruptly, brings his hammer down. 'Sold . . . for a new world record of $10.2 million dollars.'

The crowd erupts. Those who do not realise the significance of the event roar their approval and stamp their feet, simply carried on the swell of emotion, the euphoria. The Sheikh confers, briefly, with his advisers, turns on his heel, and without glancing at the losers leaves by a side exit to a waiting limousine which will whisk him to the airport. While people are still making their way to their cars, shaking their heads in disbelief, dazed by the events they have just witnessed, the Sheikh's private 747 jumbo jet is taxiing ready for take-off. Ten minutes later, as the plane known as the Flying Carpet takes off, Sheikh Mohammed is out of his Western clothes and is wearing his flowing Arab djellaba, relaxing in his private quarters.

The world's press are still mopping up in the Pavilion. Dick Warden is surrounded by reporters answering their many questions, slightly bewildered by the fuss, looking up now and then to smile or mouth words at the pats on the back, the touches of his arm, from dozens of well-wishers who want to make physical contact with him like kissing the Blarney Stone, hailing the new Emperor's emissary.

Robert Sangster has been defeated, brushed aside on the very stage where he has savoured victory on so many other occasions. He knows that this is a milestone, a flavour of things to come. Perhaps he has had his own way too long, always been ready, willing and able to fight the Americans in their own backyard, matching the might of the dollar with the wealth created from his own, quite fantastic and unique international commodity holding – a large and influential stake in the best thoroughbreds in the world no matter what the country. This is something he thought of, dreamed of and finally put into operation in a multi-million-pound project of spectacular nerve, a scale never before contemplated by the ruling class of the bloodstock industry. It was his revolution those eight years ago, his foresight, his gamble. Now someone else is here to challenge. With vast financial resources the Arabs can buy their way in, following the Sangster formula to a degree, improvising with their own ideas where necessary, but, whatever the logistics of it all, aiming for the very top.

Sangster will continue the fight, though. He has taken knocks before on the way up, learned from hard experience that, in spite of any luck that has come his way, there is no quick route. The Arabs will discover that for themselves. Speaking in short, almost staccato sentences and with a familiar note of hesitancy in his voice, Sangster says he is sorry the team lost but he takes sporting consolation that the colt will be trained in England and therefore be seen in the top races of Europe – any boost to European racing is an indirect boost to the Sangster operation – and he adds what some observers think is one of the most salient points of this emotion-sapping battle: 'At least we showed them we've got balls.'

He is wrong, however, when he says that the colt will be seen on the racecourses of Europe and, in retrospect, not taking the fight beyond $10.2 million is one of the smartest moves he has made.

For the 1983 world-record-priced son of Northern Dancer, subsequently named Snaafi Dancer, proves to be totally useless and never sets foot on any racecourse. To compound matters it proves just as worthless at stud – infertile as a stallion. It is a salutary example, one inherent in the very nature of this sporting business. Money, no matter how much, is no guarantee of success.

TWO

X Marks the Spot

Robert Sangster was given the middle name of Edmund after his grandfather, a Manchester-based businessman who was involved in wholesaling from several warehouses in the city in the early 1900s. His only son, Vernon (Robert's father), who was also an Edmund, was a teenaged member of the Manchester Regiment within the 55th West Lancashire Division during the First World War and returned from service on the Western Front to help run the comfortable family business. Vernon, however, was not totally enamoured with the wholesale trade, flourishing though it was now the country slowly began to recover from the shocking aftermath of the horrific conflict. By the dawn of the new decade of the 1920s, and at the age of twenty-one, the entrepreneurial hunger that was inherent in the family began to gnaw at Vernon just as it would a generation later when Robert would seek a new challenge. There were new opportunities out there, different horizons.

Edmund Sangster had talked with his son about the idea of a form of lottery for the working man based upon that greatly supported recreational outlet for the working class, football. This was a sport which, to the concern of Church leaders who were suffering a diminishing authority from their moral stewardship of Victorian times, had been attracting the cloth-capped, muffled masses like a new religion. The plan was uncomplicated in its theory; if large enough prizes could be offered, an inducement to become rich for little outlay, and if enough people could be attracted to wager a little money each week, a football pool could prove a sound business proposition. And so, in 1923, Edmund and Vernon launched their football-pools business. It was at the same time as another young Lancashire man, one John Moores of Eccles, near Manchester, was launching his pools company, Littlewoods, thirty miles to the south, in Liverpool. There would be no easy road ahead, however, and both of these small businesses struggled in the early days. John Moores, now Sir John, recalls how, as a young telegraphist with two colleagues (after one of whom the company was named), he started off in a top-floor office in Liverpool's Church Street. They handed out 10,000 of their new coupons at an important football match at Hull – and received only one back. Their first payout had come after a similar hand distribution outside Old Trafford, home of Manchester United, when thirty-five coupons from a total of 4,000 were returned. The grand sum of £4 7s 6d was accumulated with a dividend of £2 12s. Moores continued the business after his two partners had decided the going was too tough. He became a billionaire.

Two years later, buoyed by their own modest success and that of their rivals, the Sangsters decided that competition was the spur they needed, and moved the operation to the same Merseyside city. The pools firm from whose wealth Robert Sangster would launch his assault on the world of thoroughbred racing was a £135 private company and was called Vernons. Its founder shareholders were Vernon himself, his wife Margaret Martha (always known as Peggy) and John Moody, Vernon's close friend who had served with him during the war. Following the death of Edmund, it was the period of the thirties that saw a boom in the pools business with a proliferation of companies opening up and competing with each other to attract the working man's few weekly pence. Vernons established their headquarters in Liverpool's northern suburb of Aintree, a stone's throw from the Grand National course.

Vernon was thirty-five before he experienced something new on a personal level, for on 23 May 1936 his wife Peggy gave birth to their only child, Robert. He was elated. Now he had an heir to the business he was rapidly expanding. Vernon put his business acumen to the test with renewed vigour. He was a good wheeler-dealer, cultivating his relationship with the Establishment and with Liverpool City Council as well as becoming a director of several other businesses.

With the advent of the Second World War, Vernon foresaw a curb on football pools, so he launched Vernons Industries. And while his Aintree headquarters and staff were put at the disposal of the War Ministry, with the building being used as the Post Office sorting HQ and the War Office forms store, a factory was opened at Macclesfield in Cheshire, quickly followed by four more, producing a variety of war-effort goods from parachutes to what German children called 'Angel's Hair' – strips of aluminium foil which were dropped by Allied aeroplanes to disrupt German radio-location instruments. Although pools betting was suspended in the early part of the war mainly because of a shortage of paper to print coupons, a Unity Pool was subsequently established by the major operators, including Vernons – 'for the public morale' – and coupons were printed in the national newspapers and returned to each of the operators by post for processing.

By the resumption of normal pools service some twelve months after the war, Vernon was devoting more energy to his industrial conglomerate and was overseeing boardroom developments as his factories switched to a range of domestic products with the accent on goods for export – items such as aluminium kitchen equipment, meat 'safes' and an array of articles from a new and exciting material known as plastic. Founding another factory in the overspill New Town of Kirkby in 1946, Vernons Industries also began producing a range of children's toys. By now, Vernon Sangster was a director of more than ten companies and his Vernons Industries had expanded to embrace more new factories, across the River Mersey at Birkenhead and Bidston in the Wirral, not far from the family home on the Golden Mile of Meols Drive, West Kirby.

Vernon was a quiet, private man. He lived for his family, his business and his golf. Outwardly serious with his thinning hair swept straight back, and always wearing half-hornrimmed spectacles, there was underneath a sense of humour coupled with a kind, disarming disposition that earned him the nickname of Mr Modesty. Every day he was rarely away from the office and would take lunch in the city at the Rembrandt, a private dining club for businessmen. There, unobtrusively seated at his favourite table for lunch, and often for dinner with Peggy, he appeared unassuming, 'just an ordinary businessman', friendly, with simple tastes in food, never caring to complain should the Dover sole not be cooked quite to perfection.

The family home was called West Lodge, a grand, imposing house in a road where nothing as vulgar as simple house numbers would suffice. These were the homes of the prosperous, people who called their houses 'Roseacre', 'Hatherleigh' or 'Redcroft', and their homes had the hallmarks of Victorian and Edwardian grandeur – large bay windows, mock-Tudor turrets, multiple towering chimneys, portcullis windows and tiny attic skylights where the domestic staff lived. West Lodge had its own stable block and cottage within its grounds, the name carved into the red sandstone pillars. It had multiple roofs and white stuccoed upper-half exterior walls, neat privet hedges and pristine lawns with rosebeds, even a 'bowling green' side lawn featuring a flagpole from which the Union Jack could flutter on days like the Monarch's birthday or St George's Day. West Kirby itself could have been a Southport or a Bournemouth, what could be best described as a 'sedate' resort, the 'sea' of the wide River Dee estuary visible beyond the golf links of the Royal Liverpool Club, which lay at the bottom of the Sangster garden and of which Vernon and Peggy were members; they would later become one of the very few husband-and-wife captains. Vernon loved his golf and played off a 12-handicap. He would later become a member of the Royal and Ancient Golf Club of St Andrew's.

His prosperity would lead to the acquisition of a 300-acre dairy and mixed farm a few miles away on the Wirral peninsula, and a grand holiday home at Sandbanks, Bournemouth, which was known locally as the Diamond Shore, where schoolboy Robert would spend summer holidays fishing or tinkering on the family motor launch. The many charity deeds that Robert would subsequently perform followed the example of his father, who gave generously to many local charities – often anonymously because he did not like the fuss.

Long before Britain's towns and cities had their present-day sports and leisure centres, Vernon gave thousands of pounds to Liverpool City Council to build the Vernon Sangster Sports Centre, a facility for the city's youth which thrives today in Stanley Park, diplomatically halfway between the stadia of Liverpool's Anfield and Everton's Goodison Park football grounds. There was one occasion, though, when Vernon did uncharacteristically break cover to delight children in several Liverpool hospitals and convalescent homes by leading a retinue of a Father Christmas, a trumpeter, a jester and a band of fairies to distribute several dozen pedal-car jeeps and tricycles made at one of the Vernons Industries factories.

By the end of another decade, the Vernons organisation was a truly diversified operation employing something like 6,000 people. The pools side had vigorously defended and expanded its position to become the joint market leader where formerly there had been 230 other pools companies. By shrewd and innovative management, Vernons had introduced the fortune-winning treble-chance pool and had strategically absorbed the shattering impact of betting duty, which was introduced by the Government at a rate of 10 per cent of gross stakes in January 1948, increased to 20 per cent two months later and 30 per cent a year after that. In 1951 a Royal Commission on Gambling stated: 'Three companies, Littlewoods, Vernons and Shermans, account for 85 per cent of the total pools turnover.' The Cardiff-based Shermans was eventually taken over by Littlewoods. In many quarters, Vernons developed a reputation for looking after its workforce and became the first pools firm to recognise its clerical workers' trade union. The company established a social welfare plan which included a 'civic consciousness' scheme enabling any employee to make visits to see the workings of government, justice and industry.

Conditions for the employees of the pools firm and of a subsequent mail-order business, the vast majority of whom were women, were highlighted when Vernons pulled out of Macclesfield under pressure from the Board of Trade in order to help the local silk industry, which was complaining that the pools firm had taken most of its workers. The local Vernons girls protested that they had never had such good working conditions and said they would not be returning to the mills until the silk industry offered them similar facilities. There was a generous 'Liverpool' spirit among the workforce, too, started during the war and continuing afterwards, when weekly subscriptions were raised by the 'Vernons Girls' to provide entertainment for the war disabled.

So it was against this Vernons background, one that provided a privileged existence, though not a spoilt one, that Robert Sangster was reared. His early education was as a weekly boarder at the private Leas School, set in its own grounds of twelve acres about a quarter of a mile away and in the same road as the Sangster home, right next door to the Royal Liverpool (Hoylake) Golf Club. These days, Leas School is no longer in existence as a school, and its large Victorian building and grounds are on the market for redevelopment as a residential care home.

A few days before his fourteenth birthday in May 1950, schoolboy Robert was sent to public school at Repton, one of Britain's oldest (established 1557) and situated between Burton-on-Trent and Derby. Sangster was an enthusiastic pupil, although he was not academically gifted, and it became apparent that he and his housemasters were not going to set their sights on further education at university. But the school that has produced four Archbishops of Canterbury (Ramsey being the latest) and ten England Test cricketers, including the renowned C. B. Fry, encouraged its pupils in the sporting sphere of cricket and football, which suited him just fine. Although not good enough for the soccer First Eleven, Sangster was considered a good keen player in his house team, the Hall, and he was thought responsible enough to be made a school prefect.

It was while Sangster was still at Repton that the name of a man with whom his future would be inextricably linked was hitting the headlines. It was the period of Vincent O'Brien's remarkable Grand National treble, three consecutive winners of the marathon which is run just over the road from the Vernons Pools headquarters and from whose office windows could be seen the towering Liverpool Racecourse grandstand. In 1953, 1954 and 1955, O'Brien sent over the winners from his Cashel, County Tipperary stables, Early Mist, Royal Tan and Quare Times. Although Sangster up to this point had not shown a particular interest in horseracing other than to note the results of the big race as a matter of sporting record and to admire the achievement of this small Irishman who seemed to have a unique ability in handling racehorses, only a crystal-ball reader would have been able to tell him that fate would throw the two men together twenty years on and that, together, they would launch a racing revolution – and conquer the world.

Although Sangster is still on the mailing list as a member of the Old Reptonians Society and the family donated a sum of money to Robert's old house, one of the rare contacts he has made in recent times is when several old boys looked him up in the Melbourne cricket ground pavilion during a visit to Australia several years ago while Sangster was on his usual November visit to the Melbourne Cup.

Leaving Repton in 1955, a month before his nineteenth birthday, Sangster then went the way of all young men of his age in these times, and for his two years' National Service he was drafted into the 1st Battalion, the Cheshire Regiment. It was here that the Army provided him with one of his first disappointments. They turned him down for a commission after he had undergone the three-week leadership initiative course for POMs (Possible Officer Material) before the War Office Selection Board.

But Private Sangster of the batallion's intelligence section need not have worried about his inability to impress the board with any qualities of leadership, for he was in good company, as time was to tell. His fellow squaddie and room-mate was Andreas Whittam Smith, founder, proprietor and editor of Britain's quality daily newspaper, the *Independent*, who was known then as plain Andy Smith.

Whittam Smith, a pupil of Birkenhead School on Merseyside, had lived in the Wirral too, when his father had been minister of St James's church in Birkenhead from 1940 to 1953 and, as he and Sangster were the only two middle-class young men in the battalion, both felt they ought to stick together. 'I must say that, such was our middle-class upbringing, Robert and I had absolutely no aggression, as one might have expected, from the other boys – but we did have rather more skill in coping with that aspect. Robert, in fact, got along enviably with everyone. My great advantage of coming from such a family was that I went to camp with a five-pound note in my pocket from my mother, which put me one up on the others – but Robert, well, coming from his background, he had a car.'

That vehicle, unique to the camp, soon helped Sangster on his way to become a popular comrade among his fellow intelligence-section members of this infantry battalion – especially when he was doing his stint of guard duty on a Saturday night. For as Private Sangster stood on duty at the entrance to the dismal, windswept and derelict Barnard Castle camp in County Durham, the generosity that ran in the family and was to become one of Robert Sangster's future hallmarks became manifest when he willingly loaned out the car to anyone who had a date with one of the local girls!

The two failed officers, and future millionaires, also shared a room together – 'over the quartermaster's office' – while serving in Berlin in 1955. 'Robert was enviably sophisticated and suave – mind you, he had a bit more money than the rest of us – and we toured the jazz clubs and cafés of this romantic city under its post-war reconstruction with me usually hanging on to his coat-tails. He was excellent company and was able to carry himself with considerable aplomb and charm.'

On his return to the regiment's HQ at Dale Camp, Chester, by which time he had reached the rank of lance-corporal, he was able to exhibit his sporting prowess, developing his skill at boxing. Although he fought and won for the regiment at heavyweight, the overall stocky nature of this would-be Marciano, standing a little over five foot eight inches tall and weighing in around twelve stone, was a far cry from the heavyweights of today.

Even in those days, though, Sangster's stature meant that he relied more on agility and guile than sheer punching power, something that in later life as a steward of the British Boxing Board of Control endeared him to fighters who showed a high degree of skill over brute force.

Later on in his racing career, Sangster remembered his old regiment by naming one of his horses Louisberg after the site in Nova Scotia where the Cheshire Regiment's first-known victorious battle was fought. And, not that many years ago, when the company sergeant-major wrote to him telling him that he had been the worst lance corporal the regiment ever had and that, by the way, they needed £100 for some new lights in the regimental clubhouse, Sangster obliged with two crisp £50 notes and a compliments slip by return post.

Sangster completed his two years in the Army with fond memories of some of the times, but glad it was all over, happy and enthusiastic that he could now return to the more civilised life as a trainee executive within the family firm, which was now established under the umbrella title of the Vernons Organisation.

The widely diversified group of companies was now heavily involved in the manufacturing industry, producing such things as fitted kitchens for the American market and aviation equipment, while another factory had launched a family three-wheeler car called the Gordon. Selling at £255 (including purchase tax), the 197cc-engined 'people's car' with its canvas top 'convertible' hood was the cheapest of its kind on the road with its petrol consumption as little as eighty miles to the gallon.

Not for the dashing and eligible bachelor Robert such humble transport, though. His flair for the finer things in life saw him behind the wheel of several high-powered sports cars, something which added greatly to his appeal among the suitable young ladies of the social circles in which he was mixing. Sangster was not slow to take advantage of his position as the heir to a multi-million-pound fortune when it came to the interest expressed by the opposite sex. Invariably dressed in a sports jacket and tie, or a suit to the office, with his dimpled chin and the squareness of his broad forehead accentuated by the style of his brown hair, which he swept straight back on top and at the sides so it was almost flat to the scalp, he possessed youthful, clean-cut, 'wholesome' good looks. This all made him a good catch (as their mothers probably said) for the many girls he dated.

Inevitably given the flush of youth and a fast car, there were one or two motor accidents which, fortunately, were not as serious as they might have been. While driving with his girlfriend of the moment during his first year with Vernons he managed to damage his car badly when taking up argument with a Royal Mail van in an early-evening crash near his home. He sustained a cut nose and his girlfriend minor head injuries. But the injury was nothing worse than what he might pick up on a Saturday afternoon playing rugby for the old-established Birkenhead Park Club, of which he was an enthusiastic member.

Besides, he did not have time to worry about such things because he was leading a full life with the business, the girls and his sport. Like his parents he had become a good golfer and tried to put in a couple of rounds a week at the Royal Liverpool in an attempt to improve on his handicap, which he had now got down to 12.

At this time the pools side of the business was turning over £20 million a year – about half that of Littlewoods – paying around £6 million to the Government in betting duty. Because the Sangsters, as the pools promoters, did not take out more than the

3 per cent commission limit over which, by law, they would have to declare their take, the exact amount of commission earned was never publicly declared, although in earlier days Vernon said he took out 1 per cent. (In 1958, a 1 per cent commission would have been worth £200,000.) So the gambling side of the business, which included a credit betting division, was where Sangster concentrated most of his learning. This was the very profitable backbone of the organisation, which would subsequently spread to all forms of finance and even to a major motorcar dealership.

Although there was a keen rivalry between Vernons and Littlewoods with trade secrets being jealously guarded and innovations constantly being planned to maintain the attraction which was prompting a third of Britain's population to fill in their weekly coupons, that rivalry was never malicious, never ruthless enough for one firm to attempt to put the other out of business. There was, in fact, an unspoken 'truce', a sort of gentlemen's agreement that, in Liverpool, there existed the only two major pools firms in the country and there was, therefore, no need to squabble. Both the Sangsters and the Moores had carved out a quite unique and profitable business and the cake was big enough for both companies. And so the families became friends, not bosom pals of course, but a friendship whereby they would be at ease meeting each other at various social and family occasions.

There was a future 'burden' on Robert Sangster, the young trainee executive within one of Liverpool's major employers, for no matter how hard he tried to come to terms with each aspect of the business there would always be those within the company and the general commercial community of the city who thought he had it made. Sangster knew that by the time he was thirty he would inherit a third of the company, followed by a further third when he was thirty-five, and at the age of forty (when his father, if still alive, would be seventy-six) he would receive the final tranche of shares that would make the company his own. The arrangement was carefully structured through a family trust to avoid as much inheritance tax as possible. As events were to turn out, however, that all-important fortieth birthday would be a momentous year of great change and personal upheaval. So his task now, if he was to carry out his future duty responsibly, was to learn every complexity of the business that would eventually come under his command as managing director and, later, chairman.

THREE

Serious Fun

Working life in the late 1950s for the heir to this growing multi-million-pound fortune was to some degree a novelty because Robert Sangster's schooling and his stint of National Service meant he was almost twenty-one by the time he finally joined the company. Operating mainly from the Vernons administrative city office amid the bustling commercial centre of Liverpool, and travelling the five miles out of town to the Aintree pools 'factory' only on certain occasions – sometimes in his newly acquired Mercedes sports car – it was a period of watching, studying and learning.

Liverpool itself at this time was a city only slowly on the change after the Second World War; the wreckage of buildings that had been bombed in the Blitz had been long cleared, but the bombsites remained undeveloped through lack of finance, muddied flat gaps in the landscape that served to remind the population of Hitler's parachute buzz-bombs, V-2 rockets and incendiary devices which had tried, but failed, to demoralise the cynically humoured street-wise inhabitants of this major seaport. It was still a place of cobbled streets and smoking chimneys, of clanking electric trams grinding their way in and out of the city along a myriad of shiny steel rails. It was a time when schoolkids could still get a penny return into 'town' on such trams during their summer holidays to wander within those large emporiums, now called department stores, with their newly installed escalators – a moving staircase of free and endless fun (providing you could get past the commissionnaire on the ground floor).

There were colourful street hawkers and barrow boys,

shouting the odds from their fruit-laden handcarts, signs saying 'No spitting in public places', and muffled dockers scurrying down to the Dock Road where the large red funnels of great ocean-going passenger liners peeped tantalisingly over the towering wall of the wharfs, which had names such as Albert, Huskisson or Gladstone (the former is today a redeveloped tourist attraction with shops, offices, restaurants, a maritime museum and the Tate Gallery).

Sangster came of age in the era of teddy boys and drainpipe trousers, when fashion-conscious girls were switching to their 'Sack' dresses from the hooped skirts and wired petticoats inspired by the relatively new phenomenon of rock 'n' roll. To a lot of people Liverpool still meant Arthur Askey and Frankie Vaughan, the vanguard of the subsequent sixties showbiz explosion. It meant the Protestant Liverpool and Catholic Everton football clubs (and two other official cathedrals), Tate and Lyle sugar and Scouse wit. This was the time when 'judies' waited for their 'fellas' for a Saturday-night date underneath Jacob Epstein's giant naked male statue of the Lewis's department store opposite the Adelphi Hotel, or maybe at the Pier Head for a Saturday-night dance up the Mersey on the *Royal Iris* ferry boat when they could jive to the music of Hit Parade stars like Paul Anka and Neil Sedaka, and shout in unison when Britain's latest skiffle rage, Lonnie Donegan, asked them if their chewing gum lost its flavour on the bedpost overnight.

Betting on a horse at this time was a somewhat precarious affair for punters who were not regulars at the racetrack, where they could bet with on-course bookmakers quite legally. For unless they had a credit account with the likes of Vernons Credit Bookmakers, to whom Sangster was now devoting much of his time learning the pros and cons of the gambling game (and to which he himself would become attached as a substantial punter before very long), they would have to resort to illegal gambling.

This was prior to the 1960 Betting and Gaming Act which on 1 May the following year introduced the licensed betting shop, or turf accountant as the bookies liked to call themselves. With

Vernons Credit, punters could arrange a weekly limit, subject to the company's check on their *bona fides* with the usual credit agencies, or deposit a sum of money and bet by telephone to that ceiling, much the same as opening a credit account with a large firm today. Ante-post bets could also be waged by anyone, whether they had an account or not, and the most popular form of advance betting was by postal orders, which flooded in through the post by their hundreds every week (few of the general public having bank accounts then). This racing division of Vernons called itself 'The friendly racing service' and assured customers of its speed, accuracy, secrecy and security in dealing with their 'commissions', many of which were placed by clients who preferred to use a *nom de plume*.

The average punter, though, relied on the illegal street bookie and his runner for his daily dose of excitement. The 'Mr Big' would often operate from home, the premises well secured with strong locks on the doors to delay any police raiders just long enough to flush his day's bets down the toilet or burn them on the fire. His team of cloth-capped runners would operate from pubs and outside large factories or, more often, from a back entry well known to regular clients.

There, with a minder close by and a 'douse' on guard near the street ('scannin' for the bizzies'), a constant stream of small-time punters would amble up to the runner in this mobile den of iniquity, their threepenny and tanner bets written on the back of empty cigarette packets, Players Weights, Woodbine, Craven A. The runners would take their bets and stakes to 'Mr Big' before the first race, their jobs done until they returned that evening or the next morning when all bets had been settled. And the following day the routine would start again, with punters turning up to the same spot to collect their winnings – or to play again.

There was a great deal of honour among these illegal bookies and rarely did they welch on a bet – not like the sharks who came up for the Grand National and laid illegal bets at Aintree out in the country only to do a quick dash to solvency across the canal when the big race result did not go their way. After all, these street bookies were part of the community, lived in the district, drank in the pubs. More often the police themselves knew what was going on and turned a blind eye to the proceedings so long as there was no hint of trouble such as fighting or racketeering.

Of course, every now and then a plainclothes policeman would be dispatched from the bridwell to nab the unsuspecting runner before he could dispose of the evidence required by the courts – usually down the grid over which the runner habitually stood. On such occasions, the runner would be in court the same day, pay his £5 fine (reimbursed by his bookie) and be back on the street in time for payout. The runners got 6d in the pound commission. Any punter placing a bet of more than half a crown had probably had one of the many tips that were then, as today, always readily acquired.

Sangster soon slotted into the business life of Liverpool, making contacts and attending meetings now that his settling-in period was over. As he was working in the city centre, he was able to meet up at lunchtime with several of his rugby club friends who also worked near by. Occasionally he would visit the Rembrandt with his father. But Sangster liked nothing better than to lunch with his pals at the Kardomah Coffee House in Church Street and the first-floor restaurant there became a regular luncheon club for the group of young men, sometimes up to ten of them.

The ground floor of the Kardomah was taken up by the café, the aroma of the freshly ground coffee spilling out, invitingly, into the busy shopping street. This was where the office girls and the shoppers stopped for a quick snack, a shilling triple-decker ham salad roll and a cup of that lovely fresh medium roast. So too did the poets and musicians, the members of the jazz combos and the skiffle bands who played lunchtime sessions at the nearby Cavern Club. They would linger casually over their solitary cup, drained fifteen minutes before, with a watchful eye on the white-pinafored manageress, who did not take too kindly to the poor spenders' loitering and was liable to drag them out by their hair if she felt inclined.

Upstairs was for the businessmen, those taking real luncheon, a civilised leisurely affair (none of that yuppie 'lunch is for wimps' mentality in these times). Here the walls were panelled in oak and there were thick carpets on the floors while on a central serving table large silver percolators stood brimming with fresh brew. It evoked an ambience of Victoriana, the genteel hush only occasionally broken by the whirr of the old-fashioned coffee grinders or the laughing from the busy Sangster table.

A couple of months after his twenty-second birthday, Sangster decided to take that year's summer holiday in the South of France where the chic resorts like Cannes and St Tropez were the 'in' places for the wealthy glitterati, the towns' images boosted considerably by the publicity given to France's film star 'sex kitten' Brigitte Bardot for her frolicking on the Côte d'Azur. It was here he met his first serious love, nineteen-year-old Christine Street.

This attractive dark-haired Northerner, whose parents owned the largest hotel in the Cumbrian town of Penrith near the Scottish border, was the perfect social match for Sangster. Christine had only recently left the Swiss finishing school of Brillantmont in Lausanne after her secondary education at the Queen Ethelburga's private boarding school in Harrogate, Yorkshire. So she was well versed in the etiquette that Sangster, and his parents, expected of a 'suitable' young lady. Tall and slender, Christine chose to use her middle name rather than her first name, Dorothy. Although she was elegant, it was not the gracefulness that comes with maturity, rather a youthful poise, a freshness like that of the young Diana. She was the type of girl who, though conscious of fashion, which she had studied for a period, looked good in any clothes. Christine told Sangster that she was just starting out on a career as a model. He was impressed. Vernon and Peggy Sangster were also taken by this charming young lady after meeting her when the holiday romance had begun to blossom into something deeper.

Within twelve months, Sangster and Christine were announcing their engagement, with a date fixed for the marriage in May of the following year, 1960. In the meantime, both proceeded with their careers. Christine was based in Manchester, an hour's drive from Liverpool, and carried out her modelling engagements in both cities as well as London, making several television appearances along the way.

Two months before the wedding Sangster had a chance meeting with another young businessman which proved to be one of those fateful junctures in life, an encounter that would have a profound effect on the future.

For Robert Sangster, this meeting would lead him into the exciting world of horseracing, a sport he knew little about other than to concern himself with how much profit the company's racing division was making. In other words it was a moment that would change his whole life as well as quite dramatically altering the course of a sport hidebound by hundreds of years of tradition. The seeds of a forthcoming racing revolution were about to be sown.

The young businessman was Nick Robinson, grandson of Sir Foster Gotch Robinson, a well-known racehorse owner–breeder who owned the Wicken Park Stud in Buckinghamshire and was a member of the Jockey Club. Like Sangster, Robinson had joined the family business, which was a packaging company founded by his grandfather in Bristol, where the main operation was still based, but with a sales department in Liverpool. And it was to this Liverpool office that Robinson was sent for two years, taking over from his predecessor, one of Sangster's rugby-playing friends. Although Robinson himself was not a rugby man, Sangster's friend thought it would be a good idea if he brought the boss's son along to the Kardomah luncheon club so that he could meet Sangster and the rest of the boys in the hope that this newcomer to the region would make some new friends.

So over lunch Robinson proceeded to tell the ensemble about his interests, which of course included horseracing, adding that his grandfather had a horse running in the Lincoln in a few weeks' time and that it might be worth backing. Some of the group did not know the Lincoln from the Derby, but it soon became clear, as they listened to what Robinson told them, that this one-mile handicap run at Doncaster on the first Saturday of every new Flat season in March sounded a fascinating affair. And at the prevailing odds the horse might just be worth a flutter.

The horse in question was Chalk Stream, a five-year-old gelding, bred by Robinson's grandfather, by the popular 1949 Ascot Gold Cup winner Alycidon, the champion sire of 1955. The dam was Sabie River, who had cost Sir Foster Robinson 620 guineas as a yearling and whom he kept for breeding at his stud after it had won four small races.

Chalk Stream's Lincoln attempt was Sangster's first serious bet on a racehorse. It was a loser, however, because Chalk Stream beat only two of the thirty-one runners. But he found the whole exercise exciting. It was great fun and all the better for being associated – even somewhat loosely – with Chalk Stream's connections. It sort of personalised the punt. Yes, he thought to himself, I like this. I like it a lot.

To adapt the words of the man from Remington who liked his shaver so much that he bought the company, Sangster was so impressed with Chalk Stream's promise that he bought the horse. Nick Robinson had made the perfect entrée into the Sangster circle and it was Robinson who was persuaded by Sangster to ask his grandfather if he would sell Chalk Stream. Sangster rather fancied giving a racehorse to Christine as a novel wedding present. So Robinson did the honours, Sir Foster Robinson concurred, and Sangster parted with £1,000 for the gelding, arranging that it should be sent to a trainer who had been recommended, Eric Cousins.

Like many first-time owners, Sangster put the emphasis on having Chalk Stream trained near by. After all, he and Christine would then be able to visit the stables on a Sunday morning, make a fuss of their new acquisition and feed him a carrot or two. Cousins, who was then thirty-nine, had only just moved to the Sandy Brow estate at Tarporley in Cheshire, less than an hour's drive from Sangster's Wirral home. The former RAF pilot had been training some six years from stables coincidentally near Sangster's Repton School, outside Burton-on-Trent, combining his career for part of the time with that as an amateur National Hunt jockey, during which he rode fifty winners. So it was the beginning of a beautiful friendship and a successful owner–trainer relationship. Sangster the punter would land some spectacular (unreported) coups and would rise to prominence as one of Britain's new breed of dashing young men in the racing game.

The day of the wedding was a memorable one for the people of Penrith and they turned out in their hundreds, lining the roads and crowding the front of the parish church of St Andrew's. Rarely had any of them seen such a society wedding. The previous day, Friday the 13th, had been one of incessant rain, but it was fine when the new Mr and Mrs Sangster came out of the church and stood hand in hand, their fingers intertwined, Christine in white satin brocade looking a shade bashful as she posed for pictures with her bouquet of roses and lilies. The 300 guests, who had provided a colourfully entertaining scene for the onlookers, then made a seven-mile journey in a fleet of 150 cars and taxis to the Rampsbeck Hotel on the shores of Lake Ullswater, the Lake District's most northern stretch of water. There, under rather squelchy underfoot conditions which soon had the red carpets in the entrance to the large marquee looking the worse for wear, the guests, who included members of the Littlewoods Moores family, dined on chicken while the champagne flowed (200 bottles consumed) and the debutantes danced into the night as the happy couple slipped away for an undisclosed honeymoon location.

There were two major stories of interest to Sangster in the newspapers on his wedding day. Prince Aly Khan, father of the present Aga Khan (and others), who had enthralled and amused the world with his love of women and horses, was killed the previous day in a motorcar accident outside Paris. Aly Khan was, of course, a most prominent racehorse owner and breeder, the previous year becoming the first man to top £100,000 prize money in a season, mainly due to the 1,000 Guineas, Oaks and Champion Stakes successes of his brilliant home-bred filly Petite Etoile.

That same day, Vincent O'Brien, Sangster's future partner, was banned from training for eighteen months over the doping of one of his horses, a débâcle that was to become known in racing as the Chamour Affair. Although O'Brien's ban was subsequently cut to twelve months, he was forced to swap homes for the duration with his brother Phonsie, who took over as trainer at Ballydoyle. The whole affair is seen these days as a gross injustice by the Irish Turf Club to the man who would earn a reputation as the world's greatest trainer.

Sangster and Christine took an active interest in the progress of Chalk Stream, their only horse, visiting the Cousins yard whenever possible, discussing future plans and, all the time, learning a little more about this exciting sport. While some owners never have a winner in twenty years of ownership, Sangster's first purchase proved a shrewd buy, for later that 1960 season Christine's colours were carried to victory in the Liverpool Autumn Cup at Aintree – they could not have wished for a more suitable first local win.

It was fun time on the punting front, too. And what better, if he was ever going to lose, than at least allowing his losses to pay a few of the bills at Vernons Racing. Sangster, therefore, arranged for a friend to open an account with the firm so that whenever Sangster fancied a bet he would ring up his friend to put the money on for him. Their betting secrets were often the source of much merriment later – perhaps over an early-evening drink at one of their favourite watering holes such as Walters in Liverpool's Hackins Hay (where no women were allowed within three yards of the bar) when they would have a giggle over their drinks, served by the white-coated barmen, recalling how the friend had rung up a Sangster bet for maybe £200, only to hear the manager on the other end of the telephone calling up 'Mr Robert' on the office intercom for his permission to accept such a big bet. The answers from 'Mr Robert' were, naturally, always in the affirmative.

Even though Sangster loved to have a tilt at the ring and was intrigued by the whole nature of gambling, he found the breeding aspect of the sport the most fascinating and soon began spending hours studying the bloodlines of the influential stallions through the ages. (The plethora of bloodstock information which has been painstakingly recorded within racing over several centuries is a unique historical achievement and must surely be of use to some other branch of statistical or genealogical science.) Sangster was so taken by the sport that he was now skipping his Saturday afternoon rugby match to go racing along with a gifted chum who had been playing for Cheshire but had decided he would rather cheer the horses home than turn out for his side.

Cousins had demonstrated his ability to train for the big occasion and he would later earn a reputation as a specialist at laying out a horse for a big handicap. Sangster recognised this himself and soon he was on the lookout for another horse – something that might win one of the big-betting sprint handicaps like the Stewards Cup during Glorious Goodwood week, the Portland Cup at Doncaster or the Ayr Gold Cup. There was delight on the domestic front at this time, too. The Sangsters had adapted to the routine of married life from their new home in the Wirral and Christine was now pregnant with their first child. She rather fancied a girl. Sangster wanted a son and heir.

But after four years of ownership on a fun level, Sangster came to the conclusion that he had better start taking the sport a great deal more seriously. He now knew that racing was a costly hobby, one that did not pay its way unless you were among the 1 or 2 per cent of owners who struck lucky. He decided, therefore, on his next move to further his growing interest in breeding. He now possessed a fair comprehension of bloodstock and was determined to learn more. But there was an inescapable problem, inherent in the complexities of the subject itself. It was a gnawing hunger he knew could never be sated. For no matter how far he went down that studious road to erudition, the further away the horizon appeared. Later, at his zenith, he would comment: 'I'd say I know around ten per cent of all there is to now about this businesss, but even when I'm eighty I will only know another ten per cent.' There was, however, a logical step now facing him in this quest for knowledge, one which faces any student no matter what the subject. He would turn to the practical – and buy his own stud.

FOUR

Lessons to Be Learned

For a man of Robert Sangster's means and earning potential at the age of thirty, having just acquired a third of the Vernons Group, raising the sort of money required for the purchase of a suitable stud farm was never going to be a serious problem, though he had to employ a degree of persuasion with his accountants and bankers. He had discussed the idea with Vernon Sangster, who, as his best friend and chairman of the company, he consulted first in every matter of importance. Christine had also given it her blessing, although it meant her moving from the Wirral, where she was happily settled and had made many friends in the seven years of their marriage. So the search was started for suitable premises. Sangster's main consideration was the location; it had to be within reasonable travelling time of Liverpool, because Vernons came first in his priorities and, no matter how enthusiastic he was about his new venture, racehorses could never be a full-time business – or so he thought at the time. Eventually the ideal premises were discovered in the heart of Cheshire, an old and dilapidated farm with 200 acres of land. The farm also had a grand seventeenth-century house in the grounds which, when renovated, would be eminently suitable for Christine and their son, Guy, who was now rising six years old and who would soon be joined by a new baby. The farm was called Swettenham Hall in the hamlet of Swettenham, almost in the shadow of the famous space tracking telescope, Jodrell Bank, just north of Congleton.

Sangster might have been a newcomer to the business of breeding but he was not about to rush into any transaction without first exhaustively checking on every aspect of

Swettenham's potential. The house could be made nice, sure, but what about the land? Was it loam-based, sand, clay or gravel? Did the prevailing water supply contain enough calcium to feed the susceptible young bones of the foals he hoped to produce? Was the grazing too poor or too rich? There were, indeed, a great many questions to which Sangster wanted answers before he would part with a penny. The most important of these, however, was the financial viability of such a venture.

If Sangster was nothing else, he was a figures man. His life was ruled by profit and loss, and there was no way he was going into this venture with any romantic notions of rolling up his sleeves, putting on a yard coat and helping out at the stud if he had the time – he was simply not that sort of person. He liked the glamour of horseracing, the theory of bloodstock breeding and the academics of it as an owner–breeder. The actual mechanics of the business – in other words the horses themselves – would, however, be kept at a safe distance. Indeed, he would not show any interest in watching one of his mares give birth at the stud. The spectacle of a newly born foal struggling into the world and wobbling cautiously to its feet, and the first nuzzling moments of the mare's loving nurture, was not enough of an attraction placed against the sight of the blood and the urine and the placenta.

If there was one thing Sangster had learned from his father it was that in his career in business he would be called upon to make some tough decisions, just as Vernon had himself: closing a factory, laying off staff, sacking personnel. He had often heard his father repeat the old maxim that in business there was no sentiment. In his view the right timing was the success of good business. And he felt that now was the time to embark on this course of turning his fun hobby into a business – and making it pay, albeit on a modest scale by comparison to the heights he would subsequently reach.

Sangster was not dogmatic in his approach, because he had also learned to take advice and to trust the professionalism of those he asked. He had firm ideas of his own about certain aspects of the forthcoming operation, but he had become a shrewd listener and observer, developing a philosophy to which he would always adhere: the best advice might often be expensive, but it was the cheapest in the end.

Scientists were called in from the Ministry of Agriculture to run extensive tests on the state of the pasture. When their analysis was digested the way seemed clear to go ahead and make the purchase. They advised that several of the paddocks would need ploughing up and reseeding while extensive drainage works would be required to prevent flooding from the River Dane, which ran alongside the farm.

Sangster worked on his budget as architects from Liverpool were instructed to prepare plans of the site. He wanted the stable blocks built to form a traditional courtyard, lawned in the middle with a wide gravel perimeter. A clock tower would form the focal point with an archway through to the paddocks, which would be post and railed, even around the trees (many a high-spirited foal or yearling has killed itself rushing headlong into a tree). He had already visited the National Stud at Newmarket, which had given him some ideas for his design. The offices, barn and outbuildings forming one side of the quadrant would be renovated in reclaimed brick to preserve their character, because these were listed buildings. The manor house would need gutting to turn it into the Sangster family home, and here Christine took a part in advising the architects on exactly what she wanted. She already had ideas about the interior design. But there was still no call for a pink nursery room in the house, for when the Sangster's second child was born that year it was a baby brother for Guy, whom they named Ben. There was no question of Christine being disappointed, however, and she was delighted to be mother to two lovely boys.

Before the builders, bulldozers and heavy earth-moving machines moved in, there was another most important aspect of the operation that Sangster needed to resolve; this was the appointment of a stud manager. He wanted someone of the highest calibre, a person to whom he could entirely entrust the day-to-day running of the place. Sangster's growing commitment at Vernons meant he would be leaving the manor house early in the morning and not returning for twelve or thirteen hours, maybe fourteen. After interviewing several people, he chose Joe French, a Newmarket man with racing in his blood – three generations, in fact. French, a loyal, steady family man with young children, had started his racing life as an apprentice jockey with Tom Leader at racing's headquarters, but he had grown too heavy and had turned to bloodstock. He came to the interview with top credentials, having run the third Lord Astor's Cliveden Stud for the previous thirteen years. Sangster was fortunate to get French because he had just been offered a job managing the ageing Lord Rothermere's stud at Stow-on-the-Wold in Gloucestershire. But, having considered the two positions, French decided to throw his hat in with the younger man. He knew Sangster was in racing in a quite successful way but he was starting the new venture from scratch. It promised to be an exciting time. In a way French's decision was analogous with the gentle breeze that was beginning to rustle through racing – not yet, of course, the Sangster storm, which was still some years away (nor the desert sirocco of others two decades later), but a light whisper gently caressing the creaking rafters of the sport's upper echelons. For here was young blood, new life, although even Sangster himself could not imagine how fiercely his wind of change would blow.

French and his wife Rose eventually moved into a flat within the manor house with their two sons, one of whom, Colin, would later join the stud staff. But in those early construction days, Sangster leaned heavily on his new manager, virtually giving him *carte blanche* to transform the establishment. French would tell his new boss what he wanted and why he needed it, organising the layout of the paddocks, liaising with the builders, firmly believing that, perhaps in five years, they might just have a decent stud on their hands. It actually happened more quickly, through good management, shrewd matings which produced good stock, and a healthy fertility rate among the mares.

Swettenham Stud, the name which still survives as Sangster's horse-trading company, sent its first draft of foals to the Newmarket December Sales in 1968. These were the progeny of four mares bound for Swettenham once the building work was completed, but which, in the meantime, had been boarded out to foal at Willington Hall, near Chester. One of the mares was Sangster's favourite, Audrey Joan. Very soon, Sangster had established Swettenham as a major player on the British breeding scene.

Encouraged by the early success of Swettenham, Sangster negotiated the purchase of a further 200 acres of pasture-land across the other side of the River Dane, adding fourteen foaling boxes to the original site and strengthening his breeding stock. He was learning the business fast. And enjoying it immensely. There was no time to get involved with the minutiae of the stud; French was now reporting daily occurrences of any note to Christine, who would inform her husband over dinner when he arrived back home from Liverpool (often after seven or eight in the evening), for she too had developed an interest in the mares and foals. Once a month, Sangster and French would hold a formal meeting at which all aspects of the business would be thoroughly discussed: the progress of certain mares and their future breeding plans, their transportation arrangements to visit stallions, even the price of straw bedding and feedstuff. Sangster was still running a commercial enterprise and in these early days, to some extent, he was still under the gaze of his father and his accountants – 'Just how long will it be, Robert, before you get your money back from this investment?' Sometimes at weekends it seemed that Sangster was chewing over such questions as his solitary figure meandered around the stud, giving the occasional wave to any member of the staff he saw, but not bothering to approach them; he has never been a man for the small talk and he knew where to find them if he ever had something specific to discuss.

There was one occasion in those early days when Sangster learned another valuable lesson, a practical one, following the birth of a weakling foal. It was about nature itself, something which the good stud groom or stockman recognises as his partner in this glorious affair of rearing the young. The newly born foal was a colt by the American stallion Bold Bidder, ostensibly a valuable commodity, although all thoughts of its worth were abandoned as Christine, shocked and concerned as the foal lay dying, tried to bottle-feed it with a mixture of glycerine and water while Sangster telephoned Swettenham's vet Ted Greenway near the Cousins stable some thirty miles away, then tried a couple more vets in Ireland for a second opinion. But as the colt struggled weakly for life, the mare stood unconcerned in the far corner of the box just as she had after first giving birth, recognising almost immediately that this was a runt not destined to live. Nature had decreed this early death just as she would have decreed the foal's almost certain stunted growth and subsequent uselessness as a racehorse had today's relatively simple life-saving method of changing the foal's blood been available.

Racing in Britain in the 1960s was very much an insular affair. American bloodstock, which Sangster would later exploit on a worldwide scale, was almost non-existent on the domestic scene. A foreign horse usually meant one from France, most likely from the then Aga Khan's dominant bloodlines, while Ireland was, as now, a major contributor to the British turf. If there was any trade between Britain and the rest of the world, it was likely to be one-way, with English stallions and mares being exported to Japan and the USA and very few of the latter country's horses making the opposite trip, because they were not considered good enough (quite unlike today). At the top, racing had been in the grip of the landed gentry for generations, the Lord Roseberys and Derbys, the Dukes and Duchesses all hogging the scene. Racing's Who's Who read like *Burke's Peerage*. Most were very rich and were in racing not for anything as vulgar as profit. This was for the sport, the tradition of the turf, the frisson of victory. It was a concept that tended to make it all rather amateurish but jolly good fun. As a rule these owners paid little attention to finance in the running of their studs and racing stables, rarely selling any of their stock on a commercial basis. What they bred, they raced. The general school of thought seemed to follow the old racing maxim itself of breeding the best with the best and hoping for the best. If a Classic winner came along, well, that was fine. If not there was always next year's crop about which to get optimistic.

Sir Victor Sassoon was the most successful British owner in the 1950s following on from the Aga Khan (the present Aga's grandfather), who had dominated the British turf in the three previous decades, amassing seventeen Classic successes and becoming leading owner for the thirteenth time by the end of the 1952 season. Sir Victor, a Cambridge-educated member of a wealthy banking family, had entered racing in the early 1920s, spending huge sums of money to establish himself on a par with the Aga. At one time he also had over a hundred horses in training in India and was a keen supporter of racing in his home country, importing European mares in an effort to raise the standard of the sport there. He won the Epsom Derby four times: Pinza (1953), Crepello (1957), Hard Ridden (1958) and St Paddy (1960). He also won the 1,000 Guineas twice, and the other three Classics once.

With four studs, two in Newmarket, one in Yorkshire and one in Ireland, Sir Victor's outgoings were reckoned to be in the region of £200,000 a year at the height of his success. Sangster had studied the Sassoon operation and had concluded that here was a man who could have commercialised the business. Too often, Sir Victor had refused good offers from abroad for his stallions, reasoning that the money did not matter. He was philanthropic in his outlook, preserving the best of his blood-lines for the British market, turning down those self-generating cashflow offers, and even allowing concessions on some stallion fees to home breeders who could not afford them. Sir Victor's efforts were commendable, of course, but they did not even earn him election to the Jockey Club.

By the time Sangster had taken the first step of launching

Swettenham Stud, British racing was ripe for change. The country itself had changed; Empire Day was no longer to be found on the school calendar and post-imperialist Britain brought with it a greater social awareness. It heralded things like death duties; no longer could the rich spend willy-nilly on their favourite pastime. The political climate was such that a great degree of belt-tightening lay on the horizon. A new businesslike atmosphere was about to prevail. Of course, British racing like its ruling body the Jockey Club is slow to change. There would be no overnight waving of a magic wand and many people within what was about to become a commercialised industry no doubt hankered after the good old days and buried their heads in the sand hoping the new wave would exhaust itself.

The first man at this time to recognise the need to run his racing interests as a business was David Robinson, the self-made head of the television and radio rentals company DER, whose outlets could be seen on every high street in Britain. The Robinson approach particularly interested Sangster because here was a man who understood the principles of business and commerce and was applying them to horseracing.

Robinson started in racing in 1946 when he was forty and over the next two decades expanded his string so that it numbered close on 160 by the early 1970s. Although he switched trainers quite regularly he finally settled for employing Michael Jarvis and Paul Davey on a salaried basis as his private trainers based at Newmarket. Often appearing severe and unsmiling – and certainly no friend of the Establishment – Robinson was extremely careful where the money went. Indeed, as we shall see a little later, perhaps even Sangster with all his subsequent international success should have applied a little of the Robinson logic when it came to counting the pennies over a particular venture that went disastrously way over budget.

The Robinson trainers were responsible for strict spending on feed and other training overheads. Once a week Robinson would chair a meeting at which his horses' future race entries were decided, based on his own grading system of the horses' merits. If he considered that any of his trainers were wasting money by making frivolous entries for any of the horses then the trainer was told in no uncertain terms to get his finger out.

'He ran a very tight ship,' says Michael Jarvis today. 'I often think that there are still many trainers around who have never caught up with his business methods as he applied them to racing.'

These days Northern trainers complain when a million-dollar Maktoum horse is sent up from Newmarket to contest a humble Beverley or Pontefract maiden, thereby 'robbing' them of their bread and butter. But they have the business logic of David Robinson to blame. He was never too proud to send a five-figure horse up North, for every opportunity was taken to see that they paid their way.

Where Sangster noted that he differed from Robinson was in bloodstock breeding. Sangster had a vision of changing the face of the old breeding tradition, the very purpose for which he had bought Swettenham. At this stage of what was to become a new career, he did not exactly know how. He simply knew that a Derby winner bred to an Oaks winner never guarantees to produce another of the same – very often simply a three-mile plodder.

Robinson, on the other hand, shunned breeding, preferring to have his horses bought at the sales, this being done by a group headed by Lord Harrington, from whom Robinson had bought Newmarket's Clarehaven Stables. The team was dubbed the Robinson Rangers – twenty years on Sangster's team would be called, rather unkindly but more in mischievous fun, Sangster's Gangsters.

Although Robinson was astute in his buying and won many good races, he only ever had one English Classic success, Our Babu, who won the 2,000 Guineas in 1955. If there was one salient feature of the Robinson formula that attracted Sangster most (and probably accounted for the paucity of Classic winners) then it was the preoccupation with speed rather than stamina. Robinson's Rangers had, therefore, sought out sprinting blood and turned up other top horses like So Blessed, Deep Diver and Green God who, between them, accounted for almost every major sprint in the racing calendar.

It was Green God, the winner of Sangster's own race, the Vernons Sprint Cup at Haydock in 1971, and Deep Diver who were responsible for the eventual famous Sangster partnership with Irishman John Magnier and, subsequently, his father-in-law, Vincent O'Brien, an association that would lead to Sangster becoming the first number-one world player in racing and bloodstock. Magnier, one of three sons, had taken over the running of the Grange Stud near Fermoy, County Cork, following the death of his father and in 1971 set up, with partners, the neighbouring Castle Hyde Stud. Sangster had met Magnier while racing and found that, through bloodstock, they had several interests in common. They were both young men anxious to expand and succeed in what could be a tough, competitive and rather closed-shop world. To send a mare to a top stallion was not simply a case of picking up the telephone and booking her in to the stud where the stallion was standing. Very often the stallion would be fully booked, the patrons of long standing getting first call. Nor was it that easy to bid at the English and Irish sales without meeting stiff opposition from the well-ensconced traditional buyers. Even though Sangster had raced with a certain amount of success, his recent founding of Swettenham meant that to many breeders he was still something of a newcomer whose intentions, while sincere, were viewed with a certain amount of suspicion.

Magnier was a regular visitor to Swettenham when on his trips over to England. Together they would inspect Sangster's mares and the pair would keenly discuss their futures along with that of their horses and of the likely trends in bloodstock. It was now that the seeds of the Sangster revolution were being sown. Sangster, of course, already had a share in Be Friendly with BBC Television commentator Peter O'Sullevan, and he was on the lookout to further his interest in one or two stallions. So with Magnier he entered into a partnership to buy both Green God and, a year later, Deep Diver, the latter costing £400,000, which gave David Robinson a healthy return on his inital 8,400 guinea investment. Not all the outlay was Sangster's, nor would he have wanted it to be. Even at this stage, he knew that partnerships helped spread the risk. It was the only sensible way to deal in bloodstock and this would become a major feature of all his later international deals, whether on horses for racing or at stud. Shares in Deep Diver were also held by the other Castle Hyde partners as well as Joseph McGrath, middle son of the late Irish politician and stud owner who had co-founded the Irish Hospitals' Sweepstake lottery. A couple of years later, Sangster and Magnier would cement their relationship even further by becoming involved in a deal to stand the Sir Michael Sobell-owned Sun Prince at Castle Hyde in a £650,000 syndication.

Sangster's ambition, naturally, was to win as many Classics as possible, preferably with his home-bred stock. To do this was a simple concept; breeding the speed with the stamina in the right Classic proportion on the male and distaff side. Achieving it in practice was like looking for the proverbial needle in a haystack.

The speed was the key. But it would take a few more years yet before Sangster found the right combination to unlock the door to a worldwide multi-million-dollar fortune.

FIVE

A Punter's Paradise

Sangster's even temperament allied to his naturally reticent disposition is sometimes taken for impassivity. But he is not impassive. The successes and defeats of the racing game do affect him deeply, not visibly perhaps because only on rare occasions has there been an outburst of emotion. His is the quiet style, of measured tones and deliberation, reasoning with a certain philosophical acceptance that after victory there is often defeat. Of course he would always take precautions to attempt to eradicate the reverses – 'plus factors to minimise the downside risk' – which prompted keen-edged consideration of many factors to ensure that defeat was never going to be an easily acquired frippery. He did this by maintaining a professionalism at every stage of the battle. Later in his career this approach would intensify as if by a fine honing of his experiences coupled with a personal policy of choosing the best person for the job at any given time (continuing his 'life is all about timing' rationale). This policy would apply to his trainers, jockeys, bloodstock men, even fellow owners of his future worldwide syndicates.

It was this understanding nature, a tolerance for the sometimes unavoidable downfalls of a sport which can be kind one minute and deadly cruel the next, that made him the ideal owner for whom to train or ride. He accepted defeat graciously and was a sporting winner – a fact endorsed by many of the jockeys who have ridden for him. Sometimes there would be an added edge to those defeats, too, knowing that he had just seen a major punt go astray. But in this era, when still having most of his string in training with Eric Cousins, there were some mighty touches landed, too.

As with many people in racing, Sangster loved a bet. Planning a tilt at the bookies was exciting. It was a welcome relief from the hectic life of business. Some people might bet once a year on the Grand National but would not dream of risking so much as a fiver on a horse at any other time. For owners like Sangster, pulling off a coup was simply for the crack. Of course, it was not for the money – it rarely is. Backing a horse, whether by pin, hours of form-book study or obtaining inside information of one sort or another, is all about man or woman putting their judgement on the line. Gambling is a test of skill and a test of character, for a brief moment the loaning of one's heart to the uncontrollable. Some people have the nerve for the game, others do not want to put themselves to the test. For Sangster it was fun, too. It went with the champagne, the haute cuisine, the racing high life, the good horses, the glamour. When he and Cousins got together to plunder the bookies it was Sangster the 'free spirit' at work, unrestrained by the disciplined rigours of a careful and sometimes stuffy life at Vernons.

Chester and Haydock were among Sangster's favourite tracks in these days (he would become a steward at both in the near future). At both courses he placed his bets on the rails as opposed to the ring and did a lot of his betting with an old-school bookmaker called Joe Kennedy from Wigan. Kennedy was in his seventies then, a gentleman who would take his clients on trust, a cigarette forever in the mouth even when discussing business, repeating the bet in whispers from the corner of his mouth, fag ash everywhere. He always had a homburg hat perched over his grey hair, and wore a smart tailored overcoat with its five or six buttons religiously fastened. In those early days Sangster had a reputation as quite a fearless gambler.

But it was the ante-post gambles he liked best, because there was so much planning involved, many heart-stopping moments just to get the horse to the track injury-free and fit enough to run for its life – especially with suitable ground for the horse (thousands of such gambles go astray every season because of the vagaries of Britain's weather and many ante-post punters constantly find themselves attempting to be weather forecaster). In Sangster's early career he landed several good bets on Audrey Joan, who he eventually bought as his foundation broodmare, one of which was the filly's win in the Portland at Doncaster at long odds.

A further glorious Sangster touch in this late-sixties era was with another sprinter, Brief Star. The scene of this lucrative gamble was the Ayr Gold Cup at the Scottish track's Western Meeting in late September. Sangster loved to get away from Liverpool and spend a couple of days with Christine – herself, by now, a keen racegoer – usually staying at the Royal Turnberry Hotel at the world-famous golf course. There, with a suite of rooms, Sangster liked nothing better than to entertain his friends in racing, ferrying them to the course in his Rolls-Royce, and back for a gourmet dinner to celebrate success or talk about what might have been over several bottles of a Grand Cru and a glass or two of a decent port.

The three-year-old Brief Star had been laid low with a virus for most of the summer, evident from her fitful bouts of coughing and runny nose. Come the autumn, however, she was beginning to come to herself and she was duly entered for the Portland at Doncaster. Sangster knew that if she ran a reasonable race at Town Moor her odds would be slashed for the Ayr Gold Cup. So he backed her before the Portland at 33–1. Not content with backing her in a single bet, he coupled her with a colt he fancied for the St Leger, the fifth and final Classic of the season, run at Doncaster a week earlier. This horse was Intermezzo, bred by its owner, Gerry Oldham, and ridden by Australian Ron Hutchinson for trainer Harry Wragg. The Sangster luck was running high, for Intermezzo duly won the St Leger at 7–1, proving too strong for the favourite Ribofilio, on whom Lester Piggott was generally considered not to have ridden one of his best races, leaving the horse with too much to do. Sangster now had a substantial amount piled on Brief Star, who had bottom weight of seven stone (7–7 is the minimum these days because even lightweight jockeys are better nourished!).

On the eve of the Ayr Gold Cup, Sangster hosted dinner at Turnberry. Although he was in good spirits and the wine flowed freely, he had a nagging worry about his bet coming up. This was because Cousins had another runner in the race called Salan, who was to be ridden by an apprentice. During the meal, Sangster turned to Cousins and said: 'Don't run Salan. Take him out, because I think he will win. In my book he is the only danger to Brief Star.'

But Cousins owed it to Salan's connections to run the horse and Sangster knew his trainer could not be seriously persuaded to take the horse out of the race. He was merely emphasising what he knew to be the danger. Instead he decided to have a saver on Salan.

The race turned out to be one of those times when Sangster had the form almost right. Brief Star won and Salan was second.

To a great extent the fact that Sangster enjoyed a punt and would bet big if he considered the opportunity was right reflected a side of his personality that was necessary if he was to embark on a massive restructuring of the world's horseracing industry. Here he possessed a certain amount of daring, was willing to assess and take risks when he could simply have sat back comfortably, settling for a predictable life in the well-ordered routine of Vernons.

Perhaps, too, he was being guided subconsciously deeper into a sport that was both glamorous and exciting, somewhat the antithesis of a business built on the cloth-capped working men's club image of football (even if he did own the company). Boss of a football pool was hardly comparable on a social level with that of a top racehorse owner–breeder. Racing was inherently more socially acceptable for a start. Film stars, pop stars, models, politicians and celebrities had played very little part in Sangster's life through his connection with the 2/6d weekly flutter of Mr and Mrs Joe Soap on a sport that was rapidly developing a loutish beer-swilling following. But, through racing, the 'beautiful people' would eventually become integral members of the Sangster team on an international high-society merry-go-round of parties, jaunts and high jinxs.

Sangster wasted no time in aiming for the top races in these early days. The setting up of Swettenham Stud was his first serious foray into bloodstock – though this was still on a modest scale compared to what he would later achieve – while on the racecourse his aspirations became manifest in the same year when he had his first runner in an English Classic despite still owning only a handful of racehorses. This was a grey colt called Hang On who was unbeaten at Nottingham and Haydock as a two-year-old and whom Sangster wanted to run in the Derby of 1967. The colt was not up to the class it takes to win what is still regarded as the most prestigious race in the world (though rated only sixteenth in terms of prize money). Nevertheless, Hang On finished ninth to Royal Palace.

It would be another six years before Sangster would be associated with some sort of Classic success, however. This was when Shellshock ran third in the 1,000 Guineas of 1973 in the colours of Nick Robinson, his friend from the early Liverpool days. Robinson was now a business associate, too, for he had become chairman of the Newmarket Bloodstock Agency, which Sangster had purchased, while he would later become publisher of the British-based international racing and breeding magazine, *Pacemaker*, another horseracing enterprise that attracted Sangster money. It was a particularly pleasing result for Sangster because Shellshock was home-bred, a chestnut by Salvo, the 1967 King George VI and Queen Elizabeth Stakes and Prix de l'Arc de Triomphe runner-up and himself a rare advertisement for internationalism, being bred in the USA by a French-bred stallion out of an Italian-bred mare (and owned by Intermezzo's owner, Gerry Oldham). The dam was Priddy Maid, one of the Swettenham foundation mares.

By this time in the early 1970s, Sangster had become a leading Northern owner, still with most of his horses in training with Eric Cousins. He had gained his first Royal Ascot win (the

National Stakes with Cade's County), and, in three consecutive years, had seen Swettenham Stud become established as a top vendor of foals at the Newmarket December sales – a position it would occupy several more times in the next few years as well as becoming the fifth-largest privately owned stud in the country. Already a steward of the British Boxing Board of Control, he was now appointed a director of Haydock Park racecourse, where he was a great supporter of racing (and where he had 'cleaned up' by winning five consecutive races at the last two meetings).

Soon, he and John Magnier would own their first horse with Vincent O'Brien, the four-year-old Royal Ascot winner Boone's Cabin, and this would be the first step in the partnership that would revolutionise racing on a scale of such mammoth proportions that it would leave people gasping at the sheer size of the operation – a lot of them gasping with envy because they could not get into one of the Sangster syndicates.

To many people at this time, Robert Sangster had it made. He appeared a happy family man with a lovely wife and now three children (Adam was born in 1969). He had the backing of a solid business in Vernons which would be his entirely when he was forty in a few years' time. And he could look forward to continued success in what had started as a hobby but which had now become an extension of his commercial activities.

There were faint cracks in the façade, however. Maybe now only hairline, but, as if on the foreleg cannon-bone of one of his own racehorses, enough for a certain anxiety. Christine's approach was realistic – in a way, cautious. Excited as her husband was about the future, she felt he should still keep his feet on the ground. It was important to her, and for the sake of their children, that he did not get carried away by the opportunities on the horizon which, if he was not careful, could end up changing his whole life.

Christine's worries, maybe the manifestation of a good woman's intuition, were going to be proved right. Sangster, headstrong, was going to set out on a course that would not only change the face of a major international industry, but would end up with his own personal world in turmoil.

And it all began with a visit to Australia.

SIX

Turning Point

A business trip to Australia to set up an extension of the Vernons Pools business began a course of events that would change Robert Sangster's life in the most dramatic fashion. With Vernons' joint managing director, George Kennerley, Sangster had paid his first visit to Australia in 1972. Now, two years later, the pair were back again to put the finishing touches to a deal to implement the soccer pool in the state of Victoria.

The deal was a good one for Vernons, won in stiff competition from the two other leading British pools firms, and was the result of a two-year slog by Kennerley and his Australian staff, who visited each state premier, holding numerous meetings with state officials, finally presenting a scheme which both parties found satisfactory. It gave Vernons a 3 per cent management fee of the pool, which operated in all five states but which was initially run from Victoria. From the state's viewpoint it was another gambling way of raising money in a country used to such schemes – lotteries then being the principal source of state revenue simply because taxpayers' money went to the national Government. The scheme would give the Victoria State Government in Melbourne a 30 per cent take, of which a third would go to the mentally handicapped and the rest devoted to sporting facilities.

Sangster could not pass over the opportunity to catch up with developments in the country's racing and breeding industry while he was there. Having recently been elected to the Jockey Club, racing's ruling body, he was able to avail himself of the right introductions. Consequently he packed in as much as his stay would allow, going racing, conferring with owners, trainers and fellow breeders, and visiting several of the leading studs, where he studiously compared their methods with his own operation at Swettenham and the many top studs in Ireland of which he had an intimate knowledge.

The more he learned of the whole structure of Australian horseracing, the more impressed and excited he became about playing a part in its future growth. For here in this wonderful land of clean air and sunshine was a veritable jewel, one that had seemingly lain undiscovered by the rest of racing. It was incredible, a paradox. Because of the insularity that was the scourge of practically every country in the racing world, including even Australia itself, this new land had quietly got on with the task of developing a strong, vibrant, healthy industry that few people elsewhere seemed to know about. Horseracing was practically Australia's national sport, yet little had been done since the days of the mighty Phar Lap to promote it to the outside world. But, with their prize money so strong at home, who could blame them?

When he got back to England, Sangster enthused about the high levels of prize money, the environment so conducive to the rearing of young stock, and the Australian system of betting with bookmakers who were allowed to operate only on course – the type of layers who were not likely to flinch at a decent five-figure bet (more the kind to lay 5–2 to such a bet, then chalk up 11–4 before they handed over the ticket). He thought the TAB (the Totaliser Agency Board), which was responsible for handling both on-course and the sole off-course betting outlets, a superb idea because more money went back into racing than into the private coffers of Britain's bookies (by now, Vernons had disposed of their credit betting division because of high taxation and the introduction by the Wilson Government of selective employment tax).

Sangster's overriding impression of Australia was that here was a country of immense opportunity. Just how he would grasp this, however, would take a little time to develop, for, at home, he had several more pressing matters to resolve. There is no doubt, however, that it was this vision of Australia that opened Sangster's eyes to the possibility of becoming a world player in a highly lucrative market.

Uppermost in Sangster's mind at this time was his situation at Vernons. As a consequence of his coming to own two-thirds of the company, he was owing his banks something in the region of £5 million for capital gains tax on the Vernons shares. By the time he came into the final tranche on his fortieth birthday in two years' time, his debt would have risen to more than £8 million. As a way of mitigating this liability, he had examined the possibility of floating Vernons on the Stock Exchange, finally managing to persuade his father, who was still the major force in the company, that if Vernons could go public it would be in everyone's interests.

With his merchant bankers, Hill Samuel, plans had been set in motion to float the company in February 1974. But other forces, quite insuperable, were already conspiring against him. The country, under the Government of Edward Heath, was in turmoil, mostly because the Prime Minister was in the middle of his second miners' strike in two years. It was the period of the three-day week: industry on reduced output and households throughout Britain in the Russian-roulette grip of electricity blackouts as the power stations tried to preserve dwindling coal stocks. Ultimately, Heath declared his 'Who Governs Britain?' General Election – set for the very day Vernons was to go public. There was no way the flotation could go ahead. Vernons was a politically sensitive industry, especially susceptible to the taxation whims of a Labour Government should Heath be defeated. So the whole operation was cancelled. It was a body blow to Sangster because the flotation, to some degree, would have meant he could have had his cake and eaten it. Going public and selling off perhaps a third of his shareholding would have put him in a far healthier financial position than he now found himself in.

Now he faced two choices; he could try to join up with another company in a reverse takeover which would leave him in a similar position of being able to pay off his capital gains liabilities and still hold a major shareholding in any new set-up, or he could lessen his tax bill by leaving the country and becoming a tax exile.

There might have been a third alternative to contemplate in that he could have sold the company, paid off his debts and still had many millions left to embark on his world plan for the transformation of breeding and racing. Such an idea, however, even if Sangster had loosely considered it, would have been totally impossible. His father, who was still chairman, would not have entertained the idea. And Vernon's dominance over his son and the company was all-pervading, his unwritten word a holy writ.

In fact, while his father was alive, there was no way Sangster could sell the company whether Vernon was chairman or not – simply because it would have broken his father's heart.

So Sangster was forced to look at the former option and sound out the feasibility of a marriage with another suitable partner. His efforts to do this during the ensuing months were going to lead to a double irony that would affect the rest of his life.

With his London bankers, advisers from Hill Samuel and his own relevant Vernons personnel, Sangster spent the best part of the next year visiting the City with his shopping list of suitable companies to whom Vernons could propose. So began a hectic, though sometimes laborious, round of boardroom meeting after meeting with interested parties. He saw Gordon White at Hanson Trust (now Lord White, one of whose companies, Ever Ready, today sponsors the Derby). He had talks with the Rank Organisation and the Sears Group, who then owned William Hill. Finally, most interest was expressed by two other of Britain's Big Four bookmakers, Corals and Ladbroke.

Towards the end of the year the rumours of a possible takeover of Vernons were confirmed when Corals' publicly revealed their interest, and the name of Cyril Stein of Ladbroke was linked to a possible deal. Stein desperately wanted to get his hands on Vernons, which he saw as the perfect complement to the existing betting division of his company. The former bookmaker's clerk certainly had the Midas touch in business – quite the opposite to his own betting habits, which have lost him a small fortune. From a single Mayfair credit betting office, where clerks sat on high stools in private telephone booths recording bets from their blue-blooded upper-crust punters, Stein had fashioned a thriving and widely diversified group: a national chain of betting shops, property, casinos, bingo halls and hotels, all contributing to the company's 1974 record profits of £10 million on a turnover of £250 million.

Indeed, by March 1975, it was Stein and Ladbroke who emerged as favourites to clinch the deal. While lawyers from both sides were drawing all the strands together, and Stein awaited a report from accountants Price Waterhouse, Sangster announced that agreement in principle had been reached. It was an attractive deal, worth more than £17 million to Vernons; the company was to receive £5 million cash on completion, plus another £2 million in twelve months, while a further £7 million would be payable within two years once several Vernons subsidiaries had been sold. In addition, Sangster would become a major shareholder in Ladbroke with shares valued at £3 million plus an option to buy a further 300,000 shares (by purchasing warrants at 171p). Sangster would also stay on at Vernons, as would other management personnel, and become a Labroke board member.

Within a few weeks, however, the deal was off, rejected by Vernon Sangster, who, after all, could not bear to 'part' with the company he had founded.

Stein was disappointed, to say the least, but vowed to make Vernons his own one day. Sangster, on the other hand, now had only one route to take. That was out of the country to escape the taxman.

The irony here is that it was this forced exit from Britain that would lead to Sangster growing away from Vernons, growing away from Christine, and developing his full commitment to horseracing. And some twelve years later, as we shall see, Cyril

Stein would play a fascinating game of cat and mouse – and end up owning Vernons despite Robert Sangster's wishes.

Sangster chose the rather predictable Spanish resort of Marbella as the place to make the family home for the next year. It was the 'in' place if you were living in Spain, frequented by the glitterati, the villains and the package-tour Brits who loved to goggle at the Rolls-Royces and Ferraris lined along the quayside, hoping to match the cars to the white-hulled yachts and motor cruisers bobbing at their moorings. There were two things Sangster found he could do here; he could play a lot of golf (Sean Connery was a regular partner), and he could think.

Reflecting on the failed reverse takeover, Sangster was naturally disappointed that the deal with Ladbroke had not gone through. But he had to respect his father's wishes and he was not the sort of man to dwell on such events. After all, it was his duty.

Later, at the height of his horsepower, he would look back thankfully at his father's decision. For it was this fateful moment that finally persuaded him to devote his energies to racing rather than to what he would term as 'slogging away at Vernons'.

A recent trip to Australia, which he had snatched just before the negotiations with Ladbroke fell through, saw him attending the Easter Carnival at Sydney. His visit this time had made him more determined than ever to become involved in this racing industry he found so refreshing. Now, in Marbella, away from the daily involvement of Vernons, he could take a step back and survey his whole racing and breeding portfolio in a much more objective manner.

He came to the conclusion that this should be the time when he expanded his interests rapidly. He therefore decided he would become an internationalist.

His close association with John Magnier pleased him immensely because in Vincent O'Brien's son-in-law (Magnier had married Susan O'Brien) he had not only a friend, but someone he considered to be one of the world's best young brains within the breeding industry, someone who knew his job extremely well and who had some of the best contacts in the business. As it would turn out, Magnier proved to be a very clever businessman, too.

Magnier was twenty-four when he and Sangster formulated their plan to change the traditional face of bloodstock breeding. The tall, confident Magnier has proved to be a formidable opponent during negotiations on behalf of the syndicate. Rumours that he already had his future well assured owing to the inheritance of the family farm and stud are well wide of the mark. Grange needed much work doing to it before he could contemplate breeding racehorses there on all but a modest scale – and the financial state of the operation had seen better days.

But Magnier has proved to possess a certain flair for the stallion business. Associates say he would have made a success of his working life in whichever field he had chosen to operate, although others are of the opinion that he made the right decision in sticking to horses. A less ambitious man might have been content with the life of a dairy farmer on the farm where he had worked since leaving school. But Magnier saw the potential of thoroughbred breeding and set his sights on developing a stud of international repute. And, with Sangster, he saw reality in the 'American dream' of producing their own stallions.

Along the way to realising his ambition, Magnier has been a keen promoter of Irish bloodstock in general as well as its uniquely talented workforce, always willing to speak or take action to support the home industry. Magnier, though, is little known outside racing circles, which is a situation that he prefers. A father of five, he enjoys a quiet lifestyle and travels abroad only out of necessity. He was the perfect fit in the Sangster–O'Brien triangle, though. He was willing to let Sangster maintain the high profile and the extensive travel, while staying at home to develop what has become a massive business, all the time learning from the wisdom and experience of his father-in-law.

Often it seemed that Magnier was an old head on young

shoulders, someone who had the enthusiastic ambition of youth, yet was capable of a considered judgement that belied his years. At the age of forty he was made a senator of the Irish Government by the horserace-loving Charles Haughey, who was then Taoiseach (Prime Minister). He was also a vociferous member of the Irish Racing Board, so was now able to press the case for more government support for the industry that is second only to tourism in Ireland.

Magnier, like his partners, is not averse to a punt, and has been known to put his cash down in a round of golf (which he plays off a handicap of 17) especially when playing with the renowned Irish punter, J. P. McManus.

So close have Magnier and Sangster become over the years that Magnier has been appointed guardian of Sangster's two youngest children.

In 1973, the two men had visited Keeneland Sales in Kentucky with the aim of together buying a yearling colt which they could race – as they did subsequently with Boone's Cabin – and which would have the potential to make up into a stallion that they could stand with the likes of their Deep Diver, Green God and Sun Prince. But the exercise proved a pretty disastrous one because they had set their sights on a particular son of the then top stallion Bold Ruler (who shared the same grandsire as Northern Dancer in Nearco, a brilliant unbeaten Italian-bred horse, sold for £60,000, to stud in 1938).

In an effort to blow out the opposition, Sangster and Magnier opened up the sale with an incredible $500,000 bid – just $10,000 short of the world-record yearling price of the time. It was an incredible piece of effrontery from these two newcomers before this hallowed audience of high rollers. In that one fleeting moment, however, the pair were signalling their arrival on the world stage. People had better take notice. This guy Sangster meant business.

The bid was a gamble that failed, however, and they could only flinch inwardly as a Lexington bloodstock agent, Jim

Scully, clinched the colt with another $100,000 bid on behalf of a syndicate headed by Japan's most prominent owner–breeder, Zenya Yoshida, thereby creating a new world record from the two-bid sale. The horse in question was subsequently named Wajima after a famous Sumo wrestler. It seemed that Sangster's luck was not yet running because Wajima became US champion three-year-old and was eventually retired to stud with a value of $7.2 million. Sangster had now been blown out himself. But he would be back – he was determined about that.

When Sangster left his Marbella base to attend the Keeneland Sales two years later, the partnership with Magnier and O'Brien that was to become so powerful had been established. Vincent O'Brien, small in stature, big in reputation, was literally a living legend. His eyes, a crystal blue exaggerated by the ruddy, cherubic features of his face, sparkled whenever he spotted a horse he liked, the gaze intent, hypnotic. His Ballydoyle establishment is a world-class training centre, the result of O'Brien's lifetime of dedication to the racehorse. But the Irishman's career has not simply been one fashioned out of enthusiasm, hard work, even skill. Those attributes abound in plenty in people who have never reached the heights of O'Brien. The make-up of the man has been aided by that vital ingredient of subliminal genius, the sixth sense which is bestowed on people who achieve greatness.

As conservative as he appears, the man is renowned for his fearless betting coups, never shirking the challenge not only to win the race, but to support his judgement with hard cash as he has done since his early days, building the nest-egg, developing the stables, working ceaselessly towards the goal he had set himself as a young man – simply to be the best at what he was best doing. The sixth son of a County Cork farmer, Dan O'Brien, Vincent was one of three boys and a girl by Dan O'Brien's second marriage. His father's first wife died giving birth to her fifth child at the age of thirty-six, as was 'God's way' in those dark days of 1914.

Dan O'Brien road to hounds in the Churchtown area of County Cork that was famous for horses. It was a natural progression of Vincent's upbringing and environment to join the local hunt. Dan O'Brien trained horses, too, and Vincent rode for his father as an amateur in point-to-points and then in National Hunt races. Although it was not a poor family, O'Brien, like his two brothers Dermot and Phonsie, was expected to pull his weight, being brought up with the ethic that nobody earns anything without grafting for it.

O'Brien's nerve (and verve) for gambling started early. This was in an era when, like many trainers, a couple of decent winning bets a season were necessary in order to survive. He dabbled with a few greyhounds, selling one for £4 and putting the lot on a horse he had trained himself which came in at 10–1. At the age of twenty-seven, in 1944, he picked up £1,000 when he landed a double by saddling Drybob to dead heat in the Irish Cambridgeshire and Good Days to win the Irish Cesarewitch. O'Brien the punter and the trainer had arrived.

Then came those National Hunt golden years of the late 40s and early 50s; four Cheltenham Gold Cups (three with the same horse, Cottage Rake), three Grand Nationals, three Champion Hurdles, as well as many other races at the Cheltenham Festival.

His credentials on the Flat were even more impressive. When he agreed to join up with Sangster, O'Brien had trained the winners of twelve Classics in Britain alone; four Epsom Derbys, three St Legers, two 2,000 guineas, two Oaks and one 1,000 Guineas.

With the young brains of Magnier and the wealth of experience that O'Brien had accumulated at the highest class in his distinguished career, Sangster felt he had the perfect partners to literally take on the world.

The master plan of Sangster and Magnier's now was to buy yearlings which the new partner, O'Brien, could help turn into decent racehorses and which possessed the pedigree to make a potential stallion – as had proved the case with Wajima. To a great degree this was a bucking of the trend, brought about by the intense competition Sangster and Magnier had encountered for truly fashionable potential stallion stock at home in Britain and Ireland, as shown by the prices they had had to pay for Deep Diver and the others.

The chances of a colt, perhaps exemplary as a racehorse, becoming a top stallion are about as imponderable as those of a good-looking, well-bred yearling becoming a top racehorse. Many a macho racehorse has proved a disaster at stud simply because he has turned out to be infertile. Even those young stallions seemingly with everything going for them might produce useless stock.

But this new partnership would be looking for potential stallions, for no stallion can prove himself through his progeny for at least three years – when his stock are running as two-year-olds. By then, the stallion is revalued up or down, his stud fees increased or lowered.

If a colt possessed the right ingredients of pedigree and racecourse performance then, simply as a potential stallion, the Sangster partnership would hold a very valuable asset to the business. Before the horse ever proved himself at the stud, Sangster and his two partners could have cashed in well by selling off as many of the forty shares (the standard stallion syndication apportionment) as they desired. There would be no shortage of breeders and bloodstock players anxious to snap up a share of the latest racecourse rage before he was packed off to stud – such is the glorious uncertainty, not only of racing, but of breeding too.

The canny O'Brien had recommended they should switch tack and try for the yearling sons of Northern Dancer. It was hardly surprising O'Brien should pursue this direction, for it followed the success he had gained with Nijinsky, another son of Northern Dancer, with whom he had won the Classic triple crown of the 2,000 Guineas, Derby and St Leger five years earlier.

Sangster and Magnier had envisioned that the key to future growth of their new business lay in the syndication of the yearlings they were going to buy. No one in Britain had previously syndicated horses to any large degree – certainly not racehorses. It was a common feature of breeding, of course, with colts traditionally being syndicated in that forty-share apportionment when they went to stud – a $4 million stallion therefore selling at $100,000 a share, with each shareholder then holding the right to send his mare to that stallion, a right which he could sell. As a general rule of thumb, investors in a stallion could expect to start making money after four years, providing all went well.

Sangster had sought his father's permission when he borrowed money to set up Swettenham Stud and, even though this venture had shown something approaching an £800,000 deficit in its first year, it was now proving profitable. So once more he had outlined his plans to Vernon, explaining that, even after his time out in Marbella, his involvement with Vernons would be on a much reduced level – perhaps only 10 per cent of his time in future. Sangster also wanted to borrow money to finance this new expansion and found it rather tough going trying to convince his financial advisers that his international vision was a viable proposition. He succeeded in raising something like $2 million for this initial assault on Keeneland but, at the same time, bankers thought it all a rather odd business – horses! My God, the risk!

It could be said that this new partnership comprised Sangster's cash and Magnier's and O'Brien's skills. Sangster was learning all the time, of course, but even he had to bow to the superior knowledge of his two partners, certainly someone like Vincent, who was then fifty-nine, and whose experience was priceless.

The partnership was duly established on a basis of 40 per cent to Sangster, 20 per cent to Magnier and 10 per cent to O'Brien. All were in agreement that the remaining 30 per cent of the yearlings they purchased should be spread among a clientele selected from an international set of owners wealthy enough to play the game at this top-class level. The safeguard in the syndicate's composition was that Sangster had overall control.

And he would ensure that disposal of the 30 per cent 'free float' was on such a basis that the founders would always retain control over any of the horses they owned.

At the same time, another scheme was under way to produce what it was hoped would become the most powerful group of stud farms in Ireland. This was the amalgamation of Magnier's Grange and Castle Hyde studs with that of the Coolmore Stud, near O'Brien's training centre at Cashel, Tipperary, which was then owned by Tim Vigors, and in which O'Brien had an interest. The group would be known as the Coolmore, Castle Hyde and Associated Stud Farms, incorporating several other smaller studs such as the nearby Longfield stud and, near to Castle Hyde in Fermoy, the Dunmahon and the Beeches studs. Magnier became managing director of the new company while Sangster's cash bought him a 32 per cent holding. Such an operation was required, of course, to house their future stallions.

The Coolmore group has grown into a huge commercial conglomeration of studs in the south of Ireland, under the general managership of Bob Lanigan; there is Coolmore itself, Castle Hyde, Grange, Sandville, Beeches, Longfield, Thomastown Castle, Lyonstown, plus its holdings in two Kentucky studs and interests in Australia. A visitor to the main Coolmore Stud three miles north of Fethard, County Tipperary, is likely to be struck by the admistration block, an efficient modern office complex, computers abounding, a virtual green-field site as if housing some high-tec industry. It could be a planning company, a design office or a firm of financial consultants (it is probably a mixture of all three), the silence broken only by the sounds of keyboards and computer printers, hardly discernible above the low whirr of the air conditioning, which occasionally sends wafts of cool air to sway the leaves of the potted plants dotted about the office in large tubs.

Outside, the Coolmore fields stretch for as far as the eye can see, mile upon mile of picture-book lush green paddocks, pristine post and rail. Then there are the buildings, large American barns, where all the boxes are housed under one roof, traditional yards with names like Walsh's, King's Lake, the blue doors and pitched roofs of the stallion boxes, which look like a row of pretty dolls' houses set around a manicured lawn and rose garden. The place exudes class, a certain expensive exclusivity that is reflected, like a prestigious hotel, in the price the customer has to pay for the product.

The likes of Magnier and Lanigan brought a new meaning to stallion promotion. It was a pretty dour product before they came along. They gave it a high-gloss definition, transformed the art of advertising and marketing, introduced promotional videos, slick brochures, impact colour advertising. Coolmore might be in the middle of nowhere run by country folk, but the sales material is out of the top drawer of any capital city. It was as if Magnier, having blown away the cobwebs of Grange's old dairy sheds, banished any thoughts, too, of the traditional way of promoting bloodstock – the sort of 'If they're interested let them find us' type of attitude. This Coolmore operation is up-front, aggressive and totally commercial. It is about investment and returns, maximising the product. The most famous sire of National Hunt horses, Deep Run, was soon covering 150 mares, then 200, and at a high point covered 231 mares in one season. It became a highly profitable organisation and made the partners wealthy men. But Coolmore has had its critics, too. Not everyone within the racing and breeding industry was happy about the commerciality. As we shall see, the criticism came in the form of the familiar clash between traditionalists, conscious of horseracing's sporting heritage, and the progressives, who were running a business, trying to adapt to the increasing pressures of commercial reality.

There were several factors persuading Sangster that, in this new and exciting gamble, he was making all the right moves. Australia and America had opened his eyes to the fact that there was another world out there capable of being commercially exploited. The world itself was becoming a 'smaller' place due to the advent of Concorde and the improvement in flight times of subsonic aircraft. To the likes of Mr and Mrs Average, the most prohibitive factor of all travel is not the time it takes to fly anywhere in the world, it is the cost. To Sangster it is not the cost but the time. Thanks to Concorde he could now go racing in New York, hold several business meetings, and return – all in twenty-four hours.

There was also a new pattern to be set, a trend that, almost inevitably, embraced America and either its culture or its ideas. As post-war history has shown, Britain's unique relationship with the United States has led to a dominant influence – one way across the Atlantic. Sangster realised that if this was occurring in all aspects of life in Britain, as it was, then it would not be long in permeating through to the home of thoroughbred racing.

O'Brien himself had recognised the emerging influence of North American-bred sires on British bloodstock – Sir Ivor and Nijinsky, whom he had trained, were the living proof. But the odd trickle was nowhere near yet a flow. That great English tradition of snobbery had for years treated American stallions with a peculiar disdain – well, after all, they were *our* cast-offs in the first place, weren't they? These American stallions, refined through decades of 'speed' racing, were regarded as simply out of the English second and third division. Give or take a couple, we kept the best at home and let our 'colonial' cousins pay heaps for what we did not want. So how could they be any good?

From O'Brien's point of view the timing was right for this new venture. Even someone of his tremendous expertise needed the financial ammunition of a rich owner to launch an assault on the Americans in their own back yard of Keeneland. Charles Englehard, one of America's richest men, for whom O'Brien had trained the winners of six Classics, had died in 1971 at the age of fifty-four. No trainer can afford to lose his mainstay. Comfortably off as O'Brien was, a lot of the money he made – much of it from successful gambling – had gone into developing his Tipperary training base into one of the finest in the world. So he was at a stage in his life where he could have taken a back seat and begun preparing to hand over the reins of Ballydoyle to his elder son, David. Instead, he chose to 'kick on' with Sangster.

It was another Americanism, too, that would make O'Brien a rich man as a consequence of the Sangster connection. For, up until a couple of years before the syndicate was established, O'Brien was training the horses of Classic races galore and picking up no more than his percentage of the prize money and the odd present. Basically, he was underselling himself, still stuck in that non-commercial time warp when owners gave their trainers a pat on the back, told them that they were 'a jolly good fellow', and waltzed off to the bank with the takings from the Derby and their horse's stallion syndication. The fact that, up to then, he had never marketed himself by negotiating a piece of the action – receiving a small percentage of an owner's horse for training it – had never occurred to him. This so disturbed owner John Mulcahy when he joined the stable that he persuaded a rather reluctant O'Brien that he should demand 5 per cent of any horse he trained simply because he was one of the best, if not the best, in the business.

Mulcahy, an Irishman who had made his fortune in American industry, knew that this practice was prevalent in the States in many areas of business and sport. It was only right, he thought, that O'Brien should do the same.

Sangster, too, thought this type of arrangement a fair one, so much so that he subsequently extended the principle to his jockeys, creating what is common practice today: a rider of any of his horses which wins a top-class Group race and eventually goes to stud automatically receives one share – a fortieth – in the stallion (a jockey would therefore hold a share worth $500,000 in a stallion syndicated for $20 million). This practice, never quite given the same publicity as the earnings of Formula One drivers or tennis players, catapulted top jockeys into the big-money league. Through Sangster they not only became super-stars but millionaires.

Sangster's initial philosophy was that he would give this partnership three years to succeed, possibly four years at a push.

For whatever yearlings they purchased in America now, it would be another year or two (when those horses were racing as two- and three-year-olds) before they could discover the merits of that stock. In the meantime, of course, they would need to return to Keeneland each July, thereby maintaining the financial outlay on more stock. So, if the partnership's combined resources of money, skill and experience could not turn up a decent horse in that time, then Sangster would bring the partnership to an end, lick his wounds and reconsider his future.

He need not have worried, however. For the success that was still merely an idea on the drawing board would manifest itself not in four years or even three, but in two.

SEVEN

A New Sheila

Robert Sangster's growing fascination with Australia was not confined to horses. During his visit to the Sydney Easter Carnival in 1975, he had attended a private luncheon party at Randwick Racecourse where he was introduced to the leaseholders of a very good racemare called Leilani, who had been second to Think Big in the 1974 Melbourne Cup, and who was voted Horse of the Year the following season. The couple were Andrew and Susan Peacock.

He was the Australian Liberal Party's spokesman on foreign affairs, their great hope for future political supremacy. Friendly and rather dashing, he carried the sort of good looks that would often elicit an interested second glance from women (his name would subsequently be romantically linked with the American actress Shirley Maclaine). Many people, too, believed he would one day become Prime Minister. Like several of his fellow politicians, he was passionately involved with horses, an interest he had inherited from his father and his grandfather, though his hobby was on a much more modest scale than that of Sangster. He was also an avid follower of English soccer, having been an Arsenal supporter from his boyhood days when he used to read 'Bobby of the Dazzlers' in the *Champion* comic – the Dazzlers playing in a red and white strip similar to Arsenal's.

Susan was the darling of society in Melbourne, her home city. Glamorous and vivacious, her natural effervescence, which sometimes appeared to encompass a shade of vacuous joie de vivre, readily appealed to Sangster.

The daughter of another politician, John Rossiter, who held several positions in the Victorian state parliament before becoming Sir John, Victoria's Agent-General in London, Susan's gregariousness meant she was a natural 'people person', ideally suited to her job as a journalist. She started her career on the *Melbourne Sun* where, for a time, she worked on the women's pages, taking a particular interest in fashion and society. Occasionally she turned her hand to more serious writing, once interviewing infamous US teamsters union boss Jimmy Hoffa, who had been sentenced to a thirteen-year jail term (following a Robert Kennedy investigation) for receiving illegal payments from employers. Susan had also worked as a television reporter on two Channel 9 programmes, *No Man's Land* and *A Current Affair*.

But it was as a socialite that she excelled, photographs appearing so regularly in newspapers and magazines that it was a toss-up as to who was most in the media eye, Susan or Andrew. When she was not on the front pages of every newspaper in the country dressed up as Jane Russell while taking part in a charity review, she was appearing in the features pages showing off her latest fashion acquisitions from Paris – outfits from Courrèges, Yves Saint Laurent or Lanvin, in some of which, quite frankly, she looked dreadful.

The Peacocks had by this time been married twelve years and had three daughters. They appeared the perfect couple, an aspiring politician and his high-profile socialite wife. But, for some time, it had not been a happy marriage.

Perhaps this disenchantment with her husband showed in Susan's deep-brown eyes as she and Robert exchanged more than friendly glances across the luncheon table. Certainly he was captivated, enthralled enough to show his interest which she could not help but notice. She wondered what sort of marriage he had as they talked about their respective lives and families; a few fleeting moments of intimacy between the polite chat of such a social occasion, he displaying a quiet warmth and kindness, she, receptive, amusing, gay (in the old fashioned sense).

Afterwards, when reflecting on their meeting, she could tell she had made an impact. It made her feel good, gave her that buzz of excitement that is the pleasing result of knowing there had been a mutual attraction. While she had to admit to herself that she had found his attention interesting, she had not been captivated by him, more the other way around, she thought.

It would be another several months before he would see her again. In the interim he would think of her often. Until they did meet again and he revealed that he had fallen for her, Sangster's life would be in turmoil.

By the time the three members of the new partnership flew together to the 1975 Keeneland Sales and the sultry July heat of Kentucky, Sangster had become disenchanted with Marbella. He was fed up playing golf all day and, besides, he was too English – he missed many of the things from home. He was one of those casualties of Spain, part of that often stultifying ex-pat social set, hardly any of whom spoke Spanish (or wanted to learn) and who clung to their Englishness with a club mentality that was almost suffocating.

By now the Sangsters' eldest son, Guy, was at Harrow (where all three sons would be educated) because Sangster, the Old Reptonian, rather liked 'the type of people' Harrow produced. Christine, who was pregnant with their fourth child, was not totally enamoured with Spain either. So a decision was made to move to the Isle of Man, that small Irish Sea island halfway between Liverpool and Ireland which is famous for its kippers, its annual motorcycle TT races and for the number of wealthy people who live there because of the independent Government's low taxation.

The Isle of Man held other advantages too. It was, of course, only a half-hour's flying time to Liverpool and Ireland, therefore making it an ideal base both for Vernons and for Sangster's new Irish connection. And, more importantly, with the ever-increasing threat from the IRA, there was an in-built safety factor about living on such an island. The IRA, of course, had got the act of kidnap and ransom down to a fine art and there are many victims around today whose family fortunes are a million pounds or two lighter as a result of being kidnapped – all ransoms settled without the involvement, or knowledge, of the police. Sangster felt that, as there were only two ways to get off the island – by boat or aeroplane – the odds against becoming one of those terrorist victims were very much reduced.

For the syndicate's inaugural swoop on Keeneland, Sangster chose a suite in Lexington's Hyatt Regency to use as his base, travelling to the sales complex in a hired chauffeur-driven limousine. Magnier and O'Brien, like Sangster, had gone through the sales catalogue with a fine-tooth comb in their effort to select a batch of yearlings strictly on pedigree. On the plane over they had discussed the ostensible merits of all the horses they had picked out, each man speculating as to how much each yearling might fetch at the auction. This way it gave the syndicate an approximate band in which to bid, a high and a low, based on their experience of previous sales and especially O'Brien's here at Keeneland.

But there was still some time to go yet before the two-day sale got under way. Now began the stamina-sapping hours of pre-sale inspection of the living produce in the vast barn areas, each barn decked out in the colours of the consignor stud, the stud staff wearing matching uniforms (usually topped by a baseball cap).

It is here, in the lawned areas between barns, where the consignors have erected green-and-white-striped awnings to protect people from the blazing overhead sun, where patrons can sit and recuperate for five minutes with a plastic cup of the ice-cold soft drinks on tap. For others who prefer a coffee or iced tea with lemon, white-coated waiters (old habits die hard, so they are black) are on hand to bring out the best china.

These days in this vast barn complex there are dozens of British and Irish trainers, bloodstock agents and owners – Newmarket in the sun. Champion trainer Henry Cecil, looking cool in an open-necked, short-sleeved shirt and accompanied by the new young love of his life, watches a yearling being trotted up and down the walkway by its handler (for the umpteenth time). His former wife, Julie, is just yards away doing her own thing. Top trainer Michael Stoute, who is recently divorced, is here with the ex-wife of another Newmarket trainer. It's not all work without play. The gangly Peter Walwyn walks around inelegantly, almost comically, in polo shirt and baseball cap. If only the boys back home could see them now – the English conservatism seen every day on the racecourse is, literally, 5,000 miles away. Some trainers are here, all first-class flights paid for by their Arab patrons, not specifically to buy, but to join the 'team', pass their judgements on various yearlings which may or may not be bought once the Maktoum machine swings into action. Other trainers are here having paid their own economy-class ticket, taking valuable time off from their daily training routine at home, simply in order to be seen here. Keeneland is now this important. A trainer or bloodstock agent not at Keeneland either has a very good excuse – or is not an important player in this multi-million-dollar game.

In 1975, however, Sangster, Magnier and O'Brien, plus one or two agents, were virtually the only Europeans around. The Americans knew Vincent, of course, but the other two guys? This relative obscurity made the whole Sangster sales assault that much easier, simply because they were not seen as a major threat to the home-based high rollers. Therefore there would not be mass interest whenever one of Sangster's men bid for a yearling, no 'follow my leader' attitude either from the opposition which would push up prices, making the whole task of buying untried horses that much harder – and more expensive.

But the Sangster team was up and running and the syndicate had come to Kentucky with their own technical support; veterinarian specialists in horses' hearts, lungs, and knees. They did not broadcast the fact, naturally, but the triumvirate were here fully wound up and ready for business. Sangster might not know if the horses they were buying could run fast – that was the imponderable bottom line. But by thoroughly dealing with every other factor, the risk of buying a dud was truly minimised.

The sire Northern Dancer, whose stock the syndicate had set their sights on here, had topped the 1974 Keeneland statistics for this Selected Sale; five of his yearlings selling for an average of just over $130,000 each. O'Brien had been taken by one of Northern Dancer's sons when he had inspected him in the barn area. This was a smallish, stocky chestnut with four white socks, an appearance guaranteed to put many people off buying him (flashy would be the best description). But O'Brien had looked the horse over several times, had returned to it again and again, once spending fifteen minutes or so gazing at the animal, not moving, not talking, but simply staring with an intensity in those crystal-blue eyes almost as if he was trying to communicate with the horse itself. This was what Sangster would later describe as the Irish 'tinker' skill with horses. But O'Brien had this attribute in abundance. He had it in his soul, almost as if, in this one man, there was a refined concentration of the empathy with horses that has evolved with the Irish over generations. He disregarded the vulgarity of the horse's appearance because there was something else which attracted him to the colt. There was a certain athleticism within this small frame, O'Brien thought. So he recommended they bid for the colt. 'We must have this one,' he told his two partners.

They met some opposition during the bidding, but not serious enough to dissuade them from pressing on, eventually sealing the sale with a final bid which saw the colt knocked down to them for $200,000. This was not cheap but the figure was still two-thirds less than the current world record and it would lift the six yearlings by Northern Dancer sold at the sale to an average of over $143,000.

By the end of the two days, the syndicate had bought eleven other horses, spending over $1 million. Now, after the yearlings had been flown to Ireland and brought by road to Ballydoyle, it was O'Brien's autumn and winter task to have them broken and backed before they had their second birthday on the first day of

January (all racehorses in the northern hemisphere being conceived to be born between mid-January and mid-June and having their birthday on 1 January). By the spring they would be cantering, the sharper 'early' types being given more work in the hope of racing soon, while other slower-maturing horses would be brought along steadily. No rush, no forcing. Just plenty of patience, kindness and care. This is where O'Brien and his well-trained staff excelled, and it is no wonder, years later, with thirteen grandchildren, that O'Brien is thought to be so good with children – he has been training 'children' for over fifty years. He would probably have made an excellent school-teacher.

Shortly after returning from America, Sangster and Christine decided to quit Marbella and move to the Isle of Man. In the autumn they moved to a new house in an up-market area called Derby Haven, nothing as splendid as the home in which he now lives, The Nunnery, but comfortable enough while he looked around various other properties on the island for a more fitting base.

It was during this period that the rhythm of Sangster's life started breaking up. There was now a dual and conflicting aspect to the most important parts of his life. He was happy with the direction he had taken with his horses, which meant less work at Vernons. The founding of an international approach to the buying, selling and rearing of bloodstock was something to which he was eagerly looking forward. He knew that to promote his syndicates there would be a great deal of travel. He would have to raise his public profile if he was to be the syndicate's front man, its travelling salesman. That was fine by him. He had a zest for foreign travel, had the stamina for what some people might call the high life of wining, dining and socialising even if he was still rather shy. In his position, of course, he did not need to knock on any door unannounced. He was no cold canvasser trying to sell double glazing. The introductions were arranged for him. Soon, he hoped, suitable shareholders would be approaching him. This was all very genteel, civilised. He loved a good lunch or dinner with the best of them.

It was in his personal life that he felt out of step. He had never been the epitome of a family man. The children were, well, just around. Sangster himself had been sent to boarding school at the age of eight then on to public school and that was where his children were going. Even when the children were small, his business commitments meant he was not at home as much as would be called normal. (Ironically, it would be much later in his life that he would be 'educated' in the delights of parental involvement.)

All was not right, either, in his relationship with Christine. Sangster considered himself a romantic, others thought him something of a ladies' man. But he appeared to possess several hang-ups straight from his public shool upbringing. He once told an Australian magazine that he did not like wearing any sort of ring on his finger – even a wedding ring – nor a fashionable chain around his neck. To do so, he thought, made a man's masculinity appear 'sus'. Nor did he ever like sending a woman flowers. He also thought Frenchmen and Italians somewhat 'cissy' because they kissed ladies' hands. It was the sort of 'man's thinking' synonymous with some of the worst aspects of the average rugby club, a rationale of the male-female role in society not surprising given the various aspects of his upbringing.

This kind of traditional machismo made him popular in Australia, where many of the men who met him thought he was what is often referred to there as a 'good bloke'.

When he returned to Australia again in November – leaving Christine at home with their new baby Kate – it was to visit Melbourne for the Cup week festival, for which he booked into the Hilton Hotel. He desperately wanted to see Susan Peacock again, the woman who had made his pulse quicken on that first meeting. He was intrigued as to how she would greet him. When they met up again this time the attraction was totally reciprocated. The sparks flew. So began a passionate love affair that rocked them both. During their time together she repeated how unhappy she was with Andrew. It was now, as she poured her heart out to him, that they fell in love.

Soon afterwards they began thinking of their future, both agreeing that because of the distance that kept them apart and their own respective situations they would have to wait a little while yet before they could be together. While this was going on, the rest of Australia still accepted the Peacocks at face value, Susan appearing in public at Andrew's side for appearance's sake, for the obvious political reasons, and for her three young girls, aged nine, ten and eleven.

But, as far as Sangster and this new woman in his life were concerned, their respective marriages were almost over. Within a few months they were spending time together in Hong Kong at the island's finest hotel, the Peninsula, where Sangster had booked a suite. Several weeks later, Christine confronted her husband about his affair and, distraught, left with the children for a house subsequently bought for her by Sangster in Virginia Water, Surrey. Until Sangster decided his next move, he and Christine would be seen together socially, like the Peacocks, for appearance's sake only. The marriage was already over.

It was be another two months before Sangster's name hit the news headlines for the first time on a national level. It made great copy for the popular press, of course: 'Pools chief and the runaway Foreign Minister's wife'. (The Liberals were now in power there). Susan was so smitten by Sangster, so unhappy with Andrew, that she had left her daughters behind in Australia where they were attending boarding school.

Susan first wanted to explain her actions to her mother and father which she did over lunch in London where they were then living. She was naturally saddened at the thought that she would not have regular close contact with her daughters other than speaking to them on the telephone and writing twice a week. But the self-doubts and occasional depression she felt about leaving them were somewhat offset by the knowledge that she and

Andrew's lifestyle had meant that one or the other was often away from home for fairly long periods and the family had, therefore, not had the luxury of a normal routine. She had already insisted, however, that the girls would spend their holidays in the Isle of Man. And she and Sangster had worked out that she would be able to devote extra time to them on her twice-yearly visits to Australia accompanying the new man in her life.

Sangster and Susan had, in fact, already been away together, visiting Singapore and the Philippines. Then, after a trip to France where they visited the training centres of Lamorlaye and Chantilly, outside Paris, they flew to the French Riviera (where Sangster had honeymooned with Christine sixteen years earlier). It was here that the media first got wind of the story.

This was the start of a new life, and style, for Sangster. With Susan's influence, this was going to be public, high-profile, glamorous, seemingly the epitome of a couple leading a 'jet-set' existence. It was all unavoidable to a great degree because Susan thrived on publicity. She simply adored it. Even Sangster soon publicly announced his new love's 'credentials'. It had been said in Australia, he proudly announced, that Susan was one of the country's two most famous assets – the other being the Sydney Opera House. Whether he was moved to say this to maintain, maybe enhance, his credibility, or merely to have a little fun in establishing her status with the rest of Britain's horseracing society, there was no doubting that Susan was a leading social personality in Australia. It would not take too long, either, before she made her mark in Britain.

There was another reason, too, why the 'shy' Sangster would subsequently agree to go along readily with the countless interviews that would thrust him into the public eye. This was the high profile he felt he needed to achieve if he was to attract successfully the right people into the various racehorse syndicates he was setting up. Operating in such a manner would make his job so much easier because people interested and wealthy enough to seek a share of the action would know who he was and have a fair idea of what his syndication plans were before they even met him.

But the extent to which the publicity would not only be welcomed, but sometimes sought – even many years later when he was well established – perhaps suggests that, quite unlike the lifestyle of his very private father, Sangster liked spreading his public persona. As one of his former aides said: 'Without doubt, he likes all the publicity. He just does not like the idea of other people knowing he does.'

So, for Sangster, it was now a case of 'life begins at forty'. He and Susan moved into The Nunnery Mansion House, a large estate barely a mile outside Douglas, which Sangster had purchased at the end of 1975 for £150,000 and then spent a similar amount renovating. The Nunnery is a fine castellated, mainly Victorian building though parts go back to Elizabethan times and some areas of the site are from the original nunnery which was built in the twelfth century. It has six main reception rooms, eight bedrooms including six guest suites, a magnificent hallway with marble pillars, a library and study, while in the eleven-acre grounds are a chapel, a salmon stream, large formal gardens and paddocks. (These days the roof holds several large satellite dishes to enable Sangster to keep up with his international racing.)

The sight of the recently-renovated house was sheer delight to Susan, for most of the decorative work had still to be carried out and she was therefore able to begin what she would call eighteen months of hard graft putting her stamp on the decor. They would have domestic staff, of course, including a cook, which was just as well because, by her own admission, Susan was no cordon bleu – nor was Sangster who did not know one end of a saucepan from another. But as Sangster was basically a steak man (well cooked!) there was little incentive anyway for Susan to do more than throw a piece of fillet and a tomato under the grill for him.

By the time the public furore had subsided over what was termed the 'runaway romance', Sangster and his team had paid another visit to the Keeneland Sales to replenish their stock with a new batch of yearlings. Although some of the previous year's intake had not yet made their racecourse appearances, O'Brien was pleased with what several were showing him on the Ballydoyle gallops in their daily workouts. Among them was a good-looking bay colt called Artaius who had cost $110,000 and was by the US sire, Round Table, while their most expensive purchase – that $200,000 flashy chestnut had been named The Minstrel – was also catching the eye. Another son of Northern Dancer was pleasing all who saw him. He was called Be My Guest.

The stone-faced maestro Lester Piggott was O'Brien's stable jockey at this time, travelling from his home in Newmarket to ride in Ireland and, on specific occasions, to do work riding at Ballydoyle. Piggott, of course, was one of the most famous jockeys in the world; a curious mix of dedication and single-mindedness to the point of obsession. This classic association with O'Brien had gone back ten years to the time he had given up his retainer with Noel Murless and ridden his first Epsom success for O'Brien on Valoris in the Oaks (Piggott had won the 1958 Ascot Gold Cup for the trainer, too, aboard Gladness). The partnership had been successful many times since with horses of the calibre of Sir Ivor, Nijinsky, Roberto, and Thatch. Piggott had been riding on a freelance basis until the Sangster syndicate was established. Now he was under contract with a retainer and all the perks, stallion shares, and high rewards that went with it.

O'Brien had almost a love-hate relationship with Piggott at times. No-one could deny this jockey was the best, but he would infuriate the Irishman on the gallops by doing his own thing, riding a horse the way he wanted in order to find out its ability rather than the way he had been told. This would upset O'Brien because it threatened to undermine the carefully-structured training programme which he applied to his horses, treating them as individuals, naturally, and organising their amounts of food, work and care accordingly.

It was for this reason that Piggott, despite all his brilliance, was not as regular a work rider at Ballydoyle as some might have thought.

At the end of the 1976 Flat season Sangster was filled with optimism. The syndicate's plan, so far, seemed to be going to perfection. They had brought in several partners on some of the horses for the smaller percentages and, more importantly, they had several horses who looked like justifying their enormous outlays and who could turn out to be crack three-year-olds for next year.

There was The Minstrel who had swept all before him in three races. The colt had finished his two-year-old career by coming over to England to run in the Dewhurst Stakes at Newmarket, a race that was increasingly becoming the best guide to the following season's classics. The Minstrel had won this in marvellous style, quickening up to produce a brilliant burst of acceleration after being held up in the earlier stages by Piggott. In the Free Handicap (a 'merit table' of weights which the top 100 or so two-year-olds would carry if they were to run against each other), The Minstrel was rated 8 lbs below the top horse, J. O.Tobin, who was allotted the highest weight of 9–7. Many observers who had seen The Minstrel's Dewhurst victory thought this an insult and reckoned, as it would turn out, that he was the best of next year's Classic bunch.

There were other two-year-olds in the stable, too, who were shaping like moneyspinners, Be My Guest, the filly Durtal, and the once-raced Alleged.

The whole enterprise, in fact, was running so smoothly, so promisingly, that Sangster's massive gamble looked as if it was going to pay off.

EIGHT

Building an Empire

The Sangster racing and breeding empire began a rapid international expansion in the latter half of the 1970s, taking in Australia, America, France, South Africa and eventually Venezuela, apart from the Irish and English connections. Much of this business was conducted in the name of Swettenham Stud, which was now a subsidiary of the Vernons Organisation.

In France Sangster owned twenty broodmares and a stud called the Mont dit Mont, outside the racing town of Deauville on the Normandy coast. In America there were connections with the famous stud farms of Claiborne and Gainseway in Kentucky in the form of twenty-five mares and holdings in several stallions. There were over ninety mares in Europe, shares in forty-five horses in training with O'Brien, twenty mares in Australia – and, of course, the large stake in Coolmore, its subsidiary studs and many of the stallions housed there. Sangster also kept a proportion of his home-bred stock to race, these being trained by Barry Hills at Lambourn.

There would be small percentages of some horses and stallions, larger percentages of mares, and around a couple of dozen racehorses that Sangster owned outright. He would enter into foal-sharing arrangements with breeders, doing a deal on the percentages of the progeny of another owner's mare from his stallion and vice versa. Almost every day he would be non-stop on the telephone, structuring deals, buying, selling, swapping. He could say one week that he owned maybe 350 to 400 horses around the world, only for that figure to be increased by ten or twenty by the end of the week with the birth of foals or the acquisition of several winning racehorses whose owners could not refuse the tempting offer Sangster made them (at the height of his success he would 'own' somewhere in the region of 1,200 to 1,300 horses).

Such was the intricate nature of the business that Sangster had turned the whole basement floor of The Nunnery into an operations room which became known as the bunker. Here was every piece of modern telecommunication equipment (later it would be fully computerised). There were files and charts, cabinets containing genealogy details of every horse owned, all going back to the umpteenth remove. Visitors to the bunker could not help but be impressed by the sheer scale of the operation.

Sangster's earlier association with Eric Cousins, who had decided to retire at the end of the 1976 Flat season, was maintained when Cousins' daughter Wendy was invited to work at The Nunnery as one of the racing secretaries. He would subsequently engage an American, Mark Glyer, as his Isle of Man-based racing manager. Glyer, a former associate of the US bloodstock agent Albert Yank, was recommended by another member of the Sangster team, Billy McDonald, an Irishman whose bloodstock business is based in the States and who, as we shall see, played a major role in the early Sangster successes. Both Wendy Cousins and Mark Glyer were still with Sangster in 1991, which is testament to the loyalty that Sangster engenders in his staff and how well he treats them. In these earlier days, Sangster relied heavily, too, on Lil Markey, known to everyone as Miss Markey, Sangster's former secretary at Vernons. The epitome of what would be called the old school of spinster secretary, Miss Markey lived in the Isle of Man all week, travelling home to Liverpool at weekends in one of the Sangster Vernair company's charter planes, which were based at Liverpool Airport.

Sangster needed his own private aeroplane, hence the purchase of the Vernair company and its six aircraft. The company was still run on a purely commercial basis, however.

It was now that the term 'travelling salesman', which Sangster would apply to himself, became an accurate description. Soon he would be clocking up a quarter of a million miles a year, hardly ever off an aeroplane, literally jet-hopping all over the world: two days in America, back late to The Nunnery where, after a glass of milk and a sandwich, he would sleep for six hours before taking the Rolls to the island's Ronaldsway Airport for his plane to Ireland to see his horses on the early-morning gallops, then on to France for a day's racing, back to The Nunnery that night, then off to a different part of America the next morning. Sometimes, in any one month, if he and Susan spent a total of one week at their home, they counted themselves lucky. To many people this was all a very glamorous way for Sangster to conduct his life. It is true, of course, that there were many fine moments, good times, within all this travelling. But, in reality, Sangster had set himself an extremely punishing schedule requiring great stamina. It was a life of which most people would quickly tire.

Now that Sangster and Susan Peacock were living together awaiting their respective divorces to come through so that they could marry, Australia loomed large in the overall plan. And it was through an association with that country's greatest trainer, Colin Hayes (known simply as C.S.), that Sangster became Australia's most important owner–breeder, a position he would occupy for at least the next fifteen years.

Colin Hayes is a lovely man; kindness exudes from him with the warmth of a loving grandfather (which, today, is what he is). He possesses that endearing quality in many Australians which is to accept a person for what they are rather than what they own, the antithesis of the superior 'pom' behaviour so prevalent in Britain and especially in racing, which is run on such militaristic lines from the top that it seeps downwards, condescendingly, and in a frighteningly unmalleable manner as practically to suffocate any initiative, enterprise or flair that is occasionally espoused by the few progressive thinkers in the sport.

Hayes had begun training in the 1950–1 season and was soon regarded as an up-and-coming South Australian trainer, starting out with only a handful of horses from a rented training base at Semaphore outside Adelaide. Occasionally, he would send a horse up to Victoria if he thought it good enough to run in Melbourne, and it was here that he struck up a friendship with a successful young jockey he often used, Ron Hutchinson (who later came to ride for the late Paddy Prendergast in Ireland and for the Duke and Duchess of Norfolk in England).

The two men formed a business partnership, as a first step buying several squash courts between them. At this time, Hayes was also renting another piece of land, a forty-acre spread called Beaufields at Gawler, twenty miles away from where he trained, where the horses were rested when they were out of training. They purchased this, too, when the property came on the market.

Hutchinson was riding successfully in Ireland by the time Hayes, three years on, found he wanted bigger and better training facilities. And the chance of a lifetime came along when they were able to purchase a 1,000-acre estate, Lindsay Park, at Angaston, an hour and a half's drive north from Adelaide, deep in the heart of the bountiful Barra Valley wine-growing region. The Hayes syndicate also included racing enthusiasts like the late Harry Cornell, Wyndham Hill-Smith, owner of the Yalumba Wines company, South Australian Jockey Club member Don McKay and, later, his son Bob, who is now chairman of Lindsay Park. Today, the enlarged 2,000 acres of Lindsay Park is one of the best training centres and stud farms in the world.

Set among gentle rolling green countryside, on limestone that goes down three, maybe four feet, with rich paddocks and fields dotted by centuries-old giant red gum trees, Lindsay Park had been in the Angas family since the first years of British settlement. In 1850 it was the home of George Angas, one of South Australia's founders, and Lindsay Park remained in the Angas family for four generations until Hayes took over. Its last tenants, Sir Keith and Lady Angas, had established a stud within the beautiful parkland valleys, and Hayes began a labour of love transforming the stud and establishing a training centre, work on which is still continuing today.

There is room at Lindsay Park for up to 700 horses, 500 of which will be mares sent there for the breeding season. The stud itself owns about sixty mares and breeds commercially, selling at public auction. Should Hayes take a liking to a particular yearling that has been raised at Lindsay Park and wish to obtain it for one of his racing stable clients, then he has to bid for it at public auction just like everyone else. This 'no favours' approach is important in order to maintain credibility, for if buyers thought that Hayes was keeping the best yearlings back the rest would fetch such miserable sums as to be not worth entering in the sales, thereby destroying what is, after all, a commercial breeding operation with shareholders to satisfy.

In fact, Sangster himself had gone through such an experience at the Newmarket yearling sales of 1976. He had previously sold only foals from Swettenham but thought he would keep the stock to discover if there was an extra profit, as one would expect, in selling them as yearlings. Sangster was most alarmed, though, when it proved a disastrous exercise – buyers thought he had kept the best yearlings of his crop for his own racing stables and that these at the sales were merely the result of a Swettenham 'cull'.

There is a certain quiet efficiency about Lindsay Park, evident from first light when the horses are brought out to exercise. This is the Hayes way of doing things – no shouting, no raised hands, no panic. It is a simple, calm, gentle atmosphere, like C.S. himself, that prevails, maintained now by his son David, who has taken over from his father. The philosophy at Lindsay Park is to keep the horses happy. Contented horses make good horses, Hayes says.

It was with this one aim that Hayes began the development of the 2,000 acres, turning it into a paradise for the horses he races, the mares and foals he rears and the stallions stationed there, some of which were owned in partnership with Sangster and Coolmore Stud. There are three gallops; the six-furlong grass gallop has turf the equal of the best racecourse. It is as wide as a racetrack, and incorporates its own sprinkler watering system so that the ground does not get too dry and hard – which produces sore shins on young thoroughbreds. The gallop was constructed on the collar so that it rises 180 feet in the last half-mile – 'This takes the strain off the horses' forelegs, but they still have to work hard at the finish,' Hayes says. 'I believe that good training is all about the power-to-weight ratio of a horse.'

Nothing is left to chance at Lindsay Park, even when the scorching sun of an Australian high summer sends a punishing run of 42-degree days that threatens to scupper the training routine. These days David Hayes takes a leaf out of his father's book and works the string half an hour earlier at 5 a.m. when it is still dark and refreshingly cool, the stillness broken only by the sounds of clinking bridles, creaking tack and, somewhere in the depths of darkness, chirring crickets.

David has his dark hair cut fringe short, which gives this man of twenty-seven a boyish look that is exaggerated when he smiles, which is often. If he has felt any pressure in taking over the 7,000-winner mantle of his father then there are not many people who have noticed it.

The training day starts high up above the all-weather track in a wooden observation office which is built on stilts. David's fingers are usually curled around a polystyrene cup of black coffee.

Two hundred yards away, in the darkness, comes that emotive rhythmic beat of horses' hooves at a three-quarter gallop. David cocks his head to listen as two unseen horses and riders gallop past, yet he is still able to name both horses from the snorting, rasping sounds they make as they travel on through the darkness.

The routine is well established; each rider trots his mount back to the observation box where the trainer has a few words: 'Everything all right?'

'Yeah, boss. My fella flew this morning, didn't he?'

David hopes this particular horse will fly on the track at the up-coming meeting in Melbourne where, in the first two days alone of a four-day meet, there are three races worth $300,000 and six worth $100,000. For this animal is Sangster's most promising two-year-old, Canonise (who subsequently won the $500,000 Blue Diamond Stakes).

Among the experienced team of work riders is Ron Hutchinson's son Peter, Lindsay Park's number-one Adelaide jockey and number-one joker, though he did get serious when he learned he had just kept the ride on Canonise in the big one. Peter's amiable brother, Raymond, the former top amateur rider in England, is one of the two vets at the stud.

All gallop times are checked on an electric timing machine, which is started and stopped when the horses run through an electronic beam at the start and finish of the gallop. Hayes is happy to explain his training methods: 'Like the Americans, we work against the clock. I think you can tell how well a horse has worked this way. We work all our slower horses together, too. It can be misleading if you don't use the clock then because you can be led to think a slow horse has done a good piece of work only to find out later on the track that it hasn't.'

C.S. has retired, but that only means an extra few minutes in bed in the morning, for he usually arrives just after the string have pulled out ready for work. He still likes to keep his eye on things too, consulting with David, advising when necessary. But it is an overview role, a friendly, fatherly one, for David is the boss now. These days, C.S. is a busy man anyway, and is a director of several companies including the TAB. Mind you, he is glad he does have a few extra minutes to take calls from such friends as Prime Minister Bob Hawkes, a very knowledgeable racing man. 'Bob is very interested in racing and likes to know what is going on here, so we talk regularly,' he says.

Each horse of the 100 or so Lindsay Park string has its work arranged twenty-four hours earlier, then logged on computer. The print-outs, from which each rider is given his or her instructions, are an essential part of David Hayes' 'tools' each morning.

The horses are taken for a swim immediately after exercise and again in the afternoon. C.S. designed the one-man-operated pool himself just as he did the stable block, the boxes – where horses are bedded on sand – the gallops, the paddocks, the feeding system (100 horses can be fed in twenty minutes), even the sandpits in which the horses have a good roll. 'I could have tried to explain to an architect what I wanted, but I reckon, even then, it wouldn't have been right. I know this sounds crazy but I believe you have got to try and think like a horse – that's why everything here has been designed to keep them happy.'

Sangster's early involvement with Australian breeding began when he started sending out Swettenham mares which had been covered to southern hemisphere time by his stallions in Ireland. In 1977 he was organising the matings of thirty-five of his mares with Coolmore stallions like Rheingold, Be My Guest, Sun Prince, Habitat, Mount Hagen and Red Alert. By then he already had thirty horses in the country. The fact that they were mainly stallions (in which he owned shares) and broodmares, with only two racehorses, indicated his preference for breeding rather than racing.

Australia's covering season is six months 'behind' that of Britain and the rest of the northern hemisphere's mid-February to mid-July period. After a mare's eleven-month gestation, foals in the north are born from mid-January to mid-June (and have that 1 January birthday). Southern hemisphere foals are born from mid-August to mid-November (and all have their birthdays on 1 August).

In order to promote his idea, the Coolmore stallions began the lucrative extra duties, therefore covering more than the normal forty-five or so mares they were servicing to northern time. But Sangster was forced to postpone continuation of the scheme when a worldwide outbreak of equine metritis – a type of venereal disease – occurred and a temporary ban was imposed on the importation of in-foal mares to several countries, including Australia.

In an effort to keep the 'production line' rolling, Sangster then tried an experiment to breed the foals in Britain, but to southern hemisphere time, in order to export them to Australia where they would be sold.

This was a totally unnatural process which, to some degree, reflected the commercial pressure Sangster was under to expand his horizons and, at the same time, make the business profitable. Foals would now be bred at Coolmore in the autumn, then returned with their mothers to Swettenham around Christmas time.

There were several hurdles that Sangster tried to overcome with this method. With the foals having been born in the British autumn, they would have to be dispatched to be prepared for the Australian sales with their long winter coats, while their southern-hemisphere counterparts would be sporting fine, sleek summer coats. To compensate for the cause of this – the lack of daylight – overhead lights in the Swettenham boxes were left on all night. But the artificial lighting had little effect. Hence several rather shaggy yearlings arrived in Australia, some bound for the sales, others to go into training with Colin Hayes.

There were other problems in this topsy-turvy time reversal, too. For it was verging on winter as the foals faced those most important formative months of their young lives, yet the mares were producing poor milk. The winter grass, of course, contained hardly any of the nutrition that comes from the lush summer pasture the mares would normally eat while suckling. In an effort to overcome this, the mares were put on a high-protein feed in the hope they would pass this on through their milk. But this did not work either, and the foals did not sustain full growth.

In the end, the experiment was deemed a flop and was abandoned.

There was a better way, however, to keep the output flowing

once the metritis ban had been lifted. Sangster would subsequently move the mountain to Mohammed and send some of the stallions out to Australia. There, they would spend a season covering forty-five mares, but return to Ireland for the northern-hemisphere season. It was literally the best of both worlds.

One of the first stallions to break this new ground was Green God, who stood a season at Coolmore and a season at Ken Cox's Stockwell Stud, outside Melbourne. Sadly, Green God died prematurely, not through any over-exertion, but because of colitis – horses cannot vomit and any intestinal trouble can sometimes result in a fatal twisted gut.

So Sangster was now taking advantage of scientific progress. Coolmore, now the biggest stud group in Ireland, had its own in-house veterinarians and a fully equipped laboratory, which is so necessary for the testing of mares in foal, the analysis of blood samples and dozens of other related areas in this often precarious business of bloodstock breeding. In earlier times a mare would be covered by a stallion during the period she came into season (every three weeks). So a stallion might have covered a mare four times or more before she conceived. Vets have perfected the examination of mares to the degree that they are now able to detect when a pregnancy is likely, so that the number of times she has to be covered has been reduced.

Sangster reckoned that, due to the kind climate in Australia, mares were in foal with an average of 1.8 services, while in Ireland it was 2.5 covers per mare.

This pioneering double-duty idea spread to ten stallions by 1977 with such as Lorenzaccio, Deep Diver and Crowned Prince being sent to Hayes at Lindsay Park and to John Kelly's Newhaven Park Stud at Boorowa in New South Wales.

Today, many Sangster stallions have gone down the same path with some, like Godswalk, Salmon Leap and Bluebird, having great success at Lindsay Park, which has produced the winners of more than $30 million in prize money from its breeding activities.

Sangster's commitment to Australia was obviously bolstered somewhat by his relationship with Susan Peacock. Her renown meant that she was very well connected, not only with high society, but also politically. This, Sangster would admit, was a very useful entrée into the aspects of the country's racing and breeding industry that he was seeking to exploit. She would prove a useful asset to the whole business, as he would later describe her, and especially to the task of attracting clients who might want to be associated with this newcomer.

Without Susan by his side, his high profile would have taken much longer to achieve. But now everyone in the media wanted to interview this multi-millionaire who was Susan Peacock's partner.

The philosophy behind the Sangster policy of expansionism was that horseflesh was an international currency, a hedge against inflation. The logic seemed to be exceptionally sound. If sterling lost its shine it did not matter because the value of Sangster's bloodstock stayed the same. And it was an asset he could always shift because of the growing number of international outlets he was opening up.

There was also an underlying element to this love affair with Australia. Although it was still commercially orientated it was one that contained a hint of philanthropy.

Sangster wanted to open up Australian racehorses to the rest of the world. He wanted the Americans to take an interest in Australian bloodlines. He wanted Australia itself to wake up to the export potential of its tough, racy stock. He foresaw an end to the one-way traffic of stallions and broodmares from the States and Europe. Sure, there were benefits from importing good stock from these places because it helped raise the overall standard of bloodstock, made the breeders international enough in outlook to take an interest in the sons and daughters of the stock they exported in the first place, thereby maybe creating new future trade.

But there was a major resistance here, one that would still be in existence many years later. It was a basic facet of human nature itself: why play away if you are content at home?

For such is the high level of prize money in Australia that owners of top horses are, rightly, loath to risk running their horses 10,000 miles away for the prestige of winning abroad. They might win more money, say, in America or in one or two top races in Europe or maybe win the Japan Cup as did the New Zealand mare Horlicks in 1989 and David Hayes did the following year with Better Loosen Up. But if they lost? Not only would good prizes at home have passed them by, but a 'flop' who returned from a failed campaign abroad, whatever the excuse, might do damage to its future reputation if it was to have a life at stud or in the paddocks.

Only a brave few would be tempted to test the overseas temperature. And, although they were usually successful, it would hardly make a ripple on the international waters.

Sangster himself in these earlier days made the first moves in doing this by purchasing Australia's top three-year-old sprinter, Luskin Star, who had won ten times from thirteen starts (including the champion two-year-old sprint, the Golden Slipper, at Sydney's Rosehill Racecourse) and had amassed $250,000 prize money. He paid an undisclosed, but substantial, six-figure sum for the colt on the eve of the 1977 Melbourne Cup in the hope of racing it in America the following season. If it was successful there, as some of his other ex-British horses had been, he was hoping to bring it back to Australia and syndicate it as a stallion for $3 million.

His plans were scuppered, however, when that metritis ban was enforced the following year. So Luskin Star stayed at home, won two more good races, and was retired to Segenhoe Stud in New South Wales' Hunter Valley at a smaller figure.

But this incident was only a minor setback in the overall plan. For everything else was going swimmingly.

NINE

The Almighty Dollar

This man Sangster was someone in a hell of a hurry to get to the top of the tree and make himself a lot of money from his new chosen direction. The international seeds of an intricate and extensive network had been sown. Now he could survey new landscapes while the young stock he owned around the world began to blossom and, hopefully, bear fruit.

And in 1977 his stock did exactly that in Britain. Only two years after the Sangster syndicate had paid its inaugural visit to the Keeneland Sales, they swept the board in a fantastic season during which, it appeared, they could do nothing wrong. This was the year that Sangster signalled his arrival in the most dramatic fashion. His racing colours of green shirt, blue sleeves and green-spotted white cap would win top race after top race.

The Minstrel turned out to be the mid-season starship. This tough, battling colt won Sangster his first Derby. It was amazing. A Derby winner from the first crop of Keeneland yearlings. People could spend millions in this quest for the Blue Riband of the turf and not get a sniff. Had luck decreed this reward? Or was it the result of deliberate dedication?

The Derby victory confounded those critics who thought The Minstrel's defeats in the earlier 2,000 Guineas at Newmarket (he finished third) and at the Curragh (an unlucky second) justified their opinion that the chestnut was something of a flash in the pan.

There were some observers willing to think that this new Sangster syndicate was flash too, that this result at Epsom was a one-off hit at a rich vein of gold. The syndicate would prove them wrong however. They had some more surprises to unleash yet, the result in the main, not of luck, but of planning, foresight, skill and hard work. If there was any good fortune around, then Sangster, for one, thought they had earned it.

It was with The Minstrel that the Sangster team showed their strength too, maybe making their own good fortune along the way. For, if O'Brien had had his way, he might have bypassed the Derby because he had entered two other syndicate horses in the race, the Nijinsky colt Valinsky and Be My Guest. He bore in mind that The Minstrel had already had three races and that the Derby, which is run less than three months into the season, might come too soon. O'Brien had, therefore, considered giving the colt a rest and bringing him back in mid-summer.

There was also a question mark over The Minstrel's stamina: could he stay the one and a half miles at Epsom? His sire, Northern Dancer, had failed to get that trip in New York's Belmont Stakes, the middle leg and longest trip of the US triple crown. The Minstrel's dam, Fleur, although a half-sister to Nijinsky (that is, out of the same mare), had only seemed to get a mile, though she was bred to get further.

But it was Lester Piggott who was the persuasive factor in O'Brien's eventual decision to run at Epsom. Piggott had ridden the horse in all his races and, as far as he was concerned, The Minstrel would get the trip – and win. Both men have, naturally, been wrong before in their judgements, despite their brilliance as trainer and jockey, and both would be the first to admit the old adage that nothing makes more a fool of a man than a horse. This situation, though, was what good teamwork was all about. One man, O'Brien, undecided. Piggott supremely confident and, therefore, tilting the scales.

For all Epsom's idiosyncratic balance-throwing camber, its downhill Tattenham Corner run and its tight turns, there is no jockey in this world who rides the Derby course in a positional sense as well as Piggott. If this great jockey had been aboard some of the Derby near-misses of the past twenty years then, without doubt, he would have greatly exceeded the eleven Derbys he has won.

And on that sunny day at Epsom, sure enough, there was Piggott, lying a close-up third on The Minstrel as the field rounded Tattenham Corner to enter the straight. With two furlongs to go there were only three horses in it. Willie Carson, on Lord Leverhulme's Hot Grove, kicked for home. Piggott went in pursuit while the French raider, Blushing Groom, the favourite owned by the Aga Khan, began to run out of stamina. It was here, in a desperate driving finish, that Piggott was unbeatable.

As they approached the winning post, both jockeys driving for all they were worth, the horses almost neck and neck, Piggott gave The Minstrel his famous quick-fire dose of the whip, that rapid succession of strikes which has proved, time after time, to be the difference between defeat and victory (and which, amazingly, has rarely been copied by any other British rider). The Minstrel, responding to the Piggott treatment, got up to win by a neck.

Such a short distance between the winner and the runner-up meant a difference of several million pounds.

Epsom with all its glamorous and social connotations also gave Sangster the opportunity to show off the new woman at his side. Susan had been accompanying him on many of his racing trips around the world, meeting his associates and business partners. Sangster thought she was marvellous at entertaining and was of the opinion that, like himself, everyone adored her.

Some of Sangster's male friends did not look at it that way, however. She did not see eye to eye with one or two of them and as a consequence the friendships cooled.

There were friends and acquaintances of Sangster who wished he would keep his feet on the ground just as Christine had hoped when the syndicate started. But there was no hope of that, for he and Susan were intent on a hectic life of small planes, big planes, twin props, helicopters, jets, tight schedules, travelling fast – and light. Susan would quickly become accustomed to this even though, quite ironically, she was afraid of flying. It was a part of her life with which she had never felt comfortable and on many occasions she felt the need to hold someone's hand at take-off.

Throughout this whirlwind existence she was devoting much energy into stamping her taste on the decor of The Nunnery.

She favoured plain, bright colours for the walls, lots of white paint to the extent that it was used on some of the wood panelling and on the black marble mantelpiece in the library. She chose thick white carpeting for the reception hall, mixed the clean-cut lines of Italian furniture with the intricacies of period pieces. She would go to great lengths to find the items she wanted for a particular room, lampshades, cushions, tables, chairs. If they could not be found in Britain, then she would shop in California or Florida, London or Paris. With the Sangster millions behind her, the world was her shop window.

Being as gregarious as she was, Susan was never backward in coming forward. So she was always to be seen at the side of any Sangster winner leading in the horse. And that was how the world's media first saw her on Derby day: this now-blonde, smiling, laughing, bubbling like the champagne which flowed in great quantity. This was in complete contrast to Sangster, his rather controlled nervousness almost like the great British stiff upper lip. So instead he bit his bottom lip. He smiled, of course, but his emotions did not run riot. He was never one for showing his delight in public, perhaps only to a degree afterwards when they held a celebration party for twenty guests in a private room at the popular London nightclub, Annabel's. If anyone expected him to be the proverbial life and soul, then they did not know Robert Sangster. He is a generous host, loves having fun and always tries to have the best time he can. Nevertheless, he is never the life and soul of such parties, even though, paradoxically, he is always surrounded by people.

The mid-summer test for any Derby winner is Ascot's King George VI and Queen Elizabeth Diamond Stakes at the end of July when, for the first time in a Group One race over a mile and a half, three-year-olds meet older horses. Ideally, the race presents the chance for last season's Derby winner to meet this season's, so that a comparison of the respective Classic winners can be made. Oh, if that only happened!

The vast amounts of money a Derby winner can make at the stud, a fashion that has been exacerbated these days by the Sangster success, makes it totally unviable to keep a Derby winner in training as a four-year-old. Take the Aga Khan's brilliant but ill-fated Derby winner, Shergar. He was retired at the end of his career with a valuation of £10 million to stand in Ireland (he would have fetched much more if sold to America). If Shergar had been kept in racing as a four-year-old and proved as successful, he perhaps might have doubled his career prize-money earnings of £388,970. But, at Ballymany Stud, covering fifty mares at his fee of £70,000 a service, Shergar would make £3.5 million as a four-year-old. Such is the crazy financial structure of breeding – to the detriment of the sport of Flat racing.

The Minstrel won the Ascot race by a short head, under another forceful Piggott ride, from Orange Bay, a five-year-old who had blinkers fitted for the first time in an effort to sharpen up his performance. Behind this pair came the high-class four-year-old Exceller, the French Derby winner, Crystal Palace, Bruni (who went on to win the St Leger) and Lucky Wednesday. The field represented the best middle-distance horses in Europe at that time.

In between the Derby and Ascot, The Minstrel had also won the Irish Sweeps Derby.

Now there was only one more test. These days it is not the final British Classic in September, the St Leger, which Nijinsky had won for O'Brien in 1970, because Americans are not interested in horses that win over the 'marathon' distance of a mile and three-quarters. And, due in part to Sangster, the greenback dollar rules British racing. American influences are here to stay. So it is the mile-and-a-half Prix de l'Arc de Triomphe, a month later, at Longchamp in Paris, that is the final challenge for any middle-distance horse in Europe.

There was now talk of The Minstrel rounding off his racing career by running at Longchamp. But that metritis outbreak reared its ugly head, threatening the movement of stock internationally. A quick decision was called for by the Sangster partners in The Minstrel, for they had now agreed to sell half of their shareholding to The Minstrel's breeder, Eddie Taylor of Windfields Farm, Maryland, the man who had bred Northern Dancer and stood the stallion there.

Subsequently, The Minstrel was despatched to America to stand alongside his sire. The syndicate beat the metritis ban by a few days.

Before the deal with E. P. Taylor was concluded, there had been hopes that European breeders would reap the benefit of The Minstrel's services, because Sangster was talking about the horse doing 'double duty' at Coolmore and at Colin Hayes' Lindsay Park.

But the lure of the dollar proved unmatchable. The Minstrel was sold to America with a valuation of $9 million. And, as if to prove the might of the Americans, breeders were asked by the Aga Khan to help keep Blushing Groom at stud in Europe by matching the offer from the US of $6 million. There were no takers, so Blushing Groom went Stateside too.

Sangster and his partners were all too well aware that there was no substitute for a fashionable pedigree in the get-rich-quick stakes. As a son of Northern Dancer, The Minstrel had vindicated the whole philosophy, choice and timing of the Sangster syndicate. To prove the point of the wide disparity between fashionable and unfashionable bloodlines, Orange Bay, the horse beaten only a short head by The Minstrel in that epic Ascot battle, was retired to stud himself.

He stood at the Beech House Stud in Newmarket with a valuation of £168,000.

If anyone thought that The Minstrel was a one-off wonder from the O'Brien stable that season then they were in for a rude surprise. And if there was resentment and a certain amount of jealousy from some of the stuffier sections of British racing that this man Sangster, someone from the nouveau riche, had waltzed in like a Johnny Come Lately and stolen the thunder, then it was only going to get deeper.

This was because there was another three-year-old middle-distance colt in the stable at Ballydoyle named Alleged. He would turn out to be even more valuable than The Minstrel.

The American-bred had originally appeared at the same Keeneland yearling sale as The Minstrel, but had looked such a weak individual that he had been led out without a buyer after the bidding stopped at $34,000.

Enter one Billy McDonald, a member of the Sangster team. Belfast-born McDonald is a former car salesman, which makes him ideally suited to the tasks of a bloodstock agent. There is not much difference between the two worlds, both requiring a gift of the gab and a sharp eye for wheeling and dealing. If the rotund McDonald is ever invited to appear in Who's Who, it would come as no surprise to those who know him if he listed his hobbies as drinking and gambling.

His quick-fire chat and slick sales technique endeared him to the Americans and it was in the United States that he decided to set up business after a period as a bloodstock agent in England, renting an office in Los Angeles, not far from the Santa Anita Racecourse. He was good for contacts too, and was instrumental in alerting wealthy clients to the Sangster racing syndication such as the late Bob Fluor, who had made his fortune in chemicals, and the Palm Springs builder and publisher Danny Schwartz, who has been the longest-standing member of the syndicate's 'free float' percentages.

In fact it was Schwartz who remained loyal to Sangster and the idea of taking percentages in certain of the Ballydoyle horses – usually 15 per cent – when other people dropped by the wayside. This was a particularly evident when Sangster and O'Brien had to revisit the Keeneland Sales in 1976 and 1977 without any of the initial 1975 stock having really proved themselves. Some of the shareholders wanted to play a waiting game and see how the 1975 yearlings turned out before committing themselves further. But Schwartz hung on in there and was suitably rewarded in the forthcoming years.

If McDonald never discovers another decent racehorse in his life, he will always be remembered as the man who found Alleged.

The Ulsterman's discovery of Alleged was no fluke because he had a hand in the yearling's private purchase by an American trainer after it had been led out unsold at the Keeneland auction. He then followed the colt's development over the ensuing months and when the colt was offered at the Hollywood Park two-year-old sale the following year, he attended the auction on Sangster's behalf.

It was a pure fluke, however, that Sangster ended up with the colt – and he has McDonald to thank for that. In Irish writer Raymond Smith's excellent biography of Vincent O'Brien, Sangster reveals how he instructed McDonald to buy the colt privately before the sale started. McDonald did this, paying $120,000 to its owner. On Sangster's instruction, the colt was then allowed to be put into the sales ring when McDonald's orders were to let the colt go if the bidding reached $200,000. But the bidding did not go that far. In fact, it was McDonald who was left with the final bid at $175,000. When McDonald was then approached by the underbidder, Hoss Inman, and asked if he would 'take a profit on the colt' McDonald telephoned Sangster and asked him the same question. 'Tell him it's his if he comes up with $200,000,' Sangster told him.

But in an effort to obtain an extra profit for Sangster, McDonald asked Inman for $225,000 – a figure that was refused. So Sangster was left holding the colt, which he kept, and which subsequently furthered his dramatic impact on the world stage. This incredible stroke of good fortune ended with Alleged being syndicated as a stallion for $16 million.

Alleged was a slower-maturing horse than The Minstrel and ran only once as a two-year-old, winning a seven-furlong maiden race at the Curragh in the November, just over a month before he became a three-year-old. In fact, Alleged would have been kept to race in America but he had shown a tendency to suffer from a slight knee problem during the several workouts he had on the dirt tracks which the majority of horses run on in the States.

Although O'Brien had entered Alleged for the Derby and the Irish Derby it was felt he would be a better horse in the second half of the season and would therefore be brought along without undue pressure and with a shot at the Arc as a possibility.

Sangster, who had by now brought in Bob Fluor as a partner along with another American, Shirley Taylor, was convinced quite early on in the season that he might have another real racehorse on his hands.

Alleged had run in Ballydoyle Stakes at Leopardstown in April, winning comfortably by two lengths, then reappeared three weeks later for a race at the Curragh. This was an interesting contest on paper because O'Brien had two other much more fancied syndicate horses in the race, the Piggott-ridden Valinsky (who was subsequently to run unplaced against The Minstrel at Epsom) and Meneval, who was also being thought of as a Paris-bound horse in October. Valinsky started the 5−4 favourite, despite Piggott putting up 5lb overweight at 8−12 instead of 8−7, while Meneval was a 4−1 shot. Piggott tried to make all the running in the twelve-furlong Royal Whip Stakes (something the horse had not been asked to do before) but was outbattled by Alleged, who won by a length at 33−1.

It was a great night for the O'Brien outsiders, an even better one for Sangster's Classic aspirations, because another of his string, the Sir Ivor filly Lady Capulet, won the Irish 1,000 Guineas at 16−1. Sangster even had the third horse, too, the Barry Hills-trained Lady Mere.

Fluor had not been too pleased when O'Brien decided to bypass the Irish Derby with Alleged (and run The Minstrel), because he had been expecting to bring over a group of friends to watch the horse participate and it was to have been the highlight of their trip.

So Alleged made his next appearance two weeks later in the Gallinule Stakes, again at the Curragh, when he won again, only this time with Piggott in the saddle and the horse a firm favourite. It was now that Alleged was given a brief rest before being taken over to race in England for the first time, appearing in the Great Voltigeur Stakes at York's top-class August meeting.

This proved to be something of a revelation. Alleged slammed his opponents by seven lengths with the 2—1 favourite Hot Grove, who had been narrowly beaten by The Minstrel in the Derby, a well-beaten fourth a further three lengths away. On this form line through Hot Grove (who was beaten a neck at Epsom and had not raced since) it was a tremendous achievement, one that made Alleged a better horse than the Derby winner on the form book.

Another piece of incredible good fortune was now to come Sangster's way. This time, however, he would end up several million pounds the richer because Alleged lost a race.

In 1977, the St Leger was a lot more fashionable than it is today. This year's final Classic also looked a weak contest. It appeared to rest between Alleged, the odds-on favourite at 4—7, and the Queen's filly Dunfermline, winner of the Oaks at Epsom, England's fourth Classic. Many observers thought Lester Piggott did not ride one of his best races here, taking up the running quite early on Alleged, just after the turn into the straight in fact.

Willie Carson rousted the Queen's filly for a challenge with two furlongs to run so that it became a neck-and-neck battle inside the final furlong. Dunfermline's better stamina over this mile and three-quarters won the day, Alleged buckling under by one and a half lengths.

Soon after the dust had settled on what was a popular Royal win, Bob Fluor and Shirley Taylor were so disappointed at losing the St Leger that they sold their shares back to Sangster for an undisclosed amount (perhaps they could not read a form book, so did not realise they still had a colt of immense talent). Sangster, therefore, became the main shareholder in Alleged.

This was business after all, the very business he had set out to conduct in the first place. He was much closer to Alleged than Fluor and Williams and, by now, knew exactly what O'Brien thought of the colt as a racehorse and what John Magnier believed of the colt as a potential stallion.

So when Alleged lined up for the Prix de l'Arc de Triomphe in October in Sangster's colours – it had previously run in Bob Fluor's silks – it was no surprise to see the colt installed as favourite at almost 4–1. Piggott dictated the pace from soon after the start, much to the annoyance of O'Brien, who had issued waiting-tactic orders. Alleged won handsomely, however, defeating a rare runner from Australasia in the top-class five-year-old Balmerino, who was ridden by Ron Hutchinson and whose enterprising owners had campaigned successfully in New Zealand, Australia, America and Europe, winning twenty-one races before subsequently being retired to stud in his native New Zealand.

In the following season, Alleged again won the Arc, thus becoming only the third horse since the war to do so twice. He had undergone a light, three-race unbeaten season as a four-year-old which had been disrupted by a virus in O'Brien's stable during the summer. Although Alleged had raced only ten times in his life and it had been mooted that he might finish off his racing career in some of the back-end top US races, Sangster then retired him him to stud as the winner of nine of his races, amassing £327,000 in win prize money.

His syndication fee (forty shares at $400,000 per share) valued Alleged at $16 million to stand at Walmac Farm, Kentucky.

Whether Alleged might have followed The Minstrel to Kentucky a year earlier, if it had been possible, is conjecture. By the time of the colt's first Arc success, the metritis ban had put paid to that opportunity anyway.

What it all meant was that the Sangster partnership had syndicated two colts for $25 million with their first crop of 1975 yearlings. It was success without precedent.

And there was still lots more to come.

TEN

A Living Commodity

Robert Sangster was leading British owner for the first time in 1977, having amassed a little over £348,000 in winning prize money, a figure that was £100,000 more than French-based Daniel Wildenstein the previous year. For good measure and to signal that he was there to stay, he repeated the feat the following year. This time, however, £160,405 was sufficient to give him that top position.

Yet neither figure made much more than a dent in the running costs of his worldwide racing and breeding operation, which was then costing £1.5 million a year. His interests in the colts with O'Brien at Ballydoyle accounted for approximately half of this expense.

So it was a case of unbalanced books from a prize-money point of view, even though he had won a quite fantastic haul of seven Group One races in this year of The Minstrel and Alleged. He had also won with the top two-year-olds of their sex, Try My Best in the Dewhurst Stakes, and the filly Sookera in the Cheveley Park Stakes, plus the sprinter Godswalk in the King's Stand at Royal Ascot.

But not everything went according to plan and there was a degree of misfortune with the top-class filly, Durtal, the winner of the previous season's Cheveley Park Stakes and who in 1977 was favourite for the Oaks, three days after The Minstrel had won the Derby. Success from this Barry Hills-trained Lyphard filly would have made Sangster's year an absolute peach. But it was not to be. Durtal became unruly at the start of the Epsom Classic, bolted in a terrifying manner and threw Piggott sideways as the saddle slipped. Even this great jockey's prowess with horses was to no avail, because his foot became caught in a stirrup and he was dragged along at speed until he was thrown clear when the stirrup leather broke just before Durtal crashed into the rails, badly cutting herself. It was a close escape for Piggott and he said afterwards that he could have easily been killed. Durtal never recovered from the injuries or from a long course of antibiotic treatment sufficiently to race again. She was retired to the paddocks.

There were other top Sangster fillies around too, such as the home-bred River Dane, while Lady Mere and Lady Capulet were among the top milers.

The economics of maintaining a large string of racehorses proved that in Britain and Ireland it was impossible for Sangster to make his racing pay. Every two or three years he would have to come up with a potential top stallion that he and his partners could syndicate if they were to return to Keeneland Sales every year and replenish their young stock.

In other countries it was a different matter. Sangster was now increasing the number of his horses in training in Australia, principally with Colin Hayes, although there were now several with Bart Cummings and Tommy Smith, while adding to the number of broodmares. There, and in America, the prize money he won did cover the costs – purely of his racing involvement as opposed to his bloodstock and breeding activities. These days, on average, Australian owners can make their racing pay by winning one and a half races, while in Britain five races need to be won to cover the cost of a Flat horse in training.

But there was plenty of wheeling and dealing going on and Sangster was a ready buyer wherever there were top horses to be sold anywhere in the world. In Britain he bought yearlings at the Tattersalls Sales in October and November. In Ireland he was active at Goffs Premier Yearling Sales at Kill, outside Dublin. There was Keeneland in July and September, Saratoga in New York State in August, Deauville in France, the Easter Sale at

Sydney. Like a stockbroker with his eyes on the screen, Sangster was kept up to the minute and received regular briefings on any worldwide 'commodity' that came on the market. And anyone privately selling a horse of any note would know it was best to offer Sangster first refusal. Then he would research the pedigree, assess the horse's racing ability, and, once having spoken to one or more of his bloodstock team, make his own commercial judgement as to the horse's worth. He bought many horses this way and in some cases bought the dam of a good horse as he did when buying out Danny Schwartz in the top sprinter Solinus, purchasing the colt's dam, Cawston's Pride, at the same time. The object here was that the dam might just produce other progeny with as much ability.

He and his partners set records wherever they went in pursuit of the best-bred stock. At Goffs in 1975 they had paid a sale record of 127,000 guineas – two and a half times the previous best – for the first yearling son of Northern Dancer ever to be offered for auction in Europe. They named him Be My Guest, ranked ninth in the Free Handicap, yet he was only the sixth-best colt in the stable of 1977 behind Alleged, The Minstrel, the very good miler Artaius, the sprinter Godswalk and Marinsky. Such was the in-depth quality of the Sangster team that Be My Guest was another potential stallion at the end of a three-year-old career which was curtailed through injury. Nevertheless, Be My Guest was still retired to stand at Coolmore with a value of £800,000 which, though not in the multi-million-dollar league of Alleged and The Minstrel, was still a very healthy profit on the original purchase price.

Sangster did not always get his own way, though, because there were several other major players against whom he had to compete. Principal of these was the billionaire, Bunker Hunt.

The Texan oil and gas magnate Nelson Bunker Hunt was one of the true internationalists of his generation. At one point his equine empire was over 700 strong, with interests in America, Canada, Britain, France, Australia and New Zealand. Bunker Hunt's European horses were trained in France, although he bought one of his best horses, Vaguely Noble, at the Newmarket December Sales of 1967, buying a half-share in the colt after being outbid in the auction at a record 136,000 guineas.

Vaguely Noble, who was trained in Chantilly by Etienne Pollet, won the Prix de l'Arc de Triomphe the following year, after which he was retired to stud in Kentucky, the celebrated breeder John Gaines paying $1.25 million for a 25 per cent share. The great filly Dahlia was a product of Bunker Hunt's support for Vaguely Noble. Campaigned at three years, four, five and six, Dahlia helped her owner top the British owners' table in 1973, the year in which his son of Vaguely Noble, Empery, won the Derby. The following year he topped the owners' and the breeders' tables, again as a result of Dahlia's achievements. The filly won thirteen times, including nine Group One races, in five countries – France, England, Ireland, Canada and the United States.

The squat, bespectacled Bunker Hunt was often characterised by his slightly dishevelled appearance as though he was just about to enter the university lecture theatre to deliver some outstanding theory and had forgotten to straighten his collar and tie. But he certainly knew his horses. In the late 1960s he had seen the potential offered by New Zealand, buying two dairy farms in North Island and spending large amounts of money to transform them into what became the Waikato Stud.

He sent out his stallions from the US, Pretendre being one of the first stallions on the double-duty trail. The chestnut colt had been purchased for $425,000 after his racing career in Britain to stand in the US. After three seasons there, Pretendre was sent to Ireland, then on to Waikato. But he was transferred to England after the Kentucky Derby and Preakness Stakes victories of his son, Canonero II, then returning to New Zealand for their breeding season, where he collapsed and died of heart failure as a nine-year-old.

The Bunker Hunt stallion influence on southern-hemisphere breeding was never better served than by the stallion Decies, sire of the great Dulcify, who was trained by Colin Hayes. Purchased at a bargain $3,250 by Hayes, Dulcify won over $568,000 in ten victories. But, in the 1979 Melbourne Cup when ridden by Brent Thomson, the four-year-old became a victim of the perils of the sport. He shattered his pelvis entering the Fleminton straight and had to be put down a couple of hours later when the injury proved beyond repair.

In 1988, the Bunker Hunt equine empire was ended at Keeneland in a dispersal sale of 580 horses, bringing to an end his thirty-five-year involvement with racing and breeding on a grand international scale. The $47 million he received from the sale was, however, only a mere swipe at his debts, which totalled hundreds of millions of dollars more and which were the result of a disastrous punt trying to corner the world's silver market. The Texan had played the silver bullion market for years with great success, making millions, and had once tipped off a legendary British jockey who often rode for him to try his luck with silver – which the jockey duly did, doubling his money in a short space of time. The final curtain was drawn some three years later when Bunker Hunt's Kentucky Blue Grass Farm was sold. The former billionaire now lives in a more modest style and drives a rather old and battered car. But, then, he often did –even when he could have afforded to make a serious play for his own car company!

Susan Peacock became Susan Sangster on 10 March 1978, some two months after Christine had divorced Sangster in an un-defended hearing on the grounds of his adultery. Susan's own divorce from Andrew Peacock had been finalised five months earlier.

The couple had hoped to marry in St Bridget's Chapel within The Nunnery's grounds, but this was forbidden by the Anglican Bishop of the island because they had both been divorced. So they had to make do with a registry-office ceremony followed by a blessing at the chapel the following day.

But even here Sangster was forced to borrow a little of the

subterfuge he used extensively in the sales ring by announcing publicly – and to all but a handful of his guests – that the wedding day was to be on the 11th and that it was to be a 'very quiet' one.

Such methods were now an important part of the couple's life, given that they had achieved almost celebrity status and that public appearances such as this had to be stage-managed correctly. While the nation's media, together with hundreds of the island's residents, were preparing themselves for a glimpse of the happy couple leaving the registry office on the Saturday, the Sangsters were already married, having performed the ceremony the day before.

Not that the marriage on the Friday went unrecorded by the media, although it nearly did. In those days the registry office in Douglas just happened to be in the same building as the Highway and Transport Board office where local residents went to renew their driving licences. A clerk there spotted Sangster entering the registry and contacted a friend on the local paper, the *Isle of Man Examiner*. By the time Susan arrived in a blue Rolls-Royce Corniche, two reporters and a photographer were in place outside to record events while the national press pack were propping up a local bar blissfully unaware of the proceedings.

Sangster even went to the extent of getting his best man, Richard Formby, a wealthy Merseyside landowner and Isle of Man resident, to act as a decoy by leaving the registry office before him with a blonde, an event that, for a second, caused a little confusion. But, as Sangster would come to realise, the best way of arousing media interest is to try and avoid it.

The happy couple finally emerged from the building to be watched by a few onlookers, shoppers and office girls, as they sped off in a Mercedes back to The Nunnery. The moment was captured and the photograph duly appeared in the popular press.

Although it was a quiet wedding ceremony, the 'unassuming' Sangster style did not extend to the evening celebrations in the

Douglas seafront Palace Hotel, owned by his friend Sir Douglas Clague. Here, carefully detailed arrangements had been made for a lavish bash to entertain guests who had flown in from all parts of the world. Susan met them at the airport, where some arrived in private planes. The guest list was a Who's Who of racing and included Colin and Betty Hayes from Australia and the Aga and Begum Khan.

Susan was now in her element. The party provided the opportunity to show off her skills as a first-rate hostess. She organised the vintage champagne, the fresh local lobster and salmon, arranged for the flowers to be flown in. This was the high life she knew from her early Melbourne days as a 'social' reporter and to which she had later grown accustomed in the world of Australian politics. Only now it was all on a much grander scale and, more importantly, she held the purse strings – she was the Queen Bee. With true *Dynasty*-style hedonism, the Sangsters would publicly embark on a merry-go-round of high-profile partying, socialising and spending.

They would buy a grand house with three acres in Barbados where they would go for several weeks of the British winter. A $6 million home in Sydney would follow. It seemed to be the product of Sangster's desire to have the best time in life he possibly could, while Susan's love of the high life, and her ability to spend money, was a natural ally.

There was nothing wrong in this, of course, and lots of people spend their money as they wish. What appeared to be a turn-off to some of Sangster's earlier friends and acquaintances, however, was that the lifestyle was carried out in such a public manner. Hardly a moment passed by without the couple having themselves in print, with pictures of their latest acquisiton in an up-market glossy magazine or in the society columns of the world's press.

Susan had to emphasise not only that their Barbados home had been built by Lord Astor (she did not say which one), but that it was situated in the best position on the best swimming beach on the island. To some people, it was not simply a case of having it, but of flaunting it too.

To be fair, Sangster had decreed that he would have to build and maintain a high profile because of his business. But great care was always taken to invite a chosen handful of their favourite journalists when it came to dishing out the party guest lists and among them were some of the most influential society writers of the time, who were willing to take advantage of a free life of luxury at a weekend house party – flight included – at whichever home they were throwing a bash.

The whirl of events forced some friends to recall Christine's wishes that Sangster should keep his feet on the ground. But, by now, there was no chance of that. Susan was deeply in love with Sangster and she was the type of person who wore her heart on her sleeve. Unlike Christine, who was quieter, more refined, Susan was brash. But it was this bolder quality that Sangster found so infatuating. She would help raise his public profile too. And that was one of the qualities Sangster found so appealing.

By now, Sangster had assembled a dedicated team of professionals to accompany him on his tour of the world's bloodstock sales. His racing manager at this time was the former leading Irish amateur rider, Pat Hogan, known to most by his initials, P.P. This darting hawk-like man of quick wit and ready smile had a wealth of experience in the sport. He was a successful trainer in his own right, mainly of point-to-pointers, born into the world of horses in Rathcannon, County Limerick, and brought up watching his father Joseph wheel and deal at Ireland's horse fairs, where a spit in the palm before a handshake was a man's bond (with maybe a little 'luck money' thrown in). P.P. Hogan was, therefore, one of Sangster's Irish 'tinkers', possessing that natural ability to 'spot a real 'oss', as well as having the fox-like guile that is so necessary at the top yearling sales, where the uninitiated would be safer walking through a minefield.

The success of Keeneland's 'Class of '75' had catapulted Sangster into the limelight within international racing circles.

The headlines over his public love life, too, had spilled over into the non-racing field, creating interest in Robert Sangster and Susan *per se*.

So it was with a certain degree of obsessive curiosity from several quarters that the Sangsters attended Sydney's Easter Sales of 1978, which had become part of their two-month business and pleasure honeymoon trip to Australia. Susan particularly wanted to spend as much time as possible in Australia so she could be with her children.

In Australia the Sangster phenomenon had now created a problem. His fame and reputation meant he was a marked man when it came to bidding in the ring. So he had to work twice as hard to outsmart his rivals.

At these sales Sangster could be found drinking champagne and enjoying the company of Susan and her friends as a diversion from the main event. Minutes later, however, he would be at the back of the sales ring, in deep conversation with Hogan, Billy McDonald, Jonathan Irwin, one of Ireland's leading racing administrators, and top vet Stan Cosgrove, discussing the merits of the next yearling to hit the sales ring.

It was at sales such as this that Sangster would have to employ the 'ducking and diving' tactics he knew so well as a boxer. It was here that the team would lay false trails in an effort to throw competitors off the scent once battle commenced in the auction.

The team would inspect maybe two dozen yearlings in a high-profile manner when they were really only interested in four. Half of these would be vetted (another step in a display of serious interest) so that it became practically anyone's guess as to which of the dozen or so they really wanted once the bidding got under way. Had they merely confined their activities to the yearlings in which they were interested, the owners of those animals would have noted this and probably have doubled the reserve figure they placed on that stock.

At the Sydney Easter sales, the figures involved were measured in tens of thousands of dollars as opposed to Keeneland's millions. Even so, Sangster spent huge sums of money only if, on his own commercial judgement, it was deemed necessary. It was a tight, sleek ship he was trying to run. And that meant being smarter than the next man.

There was always the danger, too, of being 'run up' at the auction. This is when an owner knows who is bidding for his yearling and employs his own 'secret agents' to bid in opposition, thereby running up the figure to double, maybe three times what he would have got in a straight forward duel. Such run-ups are not uncommon in the bloodstock market; in fact many people in racing would say it is prevalent.

The drawback to such behaviour, of course, is when those responsible for running up the bidding are left with the final nod because they have pushed their luck too far. Perpetrators of such behaviour play the game on a knife-edge because the rewards of any run-up can be so great. (We shall see a little later how the Arabs were run up – sometimes in the most alarming manner – when they first entered racing.)

Sangster used all sorts of ploys to disguise his interest in a particular yearling when the bidding started. After all, his reputation was now established, people knew he went to great lengths – and expense – to check a yearling's suitability before a bid was made. If the Sangster bids were not the subject of a certain amount of subterfuge, then anyone could simply match bids with Sangster, knowing that all the homework had been completed. If they won, they obviously now had a horse that had been well chosen. If they lost, then Sangster would have paid, in all likelihood, far more than he should have done.

This was the sort of situation Sangster referred to when he said he used his 'street fighting' tactics (not that his privileged upbringing in such a wealthy part of Merseyside meant he would have known much about any street). But Sangster had fought before, even if it was in a different ring and under the Marquis of Queensberry's rules.

So he would often take the preliminary precaution of attempting to stay out of sight once the bidding got under way in an effort to avert the gaze of rival bidders who would have been watching his every move. Sometimes he would arrange for different bloodstock agents to bid for certain stock. These could be agents not normally associated with the Sangster camp, and who were notified only at the last minute. They might take their cue to make a bid from another Sangster agent, situated well away from the team camp, who signals the go-ahead with a scratch of his nose, a turn of his head or a touch of his Panama hat.

When the bidding is expected to run into millions of dollars, as it does at Keeneland, such 'second-hand' agents will not be on the normal 1½ per cent commission. He or she is more likely to be working for a fixed fee or a much reduced rate because their input will be confined to the sales ring as opposed to the many other areas in a bloodstock agent's duties. It was all part of the cloak-and-dagger drama at the sales, in which Sangster prided himself on being a much sharper player than the rest of the cast.

Sangster would wheel and deal in an effort to obtain the stock he wanted. He might swap several coverings by one of his stallions for a yearling so that the seller could send his mares to that stallion free of charge. He was always willing to come up with a deal – foal-sharing, percentage bartering, anything where he felt he had done good business.

Sangster explains his philosophy thus: 'Take our operation at Keeneland, for example. They have three hundred or so selected yearlings and half of them will be colts. As we are looking for potential stallions as opposed to just racehorses, we can eliminate about a hundred of these colts on pedigree alone.

'When the team visits Kentucky before the sales start, we will usually disregard half of the fifty colts on conformation, which leaves us with twenty-five or so who comply with our criteria as potential stallions in pedigree and conformation.

We then concentrate for three days on this group of twenty-five and select around ten for further scrutiny. The team will do their examination work on legs, knees, etc., which includes x-rays and blood tests, and the yearlings are extensively walked. Out of every crop we will be looking to end up with two top-class yearlings which Vincent can turn into racehorses. We need racecourse performance allied to pedigree and conformation. When their racing days are over our expertise comes into play as to where they will stand as stallions.

'One has to keep looking and replacing stock constantly. It is the same with the amount of travelling I do. The more outlets we have the better chance of making a profit at the end of the day.'

The profit motive was strong, all-embracing. The success of the whole operation was geared to it. But not every horse they bought was a world-beater. The vagaries of the business meant that failures would surely come along, almost as an integral part of the operation. It was just a question of how much the failures would set them back.

ELEVEN

An Ill Wind

The Sangster syndicate's growing success had a dramatic impact on the world of the thoroughbred both in racing and in breeding. Records at the sales were broken with monotony as the competition latched on to the Sangster way of doing things. The competition meant that Sangster was having to pay more for his basic raw material. But, as the returns on the initial outlay were proving highly lucrative, this did not seem to matter because Sangster continued to spend heavily. He became the market leader, the trend-setter, in a new-wave attack on the traditional order.

He paid more than $8 million for twenty-one yearlings at Keeneland alone in 1978. Two of these, which had cost $725,000, had to be put down on a flight from Cincinnati to Shannon after they received injuries during the flight. The yearlings were insured, so there was no financial loss, but Sangster was obviously upset at having lost two potentially good horses and the incident served to remind people of the risks involved in transporting horses internationally. Only a small percentage ever come to grief, thanks to all the precautions and the assistance of a team of very professional horsemen in attendance. Some horses, like people, get worked up about flying. In the case of yearlings such as these, by the time that fact is realised the plane is probably over the Atlantic.

The later years of the 1970s saw a 'copycat' influx of foreign buyers to Keeneland in particular, including a fair contingent from Britain. In 1978, for instance, this helped push up the prices of the middle-order stock to more than double what they had been just prior to The Minstrel's sucess.

Sangster returned the following year, and the syndicate shelled out another $9.3 million, paying $1 million for a Northern Dancer yearling he later called Storm Bird, and $1.4 million for a son of Nijinsky who was subsequently named Sailor King. He reckoned that both were 'dirt cheap'.

Once a rarity, million-dollar yearlings would soon hardly provoke a murmur from those attending such sales.

Not everything the Sangster syndicate purchased would turn out a wise buy, however. On the contrary, the list of horses which appeared to promise everything, but which delivered hardly anything, would litter the syndicate's purchasing manifest over the next several years.

There also developed what must have been a worrying trend in the O'Brien stable concerning a succession of expensive purchases which, as two-year-olds, were high class and in the same league as The Minstrel and Alleged, but which failed miserably to train on and produce the goods. One such instance proved a costly lesson to an Irish millionaire who attempted to play the Sangster game. He ended up with his fingers badly burned.

The horse concerned was Try My Best, the top two-year-old of 1977.

The British winter time is frustrating for those Flat-racing fans who do not care for the poor relation sport of the National Hunt, which occupies centre stage in the cold months, starting in August and running through to the beginning of June – the Flat starts in the spring and ends in early November. Consequently, the close season is a cauldron of apocrypha about the progress of the previous season's leading juveniles, a sort of artificial stirring of the pot, with a liberal sprinkling of hype, in which the bookmakers join in by offering ridiculously short odds on the next season's Classic hopefuls when, in reality, nobody yet knows whether or not those horses have trained on.

It is only when they have turned three-years-old and begun the three- or four-month preparation towards the new season that they begin to show signs of sparkle; the weeks of roadwork entailing miles of steady muscle-building walking, the short gentle canters on the all-weather gallops, the increasing work-load and length of canter, the stepping up of tempo and food intake, soon a swinging canter at half-pace (horses are very rarely worked at full racing pace at home), all the time monitoring how each horse is taking the routine – this is the basic pattern in the pre-season programme.

It is supposed to build into a picture so that a trainer will have noted how each horse is progressing towards peak fitness, a process of great skill and patience, adapting procedures to the needs of each individual horse, adjusting workload and feed to suit the gross thick-winded 'stuffy' horse or the lighter type which needs less preparation to come to hand.

These are some of the skills of all trainers. In the case of O'Brien they have been refined over decades of experience with some of the best horses of their generation, any one of which a smaller trainer prays might one day come his way.

Even O'Brien was deceived by Try My Best, though. He and some of the other connections were made to look the proverbial fool over this one.

After the colt had won the previous season's Dewhurst Stakes, he was reckoned by most observers to be the most outstanding juvenile in Europe, an opinion which was also expressed by his rider Lester Piggott. O'Brien said he saw no reason why Try My Best should not develop into another Nijinsky, while Sangster himself reckoned the colt was a firm 2,000 Guineas hope before going on to the Derby.

It was in the early part of the year, before the season started, that one Patrick Gallagher entered the Sangster scene. Gallagher was twenty-seven years old, had a reputation as a sort of brooding Clint Eastwood character, and was reckoned to be something of a high-flyer in Ireland where he had taken over the property-development company of his late father, Matt, pulling off several shrewd deals. He used simple methods such as paying a percentage deposit or even a purchase option on certain parcels of land. Then he wheeled and dealed with end-users, finally selling on in back-to-back agreements so that he never had to shell out huge capital sums for the land.

In one such deal he made over £2 million by buying the Sean Lemass House near Dublin's St Stephen's Green for £5.4 million (paying a 10 per cent deposit), then promptly sold it on to a building society to use as their headquarters for £7.5 million, out of which he paid the balance of his initial purchase.

Gallagher was similar in some ways to Sangster. He too was an amiable man in private, rather shy, yet always kept out of the newspapers. He was joint managing director of a conglomerate of several dozen companies, including house building and merchant banking, under the umbrella of a holding company called Bering Estates with offshore headquarters in the Cayman Islands. He owned racehorses, as had his father, and was involved in breeding on his two stud farms in County Dublin. Gallagher had also previously done a deal with the Sangster syndicate when selling them the very good sprinter Godswalk.

Although he said he did not bet on horses, he was prepared to take a gamble when he began negotiations to buy a quarter-share in Try My Best before the season started. The colt was owned in varying percentages, by Sangster, O'Brien, Magnier, Danny Schwartz and London-based Simon Fraser. Gallagher had taken the view that the colt was worth £2 million before the 2,000 Guineas. If it won the Classic it would probably be valued at £3 million to £4 million. And if Try My Best went on to win the Derby, as connections thought he could, then the sky was the limit – anything from £7 million to £10 million for this son of Northern Dancer.

So Gallagher pitched in with an offer of £500,000 for a quarter-share, having already decided that he would eventually go as far as £600,000. The negotiations were not going to be that simple, however. Not surprisingly, Sangster and his partners wanted something extra to 'discount' the colt's potential value should it actually win the Guineas. They viewed Try My Best as worth £2 million now. So why should they part with 25 per cent?

As the amicable, but tough, negotiations continued, Gallagher soon came to realise he would have to part with more than he had originally bargained for. Ultimately, he agreed to pay £750,000 for the quarter-share.

As the season approached there were extremely bullish statements emanating from Ballydoyle. O'Brien declared himself 'very pleased' with the colt's development and thought he was a live Guineas contender. Britain's bookmakers thought so too, because they had Try My Best as low as 3–1 a few weeks before the start of the season. For the colt's preparatory race, O'Brien chose the Vauxhall Trial Stakes over seven furlongs at the Curragh in early April, which Try My Best won by two lengths from Columbanus, who went on to finish third in the Irish Guineas.

At Newmarket on Guineas day, the ground was soft. Although Try My Best had shown his best form on a sound surface there was no saying his class would not see him through because he had beaten Columbanus in yielding ground first time out. All the same, instead of hardening in the betting to odds-on, he was backable at even money. There had also been rumours that all was not well with the colt, speculation that had wafted across the English Channel from France. Gallagher, however, had faith in the men around him. He said Piggott had told him the only thing that could stop Try My Best from winning was a brick wall.

Sensationally, Try My Best finished plum last of the nineteen-runner field. The winner, Roland Gardens, had cost 3,200 guineas as a yearling.

Gallagher, who had watched the race with O'Brien, understandably went white. So shocked was he, in fact, that he had to hurry away for a large brandy. The man who did not back horses had just lost something in the region of £250,000-plus.

Try My Best was dope-tested, of course, but the tests did not reveal anything. Everyone seemed mystified. A little later, O'Brien stated that in his opinion the horse must have been sickening for something. He reported that it lost weight and was listless on returning to Ireland. Although no exact cause of the

Newly-weds Robert
Sangster and the
former Christine
Street after their
rriage at Penrith in
1960.

Wife number two:
: former Australian
politician's wife,
Susan Peacock,
rling of Melbourne
society.

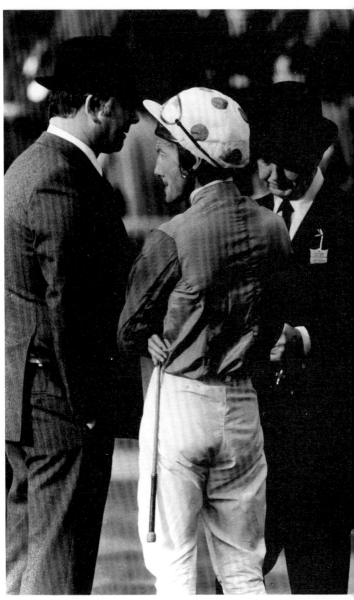

3. The winning team of Robert Sangster, Lester Piggott and Vincent O'Brien, an irrepressible combination which featured in every major race in Europe.

4. Robert Sangster with his trainer, Vincent O'Brien, the man Sangster says is simply the best in the world.

5. Sangster listens to the sales strategy as discussed by John Magnier, the third member of the famous Sangster triumvirate. The flat-capped Irishman, Tommy Stack, an associate of the Coolmore Stud organisation, joins in.

6. That 'flashy chestnut', The Minstrel, being taken to post by Lester Piggott. The 1977 dual Derby winner, who provided Sangster's first major breakthrough, was retired to stud with a valuation of $9 million.

7. Sadler's Wells, the horse which has turned into a top class stallion to continue the Sangster breeding success.

8. Melbourne Cup glory: centre stage for Susan Sangster as she poses for photographers alongside her husband after the 1980 success of Beldale Ball which was trained by Colin Hayes (left) and ridden by Johnny Letts.

9. Wife number three: another Susan, the former Sue Dean from the Isle of Man, who became Sangster's third wife (and he her third husband) at the age of twenty-nine in 1985.

10. It's the open-necked casual look for Sangster at the Keeneland Sales in Kentucky.

11. Men only: the Maktoums' entourage enjoying the English tradition of the Royal meeting at Ascot, their favourite racecourse.

12. Robert Sangster, the sponsor, hands the winning trophy to Khalid Abdullah after one of the prince's horses lands the Swettenham Stud Sussex Stakes at Goodwood.

13. Sangster with Michael Dickinson, his one-time great training hope for the hallowed acres of Manton in Wiltshire.

14. Sangster with his friend and trainer Barry Hills.

shock defeat was ever given, Try My Best did not run again. O'Brien tried to bring him back into training but the colt did not stand up to it.

Try My Best's dismal flop was the manifestation of the 2,000 Guineas jinx that haunted the O'Brien camp in this period.

When Gallagher had got over the shock and ruminated over the events that had led him into what became a disastrous flirtation with the Sangster syndicate, he calmly decided to write off a large part of his investment by selling his £750,000 quarter-share back to the syndicate at a knock-down price.

For Sangster it was purely a case of hard business. The heart sympathised with Gallagher's plight, but the head ruled that the buy-back deal had to be realistic. He too would have loved to have seen the horse win and therefore increase its value dramatically. But it showed that sentiment played no part in the running of his empire. That was why he had hedged his bet with the colt by selling the share to Gallagher in the first place. The syndicate had now made a £250,000–£300,000 'profit' on the Gallagher deal, maybe more. And Try My Best had cost 180,000 guineas as a yearling. Now they could still make money from the colt because they retired it to stand at Coolmore Stud. What was more, Sangster and O'Brien had already bought a large percentage of Try My Best's dam, Sex Appeal. She would subsequently return to Northern Dancer and produce Try My Best's full brother, a colt bought by the syndicate and named El Gran Señor, yet another winner of the Dewhurst (Sangster's fifth), who would run second in the 1983 Derby to Secreto.

Sadly, the future for both Try My Best and Patrick Gallagher was not going to prove fortuitous. The colt developed something of an infertility problem at stud, while Gallagher's group crashed dramatically during 1982 in one of Ireland's largest business failures. The company had debts of more than £50 million and gross assets of less than half that figure. Undeterred, he moved to London and began property development there. Six years later, however, he was in prison, having been sentenced to two years on charges of false accounting and company theft concerning the failed group's bank, Merchant Banking (Northern Ireland) Ltd.

If the Try My Best saga had caused rumbles in the racing world, there were more flops to come from the Sangster camp in equally disappointing fashion. One of these led to a parting of the ways with Lester Piggott in an acrimonious split towards the end of the 1980 season.

Although Try My Best's dismal performance was a setback, the strength of the Sangster buying policy allowed for a reject or two on the production line. So while plans were being made to send the three-year-old to stud, along came another top-class two-year-old called Monteverdi who, like Try My Best, remained unbeaten and landed the Dewhurst Stakes at the back-end of the season.

Monteverdi was a $305,000 yearling at New York State's Saratoga summer sale. He was a son of the promising young stallion Lyphard, who was the sire of Sangster's Durtal and the top-class filly Three Troikas. The colt started his three-year-old career with an approximate $6 million valuation. After running second in soft ground on his seasonal debut, however, he again filled the runner-up spot in a 2,000 Guineas preparatory race at Newbury, the Clerical Medical Greenham Stakes, a race he would have been expected to win to stand a chance in the Guineas.

Piggott rode Monteverdi at Newbury to find out for himself exactly what sort of horse Sangster had here. There was none of that 'tender handling' that can sometimes be employed when a horse wins well, the rider perhaps dropping his hands some distance from the line so that observers can only guess how much the horse had left to give had it been seriously put to the test.

So Piggott gave Monteverdi a most forceful ride this day. His aim was to try and get to the bottom of the horse's ability so that he could report with confidence to connections as to the best next move. There are, of course, dozens of questions that can be answered in one race. These affect a horse's performance vis-à-vis the ground, the track, the distance, the pace of the race, luck in running, the horse's fitness. It is a conundrum when the horse does not put its best foot forward after it has been working well at home.

Before the race, paddock observers felt that Monteverdi had hardly grown since his two-year-old days. The Greenham was run at a strong early pace which seemed to take the colt off his legs. But Piggott is a master at getting the best out of any horse. He held up Monteverdi as long as possible, then, in the final furlong, sent him after the leader, Final Straw, under hard driving which appeared to make the colt gallop off a true line. He went under by half a length to the Michael Stoute-trained 10–1 shot. Clearly, it was not what Sangster and O'Brien had expected, nor the betting public, because Monteverdi had been backed to 8–13.

The faces of Piggott, O'Brien and Sangster in the winner's enclosure after the race probably said it all: Piggott, stone-faced as usual, looked exasperated. O'Brien looked as though he had just lost everything as well as his shirt, and for Sangster it was time to bite his bottom lip once more.

When the dust had settled, O'Brien decided to send Monteverdi to the weaker Irish 2,000 Guineas where, in an effort to sharpen up the colt's performance, he was fitted with blinkers. This news prompted backers to make him the even-money favourite at the Curragh, but the colt's performance deteriorated. He could finish only fifth. It was now that Piggott's exasperation with the colt finally surfaced. When asked in front of racing reporters what he thought of the colt, Piggott spoke audibly enough for them to hear the important word: 'Useless.' The pack duly reported this the next day, much to the chagrin of O'Brien and Sangster.

As Sangster himself has said: 'You can criticise someone's children – but don't knock their horses.' The reason in Monteverdi's case was obvious. If someone of the stature of Piggott said the colt was useless he had probably just knocked a chunk off its possible syndication value as a stallion, whether at home or abroad.

In a final bid to salvage some of the colt's reputation, and value, Monteverdi was sent to Epsom without blinkers for the Derby, where remarkably there were still those who thought Piggott could work his old magic round Tattenham Corner, and who made the horse third favourite. Alas, it was to no avail. The colt trailed in fourteenth of the twenty-four runners in the race won by Henbit.

Monteverdi was retired to stud in America at the end of the season to stand at the Walmac Farm in Kentucky. Details of the syndication were not released.

For Piggott, though, it was the end of the line with the syndicate. In the September it was revealed that their retained jockey for the next season would be Pat Eddery. Piggott promptly announced that he would be riding for the previous season's champion trainer, Henry Cecil, a partnership that would lead to two more respective championships for both men.

It was also one that would result in a massive two-year Customs and Excise investigation into the rich rewards of Britain's top jockeys, the culmination of which was that Piggott received a three-year prison sentence for cheating the taxman, while several others were made to cough up substantial amounts to settle their 'overlooked' and undeclared revenue.

Although Sangster ended this season only in fourth place in the leading owners' table, he reaped great reward at Longchamp in October when his French filly Detroit, trained by the late Olivier Douieb, won the Prix de l'Arc de Triomphe with Sangster's new man, Pat Eddery, aboard.

The quiet, unassuming Irishman was born in 1952, one of twelve children of Jimmy Eddery, a champion jockey of Ireland who won the Irish Derby on Panaslipper in 1955. Eddery is a great jockey, stylish, strong, gentle when necessary, a man who does not enjoy the limelight, nor the attention he often receives from the racing media for his skills. At the age of twenty-two, he became the youngest British champion jockey since Charlie

Elliott and Gordon Richards half a century earlier. Like many people in racing, he has few interests outside the sport, and he 'married within the industry' too. His wife is the former Carolyn Mercer, daughter of the late Manny Mercer, whose brother Joe, a supreme stylist, took Eddery's place with Peter Walwyn. Eddery had been first jockey to Walwyn in a nine-year partnership that, today, has the ring of a golden era about it, especially when he teamed up with Grundy to win the 1975 Derby, Irish Derby and King George VI and Queen Elizabeth Diamond Stakes.

So Eddery accepted a six-figure retainer for what was now the most powerful job in racing. He would be required to ride the Sangster–O'Brien horses wherever they ran, Ireland, England, France on Sundays. It would be a hectic daily life on and off planes to Ireland to ride work where, unlike Piggott, he was an excellent trials rider. After the morning work, he would be back on the plane to England to ride at wherever the big meeting of the day was being held.

This jockeys' game of musical chairs caused quite a stir at the time. Accusations and comment about qualities such as loyalty were brought into question. In reality, however, the trend was part of the Sangster commercialisation of the sport. He wanted the best people in the business around him and would pay them accordingly. Walwyn and his patrons could not afford to match the Ballydoyle offer by a long chalk. As in all aspects of sport, the word loyalty was becoming rather old-fashioned in racing.

The appointment of Eddery was also seen as something of a snub to Steve Cauthen, the Kentucky Kid, whom Sangster had brought over to Britain as a nineteen-year-old for the start of the 1979 season and to whom he had given a retainer to ride his horses at Lambourn with Barry Hills. Perhaps Sangster and O'Brien felt that Cauthen had not yet developed into the complete rider he is today. He had ridden some 1,000 winners in America, sure. But, good as Cauthen was then, most observers felt that Eddery was the man for the Irish job. When Cauthen did mature, he left Hills and landed Piggott's job as number one to Henry Cecil, becoming champion jockey in the process.

With Sangster now establishing himself as the world's most successful owner–breeder, the pressure was on to cut his losses on the disappointments and exploit the profit-makers among his burgeoning empire. With another son of Northern Dancer, that 'dirt cheap' million-dollar yearling they called Storm Bird, there was to be a great deal of disappointment – but a fantastic amount of profit.

TWELVE

A Pot of Gold

One of the most audacious pieces of business in the history of horseracing was carried out by the Sangster syndicate at the end of the 1981 season – otherwise known as 'The Year of Shergar' – with Storm Bird, the million-dollar colt who was bought as a yearling at Keeneland in 1979. The sale of the colt would be an indication of the almost incredible heights to which Sangster had helped drive up the market.

The impact that the Sangster syndicate had made on the international scene in just five years was remarkable. But, while Sangster's foresight allowed him to talk about cheap million-dollar yearlings, it would be misleading to assume they were commonplace. Prior to 1979, there had been only two other yearlings sold at Keeneland for a million dollars or more (Canadian Bound cost $1.5 million in 1976, and Nureyev $1.3 million in 1978). There were many people among the vast army of breeders, trainers and owners within racing who could not come to grips with such ostensibly blasé statements emanating from the Sangster camp. But Sangster was unconcerned with such views. These were the thoughts of those too preoccupied with the past, never mind the present. Sangster's arrow eye was on the future. And he knew what was around the corner because he was setting a hot pace worldwide.

Like the succession of big-money purchases before Storm Bird who had proved successful two-year-olds, the colt ended his first season having won each of his five races, all at odds on, including his final start in the Dewhurst which gave Sangster his fourth success in the event in five years and O'Brien his sixth win in twelve years.

Racing experts were of the opinion that Storm Bird's form in winning the Newmarket six-furlong race was better than that of O'Brien's previous winners including Nijinsky and The Minstrel. Indeed, official handicappers rated him the best juvenile in Europe.

Unlike most of Northern Dancer's progeny, Storm Bird was a tall colt – quite different from his stocky sire – possessing a long-raking fluent action which suggested he would be suited by fast ground even though his wins had been on good or soft going. As is the usual custom with winners of the Dewhurst, Storm Bird was installed as ante-post favourite over the winter for the 2,000 Guineas in the spring.

So highly did Sangster and O'Brien regard the colt that they insured him as a three-year-old at the beginning of the year for the incredible sum of $15 million (the premium with a London broker was the equivalent of approximately half a million dollars – more than the prize money Storm Bird would have won by landing the Derby and Irish Derby). If the horse was worth that much, Sangster had indeed obtained another bargain that was going to swell the balance sheet when the colt was syndicated to stud. But the colt now really needed to prove himself as a three-year-old; it was a legitimate demand of the sport that stallions should have proved their class, toughness and ability to stand training if they were to contribute to maintaining standards by passing on those attributes to some of their progeny.

Before the syndicate could begin contemplating the new season, however, the most bizarre episode occurred when an ex-O'Brien stable lad, with a grudge against his former employer, got into the Ballydoyle yard one January night, entered Storm Bird's unguarded box and calmly began to give the horse rather more than a normal clip of his tail and mane. In fact the horse's tail, mane and fringe were hacked with a pair of scissors so crudely that stable staff who discovered the attack at first feared that the horse himself might be injured. This turned out not to be the case, although the incident was a warning against complacency.

The lush green paddocks and leafy ruralness associated with thoroughbreds conjures up a peaceful, often idyllic picture. But with horses worth millions of pounds, it was surprising that some stables, particularly in Ireland, had security inferior to the burglar-alarmed corner shop where packets of cornflakes were better protected against criminals.

Of course, the incident prompted a security review at Ballydoyle, and today there would be little chance of something similar happening again. But the lesson was not learned at the Aga Khan's Ballymany Stud in County Kildare, where Shergar retired to stand at the end of this 1981 season. He was kidnapped in 1983 after only one covering season at the stud in a daring raid by an armed IRA gang. The horse was held to ransom, and eventually shot dead when the Aga Khan and other shareholders refused to pay the £2 million demanded. It was an incredible episode and a sad loss to racing because it can take some horses several seasons to produce progeny of any real merit. Shergar never got that chance and there was nothing of any great note among the thirty-six sons and daughters he sired, although Sheikh Mohammed's Authaal raced successfully with Colin Hayes in Australia.

Storm Bird was unscathed by the attack, despite actually looking the worse for wear with a shortened tail that would take longer to grow than the mane and fringe. So he was trained with the intention of making his much awaited seasonal debut at the Curragh. The night before the meeting, however, O'Brien withdrew the colt because he was found to be slightly lame in his off-hind leg. He soon recovered from this setback and was put back in training and on course again for the 2,000 Guineas, for which he was still favourite.

O'Brien has wonderful gallops at Ballydoyle. One of them resembles Epsom's racetrack, with a sweeping bend that is similar to Tattenham Corner and on which his Derby horses are trained in order to teach them to maintain the gallop without becoming unbalanced when negotiating the cambered turn. But there is still nothing like an away trip to the racecourse for a gallop after racing. Although a horse will not work here as he would in a race, the change of enviroment helps to keep a horse interested and can sharpen it up that much better than a home gallop. Some trainers, in fact, consider that an actual race will bring a horse on in condition more than half a dozen gallops would at home.

Storm Bird was taken to Naas Racecourse in County Kildare for a gallop in the middle of April. Alas, he did not work with the sparkle that had made him such a top-class two-year-old. With a fortnight to go before the 2,000 Guineas, O'Brien revealed that the colt had developed a virus (the first signs of this are usually when a horse coughs, has a runny nose or is off his food). Racing fans, frustrated at the delayed progress of this potential equine superstar, could have been forgiven for thinking this was developing into the Storm Bird Saga, which to some extent was becoming as fascinating as the best TV serial. It was almost a case of waiting with baited breath for the next instalment.

That did not take too long to arrive because it was announced that Storm Bird would also miss the Irish 2,000 Guineas, some two weeks later. Now he was immediately taken out of the Derby betting, for which he had been one of the favourites, subsequently missing the Epsom event itself, and the Irish Derby, as well as all the alternative engagements that had been regarded as suitable. By Royal Ascot time in the third week of June, the horse's non-appearance had become something of a joke and the media comments led to strained relations – though not for the first time – between O'Brien and the press.

The whole affair, so far, did not say a lot about O'Brien's skill in the field of public relations, where the secret is to 'think like the other side'. This was surprising really, because with such high-priced animals attracting a great amount of publicity, the racing media can prove a powerful ally in the promotion of any 'wonder horse', as many a trainer has discovered. It must be said, though, that the publicity pendulum can swing too far the other way. In these instances there have been many 'talking horses' which have been hyped beyond their true ability.

As the season wore on, a break in the cloud appeared with the announcement that Storm Bird would appear after all. He would run in the Prix du Prince d'Orange at Longchamp in September, which is a recognised trial for the Prix de l'Arc de Triomphe run two weeks later. Sangster considered defeat out of the question; so did O'Brien. Over a splendid lunch at La Pré Catelan, one of the Bois de Boulogne's two restaurants much favoured by the international racing elite (the other being Grande Cascade, which is practically next door to the course), the topic of conversation was more to do with just how far the winning distance would be.

In the race though, Storm Bird severly shocked his connections by running with little zest and finishing seventh of the nine runners. Sangster, himself shattered, later said he had never seen O'Brien so devastated. The question now being asked was: had the on–off season led to Storm Bird becoming disenchanted with the game? Whatever the reason it was his only appearance on a racecourse as a three-year-old – and it was his last.

But this solitary, disappointing run did not affect his stallion syndication value. Sangster had already sold a three-quarter-share in Storm Bird for the quite amazing – some would say preposterous – sum of $21 million. He kept the other quarter himself (O'Brien and Magnier had their smaller percentages within this quarter-share).

Sangster had chosen to announce the deal at the Goodwood meeting in July within a few hours of stepping off the plane from America, where he had been buying more stock in Kentucky. There, the chequebook had been well used, for he had just bought Storm Bird's full brother yearling for $3.5 million in an assault on the Keeneland and Fasig-Tipton sales rings that cost him almost $11 million. Only a short time earlier, the Aga Khan had revealed that applications to the syndication of Shergar were oversubscribed and that his brilliant racehorse would be off to Ballymany Stud at a value of £10 million.

So here we had a horse who had raced once as a three-year-old – denting his reputation into the bargain – who had been 'sold' for more than half as much again as one of the best racehorses this century. The Aga Khan, of course, could have expected to receive more for Shergar had he decided to sell to America, but he chose to stand the stallion in Ireland for the use of his own mares and to the benefit of British and European breeders.

Even so, there was no comparison between the two horses as three-year-olds. Shergar had proved himself a tremendous racehorse, whereas Storm Bird was hardly put to the test, never mind passing it, in order to show he was a tough, sound and speedy horse of the highest class – attributes that the sensible breeder looks for when choosing a stallion for his mare. But Shergar was not by Northern Dancer; he was by the 'unfashion-able' Great Nephew, whose European (and inconsistent) blood-lines were nowhere near as attractive to the Americans.

The story of Storm Bird's syndication is a fascinating one. The repercussions of it, too, would tax Sangster's business ingenuity as he sought to benefit from a deal that subsequently went wrong.

On their numerous visits to the Kentucky sales, the Sangster team stay at the Hyatt Regency Hotel in the centre of Lexington, the town that is at the heart of a state which has more than 420 stud farms, producing nearly 9,000 foals a year. The routine, each visit, is fairly standard. The team flies from Ireland in a private jet which lands at the small Lexington Airport, from where a chauffeur-driven stretched limousine whisks them the few miles to the hotel. Sangster checks into his suite, has the champagne put on ice, and maybe has time for dinner before the work starts next day.

After breakfast in the hotel dining room, which resembles a bloodstock convention centre, Sangster heads for the sales complex for several hours of pre-sales viewing before returning for drinks and a light luncheon. Then it is either back to the sales centre for more viewing, or a visit to a stud farm to see several stallions and mares. There might be a stallion he has not seen since its racing days, maybe at his own stud, Creek View Farm in the nearby town of Paris. It can be wonderful to see such a horse, remembered best as a three-year-old racehorse excelling on sunny summer afternoons on the grandest tracks in Britain, but now at home in the Blue Grass country, in showpiece studs where one four-box stallion barn can cost upwards of $250,000 to build. This is the horse who is now fully matured, with the thick-set neck of a stallion, a gleaming, rounded body of muscle with well-developed hindquarters, and an almost strutting air of presence as he is led bouncing along meticulously manicured pathways and pristine lawns in an environment that is luxurious in human terms. No wonder his demeanour says he knows he is something special.

Someone of Sangster's stature is obviously flooded with invitations to more social engagements than he has time to attend. On some trips he has attended the annual party thrown by breeder Tom Gentry, a flamboyant character, hideously dressed in something attention-seeking like shocking pink or banana yellow, and who might look better employed handing out programmes at Disneyworld. When he is not hitting the headlines over a rather messy divorce, Gentry likes to lay on a show for his guests by hiring big names such as Ray Charles and his orchestra, or providing a party novelty like rides in a hot-air balloon from his garden – one year there was even a funfair. All in the line of duty to sell his wares at the sales, of course – an undertaking at which he has been successful, judging by the number of multi-million-dollar yearlings of which he has disposed from one of his mares called Crimson Saint.

The beginning of the incredible Storm Bird deal came at breakfast in the Hyatt Regency. Sangster, O'Brien and Magnier were just finishing their coffee when they were approached by a New York-based bloodstock agent, George Harris, who specialises in trading stallion shares and nominations. He asked them, quite casually, what sort of figure they placed on Storm Bird's valuation, and was told $15 million. After a little polite conversation about more general aspects of the forthcoming sales, Harris left for the Keeneland complex.

It was back at the hotel in the evening that Harris approached the trio again and told them he had clients who would be willing to purchase the horse at that $15 million figure. When Sangster replied that the $15 million was merely a base valuation, Harris surprised everyone by telling them that his clients were quite willing to start any negotiations from that figure – even though the horse had not yet run as a three-year-old. The clients were Kentucky-based vet and successful breeder William Lockridge and his partner in the Ashford Stud, gas magnate Robert Hefner, from Oklahoma. Harris invited Sangster and his partners up to his suite to meet them and discuss a deal.

Sangster, O'Brien and Magnier immediately went into conference to discuss their valuation of Storm Bird and to thrash out the tactics they would employ in the upcoming meeting. The three men had met like this countless times before, often when assessing a yearling's valuation in order to produce their maximum bidding ceiling at the sales (also a minimum figure so that they would know, on their judgement, when they had obtained a bargain). They also knew that there were two main advantages in their favour when the tough talking started. It was a seller's market. And Harris had approached them. The agent had not flinched, either, when initial figures were mentioned, which was always the acid test. Despite Storm Bird's absence from the track, the colt was still regarded by some as hot property, even if the mood in Britain was becoming increasingly ambivalent. But Sangster would not be selling in Britain anyway, because the commercial attraction of this horse lay in the States. So they agreed they would play cool on this deal. Cool, but tough.

They also decided they would not sell unless Lockridge and Hefner could come up with a deal that valued the colt in excess of $24 million. So with that figure firmly in mind, they left for their meeting.

The two groups met in Harris's suite and held talks which lasted a little over an hour. Sangster's side then requested an adjournment to consider the offer further – a calm, delaying move that was designed to give the impression of a certain amount of intractability. This was the important psychological denouement of the talks, at which each man played a key role: Sangster, confident and serious, Magnier forceful, formidable, and O'Brien calm, the elder statesman, whose quietly spoken words seemed to contain a supreme wisdom.

Finally they returned to Harris's suite to clinch the deal that rocked the racing world.

They shook hands on a transaction that valued Storm Bird at $30 million. Lockridge and Hefner agreed to buy 75 per cent of the colt for $21 million, thereby valuing Storm Bird at $28 million. But, within the deal, Sangster had also negotiated for himself four lifetime breeding rights to Storm Bird (the right to send four mares a year at no covering charge) which were valued at $500,000 each.

Lockridge subsequently travelled to Ireland to inspect the horse thoroughly. And the deal was finalised at Shannon Airport before his departure. Of course, such deals in the bloodstock world are rarely transacted on a basis of outright payment. In this instance, the payments would be spread over five years.

So, at the end of what had turned out to be a disastrous year, Storm Bird was flown to Kentucky to prepare for the 1982 breeding season in February. His covering fee was set at $175,000 and he was installed as the chief new stallion at Ashford Stud in Versailles, a former cattle farm that Lockridge had built up into a showpiece stud farm worth millions. At one time there were twenty stonemasons, employed full time for four years, working on the intricate stonework of the main buildings. When the Queen visited the area in the late 1980s, she said how impressed she was with Ashford.

The Texan veterinarian possessed the knack of revitalising such farms and had carried out a similar transformation with one of Kentucky's finest studs today, Walmac International, which stands such high-class stallions as Alleged, Nureyev, Bering and Risen Star. He is the breeder of the filly Crimson Saint, whom he sold for $11,000 and who was subsequently bought by Tom Gentry for $275,000. Crimson Saint, herself foaled in 1969, has proved a golden goose for Gentry. Bearing in mind that a broodmare can obviously produce only one foal a year, Gentry has sold her yearlings for a total of over $17 million. She is the dam of Royal Academy, bought by Sangster and O'Brien, on behalf of Classic Thoroughbreds PLC, for $3.5 million.

Lockridge had sold a half-share in his Ashford Stud to Hefner for $4 million earlier in 1981, and, after the Storm Bird purchase, he managed the stallion for the first three years of its career, during which Storm Bird produced fourteen Group or Graded Stakes winners, including the Group One winners, Indian Skimmer, the French-trained Magical Wonder and the US Grade One winner Storm Cat.

Fnancial disaster struck Hefner in a mammoth way, however, when the gas market slumped a few years later. His group of companies were highly leveraged and ran into big trouble when the price of natural gas dropped rapidly from somewhere around $9 to $1.5 per 1,000 cubic feet. At one stage he had reported debts of $770 million. To Lockridge's horror, he found that his own Ashford Stud assets had become embroiled in the Hefner turmoil, which became part of a further convoluted collapse of several banks which ran into billions of dollars and rocked America. Suddenly Lockridge was facing massive debts himself which were thought to be in the region of $56 million.

The stark outcome was that only $7 million of the $21 million purchase price of Storm Bird had been paid at this time. But Sangster had a contract and was willing to enforce it if necessary. Rather than be party to the massive debts he found himself facing, Lockridge was subsequently forced to part with his half-share in Ashford Stud plus his holding in Storm Bird (except for one share) to Hefner for a figure believed to be just $500,000. While Hefner came to an arrangement with his creditors, he chose to settle the debt to Sangster in full. Sangster then accepted from Hefner the Ashford Stud (value $8.5 million) and some other of Hefner's assets – including some shares in Storm Bird – as settlement of the debt.

What could have become a massive loss to Sangster, O'Brien and Magnier had become something of a gain. Neither Lockbridge nor Hefner filed for bankruptcy. In Lockridge's case he lost a substantial amount but felt honour-bound to other shareholders in Ashford Stud – apart from his belief in Storm Bird – to take the action he did. The syndicate management of Storm Bird was later transferred to the three men under the auspices of the Coolmore Stud company.

For the 1991 season, Storm Bird was still standing at Ashford Stud, which lists its ownership in the name of one of the Sangster Group's related companies, Bemak NV, which is registered in the Netherlands Antilles. But Storm Bird's covering fee, which stood at $175,000 in the opening season, was reduced each year until it reached $50,000.

While there was widespread criticism of the whole Storm Bird affair in relation to how little racing the colt had undergone compared with his selling price, Sangster could point to the deal as representing commercial reality: if someone is willing to pay the asking price – and everybody is happy – where is the harm in that? This was true, of course, and Storm Bird has turned out a pretty useful sire though not quite in the top category as several other sons of Northern Dancer.

Besides, if Sangster was willing to raise the stakes in this high-class game of poker, there were going to be plenty of instances when not every card they turned up would prove a winner.

In fact, millions upon millions of dollars of equine purchases would simply be money down the drain.

THIRTEEN

Lucky for Some

The names of the Sangster syndicate's expensive failures have now been quietly forgotten. Yearlings costing millions of dollars which never made the racetrack, or, if they did, never justified the enormous amounts for which they were purchased, evolved as the by-product of a buying machine that ground on, hoping to strike a new vein of gold.

Human nature being what it is, even the most ardent racegoer is likely to remember only the big-race successes of the group that was at the forefront, by several miles, of the international horseracing pack in the period of the late 1970s to the mid-1980s – a frenzied spiral of ever-increasing prices that drove the market to new heights.

The horses that turned out to be the lesser lights of the O'Brien stable – horses which promised much but delivered little – perhaps conjure up some hazy distant memory in the name of a horse of no particular merit. The flops, however, have been well forgotten. The agents, breeders and advisers who played their part when Sangster paid out astronomical amounts for these well-bred yearlings discreetly never refer to the failures. It is because racing is all about winning – and very little else.

These are just some of the million-dollar-plus purchases that dented the balance sheet. Sailor King ($1.4 million) never ran, Ballydoyle ($3.5 million) won a poor maiden race as a two-year-old, York Minister ($1.6 million) never ran, Empire Glory ($4.25 million) won two small races, Solar City ($1.8 million) won one small race, Father Matthew ($1.9 million) won a maiden race, Imperial Falcon ($8.25 million) won two small races.

Of course, there are many more failures in the number of yearlings bought by the syndicate for less than a million. But these big-money disappointments are an indication that, as the Sangster spending continued, it was done so on a 'bulk buying' policy in the hope that one or two would hit the jackpot – a little bit like a blind man throwing darts at the board hoping to hit bullseye. If nothing else, the flops served to reinforce what is manifest in horse-races throughout the world every day of the week – there is no such thing as a certainty. And there is no correlation between a racehorse's ability and its purchase price. Cynics might go so far as to say that, at the end of the day, choosing a yearling is only inspired guesswork.

Yet the Sangster–O'Brien–Magnier expertise was not put to use buying every expensive yearling they could lay their hands on as if on a mad spending spree. Even the failures had been most carefully researched in the painstaking style unique to the syndicate's operation. If they thought they were getting value, then they opened the chequebook.

Sangster was enthusiastic about bidding for the progeny of stallions that he owned or in which he had a holding, often creating a sales record into the bargain. Naturally, this proved of retrospective benefit to the stallion and its shareholders because, in the slick promotional material that was produced to exploit every fact and figure connected with the stallion, it could legitimately be stated that its son or daughter had recently created a new sales record. It was often difficult, too, at these sales to know just who owned what. Sometimes O'Brien might bid on behalf of the trio for a yearling in which Sangster already owned maybe 50 per cent. In such cases the final knock-down figure as recorded in the sales statistics would be more than the actual sum which eventually changed hands.

There was nothing illegal or sinister about such a transaction. The reason could be simply that the other 50 per cent shareholder in the yearling wished to sell his share anyway. In that case it would have been agreed that a public auction was the fairest way to realise a yearling's value. Even so, with the hundreds of sales throughout the world a bloodstock agent would need a microscope and an encyclopaedic memory to keep up with all the developments of the Sangster syndicate. And it could legitimately be argued that some areas of bloodstock prices were being achieved in a false market.

Sangster struck lucky once more when, in 1980, he bid for one of the first sons of the Coolmore-based first-season stallion, Be My Guest, in which he owned a substantial share. There would be no records broken here, though, because he picked up the yearling colt at the Deauville sales for the French equivalent of around £16,000. The horse was Assert, who was handled in a very brief training career by O'Brien's son, David.

In 1982 Assert won the French Derby by three lengths and the Irish Derby by eight lengths. For £16,000 virtually any Tom, Dick or Harry could have bought themselves the key to a fortune. That it was Sangster who spotted the colt and bought him was down to his belief in Be My Guest. It was also the result of his commitment to attend nearly every sale of note in the world, thereby ensuring that, merely by his presence, he was in the position to spot a likely bargain. After paying so little for the colt, he remarked there and then that he considered he had just obtained a bargain and would have been willing to pay a lot more.

So he was in the right place at the right time and had punted no more than he would in an afternoon's gambling at the races or at the roulette wheel. Yet what riches ensued. Assert won six of his eleven races, amassing over £340,000 in win prize money alone. But the prize money was, of course, irrelevant compared to the vast amounts that could now be negotiated on the American market with Assert as a potential stallion.

Several powerful groups of Americans expressed firm interest in the three-year-old towards what would obviously be the end of his racing career. Sangster, holding yet another ace, listened to them all, then finally accepted an offer from a syndicate which wanted to stand Assert at the Windfields Farm in Maryland, alongside his grandsire Northern Dancer and The Minstrel.

He sold a half-share in Assert for $14 million.

It was, once more, a case of rich pickings indeed, enough to replenish the kitty and perhaps elicit just a shrug of the shoulders at the memory of the expensive flops and disappointments of the past. They were part of the racing business. Mind-boggling losses, as they appeared to the non-players, were only part of the overall picture. In some case, too, the disappointments were not total write-offs. There was a certain amount of retrievability in the fact that, as well-bred horses, they could be sold abroad to any of the vast network of outlets now well established by the syndicate. Not everything would be worth millions to stand in Kentucky or at Coolmore. And who knew if one of these disappointments in a far-flung 'outpost' might not retrieve his reputation by siring a good horse somewhere along the line. For, in racing, anything can happen.

Although Sangster was delighted to have concluded another successful deal over a potential high-class stallion, he might subsequently have wished to have sold rather more because Assert has proved bitterly disappointing at stud, as a consequence of which his covering fee, which began at $125,000, was down to just $10,000 for the start of the 1991 season when Assert was standing at Sangster's Ashford Stud in Kentucky.

Racing and breeding is littered with swings and roundabouts. Assert's racetrack performances, coupled with that of his sire Be My Guest's other first-season progeny who proved Group class – the likes of On The House, Anfield and What A Guest – helped make the stallion champion sire in Britain. The consequence of this was that Be My Guest's stud fee was raised by Coolmore from IR10,000 guineas to IR75,000 guineas, which provided a tremendous upsurge in the revenue returned to the syndicate in a season.

For decades, a tradition had evolved whereby stallions had usually been limited to covering up to forty-five mares in the five-month season. Forty of the coverings, or nominations, would be for the use of the holders of the forty shares in the stallion, who would either use their nomination for their own mare or sell it to another breeder – privately or on the open market. The fees obtained from the other five coverings would be used to pay for the stallion's keep, his insurance and other incidental costs. No stallion has 100 per cent fertility, so at most there were never more than forty of his sons or daughters coming on to the market every year, inherent in which was the relevant rarity value of that stock. It is one of the reasons why artificial insemination has never been introduced into the bloodstock world.

But the advent of the scientific advance that has reduced the number of times a mare has to be serviced in order to become in foal has resulted in stallions now covering up to 100 mares. By the late 1980s, Alydar, the top sire in America (covering fee $310,000), was servicing approaching 100 mares a season. In other words, within five months, he would have earned for his owners the quite staggering sum of almost $31 million – on paper at least. In reality, the income would have been less than that because rarely does a breeder pay the top service fee and many nominations are open to negotiation. But a comparison with the prize money a horse could earn racing for an extra season and what he could earn at stud after being retired as a three-year-old illustrates the overwhelming odds in favour of early retirement. Of course, not every stallion is an Alydar, but even the average-to-good stallion can soon earn far more than he would ever have done in a season's racing.

Sadly, Alydar himself broke a leg in a paddock accident at the age of fifteen in 1990 and had to be put down following an unsuccessful operation. The stallion's insurers, Lloyds, faced a payout of around $30 million. After his death, figures showed that the average price of his yearlings was $466,000, yet 35 per cent of them never ran.

One critic of the Coolmore operation, the renowned blood-stock expert, writer and journalist Tony Morris, points out in his latest book, *Thoroughbred Stallions*, that the breeding industry has changed dramatically from that of the 1960s. The American invasion, and the adoption, by the likes of Coolmore, of American methods, has seriously damaged European racing, where prize money is comparatively low. Morris says that the American racing industry is far more broadly based, supported by a generous prize-money structure that offers true incentives and ensures a realistic market for young stock.

Coolmore, Morris argues, has led a new trend which has resulted in stallions being over-hyped and over-used by share-holders greedy for a quick return to satisfy bankers who have loaned money to fund the purchases at 'extortionate' rates of interest. The profit having been made, many of the stallions are then discarded before their stock is properly tested on the racecourse. Then the whole process will start again with some other 'fashionable' stallion. Morris laments the general passing of the traditional syndication of stallions, which was considered something of a sacred trust for the protection and promotion of a valuable property, organised by a band of breeders committed to furthering the interests of the stallion in preference to their own.

Morris says that breeders have been held to ransom by stallion owners such as Coolmore and are forced to pay high costs for the servicing of their mares only to discover that they themselves have contributed to the over-supply of the stock by a stallion doomed to market failure.

Others in bloodstock claim that Morris is being too idealistic in his views. While admitting he is right in certain areas, they point out that the likes of Coolmore have been 'forced' to demand high stud fees for certain stallions in order to keep those stallions in Ireland, thereby putting themselves in a position to turn down offers higher than would have been the case from America and Japan. The Coolmore stallions had then been of benefit to European breeders who would otherwise not have their services.

But there has been over-production in the British market. There were more foals born in 1990 than ever before. Although European stallion owners have cut their covering fees, some feel it had taken them a little longer than in America where stallion owners faced commercial reality with more haste.

The Sangster syndicate had received something of a boost for the 1981 season when the Greek shipping magnate Stavros Niarchos, who was by now exasperated with the competition from Sangster at the major sales, decided he would add some of his financial clout to the partnership (he had been underbidder for Be My Guest among many others). Although he continued to buy horses on his own account and have them trained in France, the Niarchos colours were carried by the syndicate's horses such as Esperanto, Father Matthew and the eventual winner of the 1985 Irish Derby, Law Society.

But the association, promising at first, eventually displeased Niarchos for a number of reasons. He later decided he would rather spend his money on his own selections at the sales and he reverted back to the role of a very rich man in racing 'for fun', as his racing manager Alan Cooper puts it. Cooper himself is the son of the late Tom Cooper, who was the much respected managing director of the British Bloodstock Agency (Ireland) and was the man responsible for many of the Sangster purchases over the years.

It was during the Niarchos partnership that Sangster had uncovered Assert. The colt's subsequent success and syndication was not Sangster's only major success of the year, though. The highlight honour went to another three-year-old, Golden Fleece, who won the Derby to make it an unprecedented three Derbys (English, Irish, French) for the same owner in the same year, while adding, of course, to Sangster's previous Derby win with The Minstrel.

Epsom provided another opportunity for Susan Sangster to revel in the glory of leading in the winner of the most prestigious race in the world. Sangster himself has never led in a winner yet; much too shy, much too nervous, much too English. He was so wound up about Golden Fleece's chances in the great race that, after a restless night at home at The Nunnery without much sleep, he forced himself to play nine holes of golf on the morning of the race to help quell the pre-race nerves before flying over to Epsom. Sangster's nervousness was exacerbated because Golden Fleece was not only the favourite but he had missed several vital last days of preparation owing to a touch of lameness in a hind leg.

But, as Pat Eddery drove Golden Fleece out for a brilliant victory, the big colt showing a tremendous turn of foot, the Sangster nerves burst into a rare display of emotion. He threw his grey top hat into the air with a whoop of sheer delight. Susan, who retrieved it, was so overcome that, with tears in her eyes, she shouted to her husband's partner in the colt, Danny Schwartz, that the prize money was his, a fact that she repeated several times. The £110,000 first-prize money was presumably mere small change now that the horse was worth millions.

Golden Fleece had already well beaten Assert in an earlier race at Leopardstown. And Pat Eddery, who had ridden both horses, considered Golden Fleece the better horse by quite some way. So if Sangster had sold 50 per cent of Assert for $14 million, what was the value now of Golden Fleece? There was no way of knowing how Golden Fleece would have fared after Epsom because the lameness which had almost prevented the colt running in the Derby subsequently returned. It meant the horse had run his last race – only the fourth of his career.

He was retired to stand at Coolmore at a fee of IR100,000 guineas which, by the 'traditional' calculation of multiplying his stud fee by forty (the number of shares held in him) would give shareholders an annual return of around £4 million. Valuing that income on the four-year basis by which a stallion shareholder could expect to see a return, Golden Fleece could be said to be worth at least £16 million.

Alas, he was never going to enhance that value or his

reputation. Early on in his second season at Coolmore, he developed cancer and died, leaving nothing of any merit to carry on his name on the racetrack.

The success of Golden Fleece and Assert reinstated Sangster as the leading owner in British racing in 1982. This was the third time he had occupied the position and followed on from three years when the top spot had eluded him (third in 1979, fourth in 1980 and runner-up in 1981).

But while he found it satisfying to be top of the tree in the country where he most liked racing, it was on a world scale that he judged his profit-and-loss account. At this period of the operation, he reckoned that in a normal trading year he was spending in the region of $18 million on horses – and aiming to sell stock to the tune of more than $21 million. The figures for the value of the disposals would be considerably boosted after a year such as this, however.

So successful was the business proving that Sangster's Swettenham Stud company was now making more money than Vernons' pools operations in Britain, America and Australia. His father, who was in his eighties, was suitably impressed with the way his son was handling the scale and profitability of the operation. Vernon was now pleased he had given Sangster his blessing along with the initial advice and encouragement, even if it was a somewhat alien business to the old man.

One year he sent Sangster a telegram to Australia congratulating him on making profits of more than £7 million. It was as if Sangster just could not lose.

This year had been an eventful one for the Sangsters on a social level, too. There seemed to be no stopping them in the society stakes where the runners trotted out of Susan's mouth like the first night of a movie premiere. She referred quite often to Frank (Sinatra). Then there was Albert (Finney), or Joan (Collins). All had become friends in the round of parties and events and functions that became so much a part of their life that

Susan was now employing a personal secretary to handle the burgeoning diary.

The biggest bash of the year was Susan's own fortieth birthday party. This was celebration with a capital C. It took the form of a ball for which the guest list and the arrangements took three months of preparation. The Jockey Club Subscription Rooms in Newmarket were hired and the three Regency-style rooms were decorated in a shade of pink which Susan described as 'hot'. A London interior designer was brought in to supervise the decor, which was modelled on an English country garden with summer yellows and greens. The bill for the flowers which trailed the walls and decorated the tables was reported to have been more than £6,000. A topiarist had crafted horses' heads, which proved an appropriate centrepiece in the alcoves around the rooms and drew much admiring comment, while Susan arranged specially-made tablecloths and napkins also in 'hot' pink. Guests flew in from Australia and America to join those representing the cream of British racing and showbusiness. The privileged inner sanctum joined the Sangsters for dinner before a further 300 guests arrived from 10 p.m. to dance until dawn when buck's fizz, caviar and scrambled egg was served.

Being such a social whirl, selected members of the media were present to record the event in their respective society columns. If Sangster had proved so successful at racing and breeding, Susan was now teaching him how to be successful at self-promotion. She made sure the media were aware that her head garland of flowers and the silk organza dress in 'hot' yellow were made for her by a Swedish designer based in Ireland. And Elizabeth Taylor was at the party, too. Not *the* Elizabeth, though. This was Mrs Taylor, the Sangsters' Australian cook, who was flown in to supervise the menu.

Two weeks earlier, the bitterness that was still lingering towards Susan from Sangster's first divorce became manifest when Christine and her second husband, Darel Carey, a former Army officer, held a party to celebrate the twenty-first birthday of Christine's and Sangster's eldest son Guy. The invitational letter to the party at the Careys' Berkshire home near Ascot specifically requested Sangster not to bring Susan with him.

The contents of the letter appeared in the Sangsters' favourite international gossip column, which made sure that its readers were told how 'deeply shocked' Sangster was by the tone of the letter.

Consequently Guy celebrated his coming of age without his father attending. On this occasion (and quite ironically, as it would soon turn out), Sangster decided that a public display of loyalty towards Susan was the better part of valour.

The day after her own birthday celebrations, Susan left for Australia, where she was to view her ultimate fortieth-birthday present – a $6 million home in Sydney Harbour's most exclusive spot, Point Piper. Sangster had bought the white-stuccoed house as their Australian summer home, making it the most expensive piece of real estate for its size in the country. Within a few days of arriving, Susan began organising another party to celebrate her birthday, 15 July, to which she invited her parents and thirty other guests.

The six-bedroomed house had been built in the late 1930s on three of the 2,400 elevated waterfront 'plots' that now grace both sides of Sydney Harbour (Port Jackson to give it its official title) almost as far as to the Pacific. Here are beautiful sandy bays, all of them public, splendid houses dotted among the low hillsides which sweep away from the brilliant blue waters of the longest natural harbourway in the world.

Named Radford after the family who had built it, the house was constructed into the hillside on three levels. On the ground floor was a ballroom and what was called a cocktail room with a bar, while lounges and sitting rooms dominated the second tier. The bedrooms and bathrooms occupied the top floor. From most aspects of the rooms and numerous balconies there were simply magnificent views: to the left the nearby Main Harbour with its famous road and rail bridge just beyond the Opera House, then the sweeping Rose Bay to the right where Sydney Boat Club held its weekly regattas and where chartered seaplanes brought in their clients. Further to the right lay the whole vista of the waterway out to the Sydney Heads.

In the grounds there were tiered terraces and gardens, a tennis court and a salt-water swimming pool near the harbour edge. As with many of these lavish properties which were similarly steeply banked into the hillside, the house had an 'inclinator' in the form of a mini ski-lift-type monorail to ferry occupants down to the pool and back rather than use the stone steps.

So now Susan had another house with which to occupy her time while Sangster continued on his exhausting international schedule. She busied herself with her ideas for the changes she wanted to make in the design and decor of the house that had now got most of Australian society buzzing. First she would consult with her Sydney architect, then with her London-based interior designer, who would be flown out with pattern books and the samples of English chintzes and colour charts. She had already made up her mind to transform the ground-floor ballroom and bar into a large sunroom and living area with a kitchen and dining room. The middle floor would become an entertaining 'complex' while all the bedrooms would be decorated to give them their own individuality.

And the Sangsters renamed the house Toison d'Or – Golden Fleece – after the horse who had helped pay for it.

In Greek mythology it was Jason and the Argonauts who captured the ram's fleece of gold from the sleepless dragon in order to win his rightful throne to the kingdom of Iolcos. Not forgetting the woman's role in the shape of events, however, it was the enchantress Medea, daughter of the King of Colchis, who fell in love with Jason and wove her magic to help him obtain the Golden Fleece. Jason then married Medea but subsequently deserted her.

In the lives of the Sangsters, the story of Jason and the Golden Fleece was going to prove quite portentous.

FOURTEEN

Gone Walkabout

When Robert Sangster walked into the foyer of Lexington's Hyatt Regency Hotel with one of the world's top models, Jerry Hall, on his arm there were bound to be raised eyebrows in some quarters. For here was the man whose reputation as king of the international horse players from the years of high-flying and high-buying at the thoroughbred sales meant he was an extremely well-known figure in town.

But he was supposedly happily married to Susan, that great hostess who was such an asset to his operation, the Sheila of the shrill laugh and high-jinks personality who just happened to be back in Australia at this time flitting between the new house in Sydney and her children and friends in Melbourne.

So what was he doing in the company of this leggy blonde who towered over him, the girl who was all but married to Rolling Stone rock star Mick Jagger?

From the couple's demeanour in each other's company at the subsequent sales and at a party, there were some observers who immediately thought that this quiet, shy man was something of a dark horse himself.

There were others, though, horsemen and women who had lived in this horse-breeding country for most of their lives and who knew the scene intimately, who heard about the Sangster–Hall appearances and were not surprised. These were people who considered Sangster something of a playboy anyway, people who had seen him in the company of beautiful women before, knew about his fun philosophy of having 'the best time in life one can possibly have'.

It brought a wry smile, too, to the faces of those who had

heard Sangster often repeat with grim determination that there was nobody in the world who could outbid him at the sales. They thought that he usually got what he wanted.

Still, it was an amazing appearance, this squat forty-six-year-old businessman and the glamorous model who was young enough to be his daughter. But then, our Robert had always had a soft spot for young models, particularly blondes.

Sangster's friendship with Jerry Hall, the Texas-born former girlfriend of another rock star, Bryan Ferry, had been on going for several months. They shared a mutual friend in Charles Benson, former racing correspondent of the *Daily Express*. The affable Benson, a world champion backgammon player, renowned gambler and Old Etonian, endeared himself to the rich and famous throughout the world through his high-blown connections and his subtle, wonderfully wicked sense of humour. The connections at fashionable clubs, restaurants, racetracks, casinos and hotels at most of the international playgrounds of the rich made him the ideal Mr Fixit for someone like Sangster, who often took Benson with him on many of his overseas trips. Indeed, in Australia, Sangster would sometimes let Benson do the talking for him when it came to after-dinner speeches or television appearances.

Susan herself had met Jerry several times, unaware that there was anything other than friendship between her husband and the Texan. Some years later, Susan would delight her friends when she did her Jerry Hall impression with a Texan drawl at its satirical best.

In an Australian interview, Susan revealed how Sangster had invited Jerry to Yorkshire for a day's racing in their private box at York races and she had 'bust a gut' to make sure the American guest enjoyed herself – even to the extent of seating her next to her husband at the luncheon table.

Susan relates: 'When she came up to me to say goodbye, she looked at me really closely, then said: "Uh, Susan, uh, d'ya mahnd if I give yo some cosmetic advahce?" Well what do you say? So, in this bright voice, I said: "Certainly, Jerry," and she said: "When yo use lipstick, I suggest yo use lip-liner 'cos, when yo get to a certain age, lipstick runs into the cracks."

'I just looked at her in total amazement and said: "Well, thank you very much, Jerry." Then she said: "That's awlright. Yo know, Susan, yo've got real nahce lips so yo should expose them more." And I thought: "I don't believe this – all this woman cares about is cosmetics!" I later discovered this was not at all the only thing of mine in which she was interested!'

It was in November 1982 that the romance hit the headlines of the world's media. This was soon after Sangster had left Susan in their usual suite at the Hilton Hotel in Melbourne, where they had been staying for Melbourne Cup week, and flown to America 'on business', accompanied by his friend Benson.

In fact a British daily newspaper contacted Benson while he and Sangster were still in Melbourne with news that they were about to run an exclusive story on the affair. Because of his friendship with Sangster the newspaper wanted to know if Benson could shed any light on the subject. But as Sangster and Benson were only hours away from jetting out of the country on their way to America, a request was made for the newspaper to put the story on hold until they were in the air so that Sangster could avoid not only the Australian press pack, who would soon pick up the story from London, but also the obvious recriminations he would face from Susan.

As it turned out, the request on this exclusive story was granted, the newspaper delaying publication for twenty-four hours. When the story eventually broke, Sangster and Benson were somewhere over the Pacific Ocean tucking into the smoked salmon and champagne in first-class seats on a jumbo jet. And it was left to a mystified and rightly angry Susan, besieged at the Hilton Hotel, to fend off the dozens of journalists who turned up there seeking her version of events. She was forced to stay locked in the Sangster suite, and on the one occasion when she tried to venture out she had to request the hotel management to clear the hotel lobby of the waiting reporters. Obviously upset at the reports which ensued, she had a brief telephone conversation with Sangster, and could not wait until she saw him again to hear what this was all about.

The news had hit her like a boxer's punch to the jaw. She felt devastated, confused, hurt. As a former journalist on the social scene herself she knew there was rarely smoke without fire. Newspapers, even gossip columns, were run by very professional people who, usually, had extremely reliable sources. And this story had now been promoted to front-page news. Oh, the ignominy of it all, here in her home country where she was the *belle célèbre*. The husband she truly loved had surely not deserted her?

Up to this time, Sangster and Jerry had carried on their relationship – one that Sangster would later describe as 'very exciting' – much less publicly than on the few occasions when they were seen at the races or at the sales of Newmarket and Kentucky. As they were both so well known, Sangster had to think up new places where they could meet around the world, taking great care in case either of them was recognised. He had occasion to use the various homes of some of his business associates, particularly the US home of one of his Australian magnate friends, as the venue for these clandestine meetings.

By the time Sangster and Benson landed in Los Angeles after their nineteen-hour flight, the media were well briefed on the story. The first thing any reporter does when he wants to find a subject such as Sangster is to check the airport flightlists, then the best hotels in town. It probably took no more than one or two telephone calls to determine that Sangster was staying at the Beverly Wilshire down on Rodeo Drive, one of the grandest hotels in town (today it is called the Beverly Regent).

Meanwhile Jerry Hall had left New York for a 'modelling assignment', also in LA. She met Sangster there in a private house and they discussed their situation. Of course, now that the story had broken, Benson, who was also staying at the Beverly Wilshire, was in a position to put the record straight from

Sangster's point of view – and satisfy his own newspaper, who were desperate for some copy virtually from the horse's mouth. For several days, Benson's position with his employers was in the balance because, as the initial story had appeared in a rival daily, they were left wondering if Benson had tipped off the opposition. The source, however, was from a New York contact who had simply seen Sangster and Jerry together. Benson's employers were further incensed, however, when he had still not filed any copy himself despite being in the front line – and yet a 'snatch' picture of himself and Sangster huddled in the back of a car leaving LA airport appeared in another opposition paper. The caption said that pictured were Robert Sangster and his unnamed minder. They were not far wrong!

The next day Benson, at last, wrote a story that was billed as a world exclusive and headlined: 'Jerry and Me by Robert Sangster, the love tangle racing king'. Benson filed a piece quoting Sangster as saying he had not left his wife. But it also quoted his other friend, Jerry, as saying: 'Who knows what any of us will be doing in the future? I have no hard feelings for Mick. I am sorry that what was intended as a private and possibly temporary parting has embarrassed him.'

While admitting that she had spoken to Jagger several times over the previous few days she added: 'Obviously he is very upset – who wouldn't be with so much wild gossip flying around.'

The 'wild gossip' she was referring to was some of the stories that had appeared in a New York newspaper which quoted her as saying, 'Robert could buy him ten times over,' in answer to the question, where could she go after Mick?

The Benson story, however, was at great pains to state that Sangster had been most upset by suggestions that their friendship had been based on his wealth, pointing out that Jerry earned a million dollars a year herself and was quite capable of standing on her own two feet.

Within days, Sangster had flown to Kentucky for the November breeding stock sales, but he went without Jerry, who had been due to accompany him. As glamorous as the relationship had at first seemed, it was now going to fizzle out.

Within a week, Jerry had flown to Paris, where Jagger was filming. It was there that the couple, who had been living together for five years until their split, eventually made up their differences. Jagger proposed and they later married and had a baby. This was precisely what observers close to the action suggested she had been angling for all along in her relationship with Sangster – to make Jagger jealous and persuade him to tie the knot, which he had, reportedly, been unwilling to do previously.

Benson later told friends that Jagger had blamed him for the whole episode as if somehow he had procured Jerry for Sangster. Benson's opinion was that Jerry had made him the scapegoat in order to shift the blame from herself. He was most disgruntled and said publicly that Jagger had lost a good friend of ten years' standing. Unfortunately for Benson, it was not the last time that his loyalty to Sangster would result in his being blamed over his close friend's troubled love life.

Sangster found himself with some explaining to do when he eventually returned to the Isle of Man, to where Susan had flown from Australia within days of the scandal breaking. She had hastily made arrangements to cut short her visit to Melbourne and Sydney, where she would have normally stayed two weeks longer in order to spend more time with her own daughters.

By now Sangster had discussed matters with his three sons and his daughter as well as with several close friends. Now he had to sit down and have a heart-to-heart with Susan and decide where their marriage was going.

Some friends of Sangster's from the earlier days felt that the marriage was doomed. They pointed to Susan's strong, sometimes overbearing personality as the main cause. They felt that what had been a magnetic attraction four years ago had been rapidly losing its energy.

One observer of the Sangsters, Australian journalist Ian Leslie, had already rocked The Nunnery with a documentary for the Channel 9 programme, *60 Minutes*, in which he said of Susan: 'She always wants to be centre stage, in the limelight. If that's ever threatened, there is jealousy. Susan Peacock was extremely attractive, she shone and had great appeal. But now she looks matronly, frumpish, and she's gone to the pack a bit.'

Causing much displeasure in the Sangster household with his blunt talking, Leslie continued: 'You wouldn't turn and look at her in the street. She'd be Mrs Anybody without the wealth. Intellectually she has little to offer but she's effervescent and can talk about the weather for hours.'

O for the bloom of youth! Once the flower begins to wilt slightly, some men seem to forget why they married in the first place – or was the love that shallow? Sangster himself was no spring chicken. Had no one suggested he might be spreading rather thickly around the waist, that with his ever-fastened suit jackets, the middle-age bulge was present for all to see?

The problem for Susan, though, was endemic in this society, especially one fastidiously geared to the glamorous lifestyle which they avidly sought. Of course Susan was attractive – she still is. But, like motor cars, last year's model can soon look dated when the new version comes out (classic models are only appreciated by the discerning). And, as Sangster had an eye for a pretty (and always younger) girl, no wonder Susan felt threatened.

After their meeting, Sangster decided to remain with Susan and give the marriage another go, his knuckles suitably rapped. Susan promptly went out and had her hair restyled, then went to a health farm for a tone-up. For Sangster it was back to the business of making money. But the marriage was on a downward slope.

The serious recession which had hit most of the industrial nations of the world in 1981–2 was still having dire repercussions for most forms of business in 1983. Yet bloodstock prices in America had been increasing dramatically throughout this period due to the intense competition Sangster and the Arabs generated among themselves. This form of money madness seemed to ignore the economic realities in the rest of world industry.

At a time when one of the prime reflectors of economic performance, the US car industry, had seen new car sales slump from a high of around 11 million in 1978 to only 7.75 million in 1982, the price of yearlings at the Keeneland Selected Sale leaped from an average price of $196,883 each in 1980 to $544,681 each in 1984. Corresponding gross amounts show the alarming heights to which the market was being pushed. The total receipts of the 1980 sale were $59.25 million (301 lots sold), while in 1984 that figure had risen to almost $176 million (323 lots sold).

Yet in other countries, untouched by the scale of the Sangster versus Arabs gladiatorial contest, the recession had bitten deeply into bloodstock values, and Sangster himself was deeply conscious of this. In Australia there were bargain prices to be found at the sales of 1983. Sangster himself had admitted that, by 1981, rising prices had led to a shake-out of the market – widespread overheating with a consequent downward readjustment. He even conceded that the soaring market had been partly his fault because of the generous prices he was willing to pay if he thought he could obtain the right horse.

To some degree, though, Sangster was a victim of his own success at whichever sale he bid because there was always the egotistical cash of the opposition, who simplistically thought it could emulate him with one or two expensive purchases. That proved a major problem for him because, like all good businessmen, he hated buying at the top of the market.

He did buy, however. The Keeneland habit became almost like a drug. He needed the best on offer to satiate the economic demands of the vast machine he had created. If someone else pushed up the price of the commodity, he just had to go along with it.

But it was not as if there was no ammunition at home in Britain to provide the resources – there was still plenty. In 1983 and 1984, Sangster was again top owner as a result of the performances by such Classic winners as Lomond (2,000 Guineas 1983), Caerleon (French Derby 1983), El Gran Señor (2,000 Guineas and Irish Derby, 1984) and Sadler's Wells (Irish 2,000 Guineas, 1984) plus many winners of the important non-Classic races in the calendar.

By the middle of this period, now almost a decade since the Sangster syndicate had set out on their revolutionary policy, estimates of Sangster's global bloodstock and racing empire were put at £100 million. From that initial £2 million investment, it was an achievement without parallel in the racing world.

A horse that kept the home fires burning was El Gran Señor, which was part bred by Sangster in that he owned the dam, Sex Appeal, in partnership with Northern Dancer's Canadian breeder, Eddie Taylor. The colt was by Northern Dancer and, being out of Sex Appeal, it made him a full brother to Try My Best.

Although El Gran Señor was beaten a short head in a memorable Derby by Secreto, who was trained by O'Brien's son David, that defeat hardly seemed to matter in the circumstances. Other than the prestige of adding another Epsom crown to Sangster's tally, it is doubtful that having actually won the race would have increased his stud valuation, which was conservatively estimated at around $30 million. He was sent to stand at Windfields Farm alongside his sire but later transferred to Sangster's Ashford Stud in Kentucky.

The fact that the horse subsequently proved to be sub-fertile and had his stud fee reduced from $200,000 to around $60,000 for the 1990 season, was another indication of the ephemeral qualities of a horse on the track and a horse at stud. However, one of his sons, Belmez, proved an exceptional colt in the 1990 season, which will have improved El Gran Senor's reputation at stud even though there will be some breeders who might not be prepared to take the risk of having a top-class mare barren for a year by sending it to the stallion. After all, the idea is to produce a valuable foal to sell, not a might-be.

The problem with the market as a whole in this period of mid-eighties madness was that it was rising from a somewhat unnatural base, fuelled by something akin to a stock market bull run, namely fear and greed. But for how long? Purchasers paying these huge sums were demonstrating their faith in the uninterrupted rise of bloodstock values. But they were sailing close to the wind and ignoring the past. They also paid little heed to the warnings that were being sounded within the industry. The bull markets had occurred in oil, in art, in gold – and now it was bloodstock. That the trade in horses would prove as cyclical as those other forms of investments had obviously not worried some people.

Least of all would it worry the Arabs who were challenging Sangster for the top spot in Britain, backed by an incalculable oil wealth that made Sangster's fortune pale by comparison.

But the years of experience, of hard-bargained trade, and of the 'streetfighting' wheeling and dealing that Sangster had amassed were a priceless commodity. He had had ten years of life at the very top, many more years before that learning the tricks of the trade. In other words he was years ahead of the opposition. His team was the best in the business, built on bloodstock, sweat and tears. No one could just waltz in and splash money around thinking they were going to be an overnight success. That was just not realistic in this tough, demanding commercial world.

But the Arabs would try, all right. They would waste millions upon millions of pounds in the process, but they would try. It might take them time, but to some extent their enormous wealth could buy that. It could shorten the years of waiting that financial prudence would otherwise force them to endure.

So Sangster, knowing that he had a fight on his hands, had two choices. He could concede now, retrench, accept the facts of life, perhaps astutely begin tailoring his operation to the demands of what was bound to become a new market force. He could streetfight, feint and bluff, maybe set up an attack which was really based on a grander defence where he could scale down but, at the same time, make money out of these newcomers before they got their act together. Or he could attack to win, take them on in something that would resemble a David and Goliath confrontation, one where there would be only one winner.

He chose the latter course.

FIFTEEN

Funny Money

The modern racehorse is the descendant in the male line of one of three Arab horses, the Byerley Turk, the Darley Arabian and the Godolphin Arabian, which were among those imported into Britain in the period 1689 to 1730. The fleet-footed attributes of these horses when bred with the sturdy English draught horse produced the thoroughbred.

Nearly three centuries later, it seemed as if the Arab princes had arrived to claim their legacy.

There were a number of Arab owners in British racing before the Maktoum brothers of Dubai came along with their open chequebooks. However, any aspirations that any of the established assortment of Middle Eastern owners might have harboured in emulating the Sangster path to success were quickly brushed aside by the sheer weight of money the Maktoums demonstrated they were willing to spend at the sales.

There are four Maktoum brothers, the sons of Dubai's late ruler, Sheikh Rashid Bin Said Al-Maktoum, who was also Prime Minister of the seven-state United Arab Emirates. The eldest son is Maktoum, the UAE's Deputy Prime Minister and Crown Prince of Dubai. Maktoum does not speak English and is not seen in Britain or America as much as his two younger brothers, Hamdan and Mohammed. From the mid-eighties he was involved in taking on more of his ailing father's role in running the gas- and oil-rich state, a country of desert lands and humid Gulf shores, 1,500 square miles with a population of around 450,000 people. With substantial foreign assets producing an annual income exceeding $2 billion, oil income alone producing approximately $7 million a day, and oil reserves of four billion barrels, Dubai is one of the highest-income countries per capita in the world.

When Robert Sangster was winning the Derby for the first time with The Minstrel in 1977, the Maktoums had just made their first entry into racehorse ownership in Britain. Horses were not new to them, because there was a family tradition of owning Arab horses in Dubai, where they raced camels too. But, on their frequent business trips to London to inspect the property they owned and, perhaps, to buy more, they particularly enjoyed a day at the races, especially Ascot.

Bloodstock agent Dick Warden, who would later join the Maktoums as one of their many advisers, persuaded Sheikh Maktoum along with the third son, Sheikh Mohammed, to break into ownership with one or two modest purchases.

Three horses raced for the brothers as two-year-olds. These were trained by John Dunlop (now the principal trainer for the second-eldest brother, Sheikh Hamdan) at Arundel in Sussex. Sheikh Maktoum owned one of the horses, called Shaab, while the other two, Haddfan and Hatta, ran in the white-starred cap of Sheikh Mohammed. And it was Hatta who stirred the sheikhs' interest in the sport. The filly cost a mere 6,200 guineas as a yearling yet she won four of her seven starts, including the prestigious Molecomb Stakes at the Glorious Goodwood summer meeting when, on paper, she had looked to have no chance of beating the odds-on favourite Amaranda.

So the die was cast and, over the next three years, they began prudently buying more. But it was still only a small-scale activity, purely for fun. The Sangster way of doing things had not yet sparked their imagination, nor their desire to follow suit. The excellent Northern trainer Peter Easterby, one of two brothers of a Yorkshire farming family, trained several of these early horses, primarily because Easterby also trained for Dick Warden (such is the north–south divide in Britain, however, that the vast majority the Maktoum horses are trained in the South of England today).

Encouraged by what they saw as a sport that was still run in an orderly fashion along well-established lines, the brothers decided that they liked the tradition attached to racing in Britain. Besides, the flight from Dubai in one of the family's fleet of aircraft was no hassle, so the prospect of regular trips to watch their horses run slotted nicely into their business routine.

By 1982, the brothers had gone their separate ways within British racing, Maktoum, Hamdan and Mohammed founding their own racing empires and employing their own trainers and jockeys (the youngest brother, Ahmed, who is Colonel-in-Chief of Dubai's Army, still only 'dabbles' in the sport). No longer would even the great Lester Piggott need to pose the question – as he did in those early introductory days: ''Ere, who's this Sheikh Mohammed bloke then?'

The brothers had begun buying stud farms and broodmares, yearlings and horses, working with vigour and something of a raw enthusiasm to set up their own teams of advisers, stud managers, racing managers et al. But it all took time. Until their respective operations could be set up, organised and refined, mistakes were bound to be made. The cost of the initial launch was something in the region of £30 million between them, but this was only a fraction of what they would subsequently spend in the quest to dominate the British racing scene. Such domination, naturally, meant that there was one main man, Robert Sangster, and his syndicate, in the way.

Sangster, though, initially welcomed the growing emergence of the Maktoums. In fact he encouraged it, reasoning that here was a splendid opportunity to transact some lucrative business. Apart from meeting them in Britain, Sangster has now paid at least six visits to Dubai. The early meetings, which were held at the Royal Palace, were carried out in a friendly and informal atmosphere with Hamdan and Mohammed – 'when they picked my brains and tried to get their act together'.

Observers of this situation, including a former close associate of Sangster, feel that Sangster thought he could maybe outwit these newcomers when it came to bidding for the choice lots at the sales. There was a belief, too, that Sangster thought his syndicate's experience with the powerful Northern Dancer blood was unbeatable. And now that Stavros Niarchos was a full participating member of the syndicate, a man who was reckoned to be worth at least $2 billion, Sangster was ready to meet any challenge the Maktoums might launch.

Of course, it was inside the pavilions of the best yearling sales in America and Europe that the sheikhs and Sangster would meet as antagonists. Here, Sangster felt his experience would enable him to duck and dive, feint and riposte, counter-riposte if necessary; it would be a bidding game of bluff so that the Maktoums and their connections just would not know if Sangster was interested in a yearling or not. The fight would only become a very public head-to-head contest a few years later.

But there were other horsemen in this large international pool that the Maktoums would have to tackle first before they even got within striking distance of the Sangster camp. And some of these horseplayers were long in the tooth when it came to carving up the opposition at sales when the big money was at stake. Those teeth could, however, be piranha-sharp to anyone who had not quite got their act together. Some, no doubt, were rubbing their hands at the thought of the money to be made at the expense of these unsuspecting Arabs who had money to burn.

Indeed, some years later, after a premier sale in Newmarket when the Arabs had dropped out of the bidding for a yearling colt which became the subject of a subsequent court case, Sheikh Maktoum's racing and bloodstock manager, Michael Goodbody, admitted that they had been run up several times in the past because of the high prices they were willing to pay.

Some experienced bloodstock agents on both sides of the Atlantic say that, in these first few years of their battle to emerge as major players, the Maktoums were alarmingly disorganised. So much so that it became almost a standing joke about the number of times certain people had been successful at running them up. Some of the stories might be apocryphal, for the rumours that abound in the bar after a sale are like flies round the muckheap. But the dealing and the double-dealing that has been known to take place before a horse enters the ring can get so convoluted that the unwary and inexperienced players are in considerable danger of bidding more than they should.

To be a successful bidder requires an understanding of the auction sales system, especially in the cut-and-thrust atmosphere of high-charged sale rings such as Keeneland. Several prominent and reputable bloodstock agents have voiced their opinion that the Maktoums got taken to the cleaners in the early years.

Said one: 'They just got absolutely carted. The Americans did a very professional job on them – they were very ruthless. I'm sure that the Maktoums did not realise that this was the case. I used to watch it happening and, very often, I could not believe my eyes. It was an absolute bloodbath.'

The Maktoums' determination to spend boldly in what can be a ruthless arena of the bloodstock business appeared to be such that, if they ever suspected they were being taken for a ride, at this point of their operation they did not really care. The vast sums of money they were prepared to spend were their way of establishing themselves. Their relative naivety, however, meant that they had none of the Sangster syndicate subtlety, which is required in myriad forms to disguise a bid or lay a false trail in order to fool the opposition.

Said another agent: 'They were very obvious when they were bidding for a particular lot, just as they were when they showed interest in a yearling before the sale started – perhaps going to see one yearling half a dozen times. All a vendor needed to do was to note this and bid for his own horse, knowing the Maktoums were most likely to eventually buy it whatever the cost. The vendor would then simply drop out of the bidding at an appropriate moment having made a mint – sometimes millions of dollars.'

To some Keeneland regulars it appeared that the Maktoums were working with no preconcieved plan of how many horses they were going to buy, what sort of budget was involved, or just what their ceiling was when buying a particular yearling. These were the tight disciplines required to make successful forays into the American market.

Such disciplines, in fact, were already being exercised within a shrewd operation that was being run by an Arab who was proving a greater opponent to the Sangster syndicate at this time, namely that of Prince Khalid Abdullah of Saudi Arabia, a man said to be richer than all four Maktoums put together. Abdullah, a member of the Saudi royal family himself, though he prefers the title 'Mr Abdullah', is married to one of his cousins, the sister of King Fahd of Saudi Arabia.

A serious, charming man, but with a good sense of humour, Abdullah's operation has been much more purposeful, often subdued to the point of apparent uninterest, but then executed with businesslike precision.

He could be described as more of a city gent, always immaculately dressed, while Sheikh Hamdan and Mohammed are fairly down-to-earth people who can be charmingly casual. The difference between them might be seen at the sales, where Hamdan and Mohammed would not be too worried about the cold or the rain. Either would happily kneel down in the sawdust of a horse's box or on the damp turf to feel its legs. Abdullah, on the other hand, is likely to be among the first to seek shelter.

Sheikh Mohammed is more ebullient than Hamdan, though both are courteous and softly spoken. Mohammed is often referred to as Action Man because of his love of outdoor pursuits, such as shooting on his 48,000 acre Scottish estate, where he also stalks deer. He has a passion for hawking with his prize falcons back home, even camel racing. Mohammed, now in his early forties, can fly an aeroplane and ride a horse, and is an expert shot, something he perfected in his days at the Mons Officer School in Aldershot.

Khalid Abdullah had had the foresight to choose one of the best bloodstock men in Britain to initiate and oversee his expansion, James Delahooke, who today runs his own stud, Adstock Manor in Buckinghamshire. Delahooke had a reputation for spotting top animals at bargain prices and many of his purchases have proved the foundation of the successful Abdullah bloodstock operation, Juddmonte Farms, today. (It was Delahooke who bought, among others, the dams of the Abdullah-bred 1990 Epsom and French Derby winners Quest For Fame and Sanglamore.)

So it was Abdullah and Delahooke who often ran into the Sangster syndicate in their search for quality at the right price, while the Maktoums were, seemingly, otherwise engaged. They were underbidders for Law Society, the Irish Derby winner who ran in Stavros Niarchos' colours. But in 1982 they snatched Rainbow Quest for $950,000 from Sangster, who was the underbidder for what was to become a class racehorse.

Abdullah, who in 1991 was reputed to be paying his retained jockey, Pat Eddery, something in the region of £1.5 million a year, was applauded for keeping Rainbow Quest in training as a four-year-old (and improving the colt's racing record), and also for keeping him at his own stud in England at the very reasonable fee of £25,000, which has enabled breeders to make a profit on his stock at the sales.

But then, as Sangster, O'Brien and Magnier would probably point out, Abdullah could afford to be philanthropic. Rainbow Quest, who was awarded a Prix de l'Arc de Triomphe (on the disqualification of Sagace in 1985), was runner-up to Sangster's own El Gran Señor in the Dewhurst as a two-year-old and in the Irish Derby at three. He proved himself a model racehorse, among the highest class over three seasons, and has already sired a son as good as if not better than himself in Quest For Fame.

Because of their buying policy, or maybe non-policy as some would claim, the acquisition of yearlings by the Maktoums generated much wastage of money and horses, far more than the Sangster syndicate and in a much shorter time. So these were crazy times, highlighted by the incredible bidding for the useless Snaafi Dancer in 1983.

This was the year at Keeneland when Sheikh Mohammed signalled that, of the brothers, he would be the biggest spender. Buying under the name of one of his studs, the Aston Upthorpe

Stud at Newmarket, he broke the million-dollar barrier six times – paying a total of $21.4 million for the half-dozen yearlings.

Here is what happened to those six products of that one sale: Snaafi Dancer (cost $10.2 million – never ran), Gallant Archer ($4.1 million – won a Doncaster maiden race), Ma Petite Jolie ($2.5 million – won an Epsom maiden race), Local Suitor ($2 million – won twice as a two-year-old, was injured, and retired at £12,000 nomination fee), Chimes ($1.3 million – never ran), Fatah Flare ($1.3 million – won twice, including York's Musidora Stakes).

But it must be reiterated that, carefree as some thought the Maktoums' spending was, it was the Sangster syndicate who were the underbidders for Snaafi Dancer. One bid less by Sheikh Mohammed's team, therefore, and it would have been Sangster and the boys who were left with the biggest flop of all time. As it was, Sangster and company would spend in excess of $60 million over the next few years in a bid to meet the Arab challenge. But the Maktoums would spend more than that in just one year.

That 1983 world-record yearling price obviously caused much comment. The sale also prompted some malicious rumours that swept America and bounced over to Britain. Sangster referred to these in an interview in his own magazine, *Pacemaker*, in answer to a question put to him by Australian racing writer Graeme Kelly. Here is how that part of the interview went:

KELLY: There have been rumours that you and your partners occasionally buy yearlings privately before they enter the sales ring. Is there any truth in this?

SANGSTER: There was a big rumour about the $10 million yearling at Keeneland [Snaafi Dancer], but the mention of litigation soon stopped the tongues from wagging. Thank goodness I had every conversation on my phone recorded because there could have been some newspapers put out of business. You know, *The Times* actually rang up – not the racing press – the Diary from *The Times* rang up and said that they had it from the best authority that we had bought the yearling beforehand.'

Such irksome and insulting rumours were only a part of the price that Sangster, O'Brien and Magnier had to pay for their success. They were no doubt sparked by jealousy of the syndicate, something that became manifest in various forms and which probably emanated from the after-sales sessions in the bars of many an international auction.

The plain truth is that O'Brien was so struck by the colt that he was determined to go for it. One of his overriding qualities is his gritty determination, a terrier-like resolve that means he simply hates to be beaten whether in a race or when bidding at the sales.

It was this sort of tenacity that made the Sangster syndicate such a tough opponent at the sales, something the Maktoums had now discovered with their hard-won fight to purchase Snaafi Dancer. That duel had now increased the will of both camps not to be outdone, drawing other players, too, into this high-stakes gamble. This became evident at the following year's Keeneland Sale when a record number of thirty-three yearlings smashed the million-dollar barrier, fetching a total of $86.35 million dollars – an average of $2.61 million per yearling.

These were almost unbelievable times for those within racing. It was if the value of money had gone out of the window. If people who had no knowledge of racing could have seen these figures, those such as merchant bankers, industrialists and captains of commerce, they might have thought they were in the wrong business.

Of those thirty-three yearlings only seven were bought by Americans. The majority of the rest went to the Maktoums and the Sangster syndicate, with only one or two going elsewhere. Throughout 1984, the Maktoums would spend over $70 million between them to purchase around ninety yearlings. Among their Keeneland haul this year were such instantly forgettable performers as Imperial Falcon ($8.25 million), Jareer ($7.1 million), Amjaad ($6.5 million) and Wassl Touch ($5.1 million). The bill for these four colts alone was almost $27 million and if they won £50,000 between them they were lucky. The Sangster syndicate, boosted by the backing of Niarchos, spent something in the region of $21 million at this sale, too, but they drew several duds such as Obligato ($5.4 million), and Professor Blue ($4.6 million).

Imperial Falcon, in fact, won his two small races in the colours of Sheikh Mohammed and was trained by Vincent O'Brien. Was this a case of some sort of truce following those Sangster visits to Dubai, maybe a softening of the will to dominate the sport in Britain? No, it was more of a token gesture by Mohammed, a sort of testing of the water to see how the colt might fare with a touch of the O'Brien magic. Unfortunately, O'Brien's wand could weave no spell with this son of Northern Dancer.

There was going to be one final year at Keeneland when the Sangster syndicate would flex their muscles and show the racing world they were no pushovers. Of course, it was born out of necessity, the very demanding nature of the syndicate's *modus operandi*; they needed the fuel to keep the fire burning.

And so at Keeneland in 1985 O'Brien fell in love with a yearling by Nijinsky. It was out of a mare called My Charmer, which made the yearling a half-brother to O'Brien's 2,000 Guineas winner Lomond, who was by Northern Dancer. The Irishman had handled two others of My Charmer's progeny in Argosy and Clandestina, who had shown fairly useful form. But the mare's greatest claim to fame was that she was the dam of the mighty Seattle Slew, the US triple-crown winner of 1976 and one of America's most brilliant racehorses. Seattle Slew himself had cost $17,500 as a yearling and had won over $1.2 million prize money.

In O'Brien's eyes, this Nijinsky yearling was perfection. He had not seen anything like it in all his years. In several pre-sales inspections, he stood transfixed, the animal filling his eye as he visualised it as a racehorse, the powerful limbs developed to muscled fitness. There was no way the syndicate were going to be beaten on this one, he told his partners. Sangster could have counselled caution had he felt the US market was soon to go the way of Australia, of which he had great experience. But if O'Brien said he wanted it, well, that was it, end of story. Sangster had relied on O'Brien's judgement before and, overall, it had proved successful.

There were several others who felt the same way, however, and would fight tooth and nail to buy the animal. Chief among them, surprisingly, were not the Maktoums but the American trio of retired magnate Eugene Klein, oil and cattle man L. R. French and their trainer Wayne Lukas. The showman was buoyant in the knowledge that by the end of the last season he had trained the winners of nearly $6 million in prize money alone, never mind some of those horses' stud values.

Klein had entered horseracing in 1982, spending some $40 million on bloodstock. The former owner of the San Diego Chargers football team, who had set up a Sangster–O'Brien-type operation with Lukas, would subsequently own the winner of the 1988 Kentucky Derby, the filly Winning Colours, which he said gave him his biggest thrill in sport. Sadly, Klein died in 1990, only months after selling all his thoroughbred interests in a 1989 Keeneland dispersal sale that brought in almost $30 million.

Klein, French and Lukas were so determined to have this Nijinsky yearling that when the bidding went past the previous Snaafi Dancer world record of $10.2 million, they were still in there fighting. But so were O'Brien and Sangster.

The fiercely fought battle of will, wit and ego finally ended because O'Brien steadfastedly, stubbornly, refused to admit defeat. So he won.

The price was $13.1 million.

It was the ultimate peak of Keeneland prices in a three-year period that was unprecedented, a price that many people thought was ludicrous then, and which, two years later, was considered total madness when this world-record yearling had won just two weakly contested Group Two races in Ireland in a five-race career that lasted just ten weeks.

Suddenly as if shocked at the extent to which this mad

scramble had reached there was a rapid sobering up, a realisation that things had gone too far. The ramifications of this roaring runaway prodigality were swift. Niarchos blew out of the syndicate, disappointed at his lack of results and probably reasoning that, at a time when he was trying to syndicate his Irish Derby winner Law Society for around $14 million, an outlay of $13.1 million on an untried yearling was simply not on.

The market itself, as if stunned by the heady heights it had reached, reacted sharply. It crashed. For many, the gravy train had run out of steam. For others it was a case of counting the cost – usually in portfolios drastically reduced in this new wave of normality.

What made matters worse for Sangster was that by the end of 1985 he had been relegated to seventh position in the leading British owners' table. Top of the tree now was Sheikh Mohammed, closely followed by Khalid Abdullah, with Maktoum and Hamdan just behind. It was a situation that would endure over the next six seasons.

With the market crashing, Niarchos leaving what some regarded as a sinking ship, and the perceived unbreakable dominance of the Maktoums along with Khalid Abdullah, Sangster had some serious thinking to do.

It appeared to most people that his own world was crashing too.

SIXTEEN

Gentlemen Prefer Blondes

Before the bloodstock market crash of 1985, Robert Sangster appeared to be riding on the crest of a wave. He thought he had it made. He had become top British owner for the fifth time in 1984 and reckoned his worldwide breeding and racing interests were now worth something in the region of £190 million. And, although there was no limit attached to his bank borrowing powers, his overdraft was a mere £14 million.

He was, it seemed, the man who had everything: 1,200 racehorses and breeding stock, stud farms in Ireland, America and Australia, multi-million-dollar houses in the world's most exotic locations, a permanent suite in London's Savoy Hotel, even his own fleet of aeroplanes, which included a Citation jet to whisk him to London in fifty minutes from the Isle of Man. He was a friend of royalty and he took his holidays in Palm Beach with the likes of Frank Sinatra, or with the 'in' crowd at his Barbados estate. And he was soon planning that a newly acquired 2,300-acre English training complex at Manton, Wiltshire, on which he would lavish millions of pounds, would become his dream version of Colin Hayes' Lindsay Park.

But, as if to prove that even successful multi-millionaires can only live their lives on a human scale, Sangster was not a happy man. His marriage to Susan was floundering on the rocks and was soon to come to an end. It appeared, however, that this would have been news to Susan.

In October 1984, she was gaily preparing for their usual trip to Australia for the Melbourne cup, planning a six-week stay for herself. Her secretary had already arranged for several carefully chosen outfits to be sent ahead by airfreight, together with a selection of hats so that Susan would need to take only one suitcase with her. She was travelling ahead of her husband to open Toison d'Or in Sydney, fill it with plants and flowers, and generally make it appealing for when he followed a week or so later. Sometimes during Melbourne Cup week they preferred to make the home their base, inviting house guests for the week, then commuting to Flemington racetrack by aeroplane each day.

It had been a busy few weeks for the Sangsters. There were race meetings to attend in England, Ireland and France and visits to several stud farms as well as a number of important social engagements. One of these was a party at The Nunnery to cement contacts with fifty Australian and New Zealand businessmen.

Sangster had also just become a showbusiness impresario by accepting the chairmanship of the Apollo Leisure Group, an Isle of Man-based company which owned several provincial theatres and one in London. One of Apollo's biggest money-spinners was the Andrew Lloyd-Webber production, *Starlight Express*. Sangster's investment gave him what he called a chance to diversify. He had previously held a stake in the company through a Vernons subsidiary, Vernons Finance, and had been represented on the board by one of his financial directors, Merseysider Ken Paul.

This move was one that suited Sangster admirably because he liked the glamorous world of showbusiness and loved to rub shoulders with the personalities in it. He enjoyed friendships with many people in the business, some of whom were regular guests at his renowned summer parties at The Nunnery or, during the winter, at Barbados, where the pro–am charity golf tournaments he hosted were now regular fixtures for many of the glitterati.

Susan was looking forward to her trip back home, especially to see her daughters and her friends. Melbourne Cup week could be so exhausting but it was such fun. There was nothing like the excitement of Cup day itself, that first Tuesday in November which is a public holiday in Victoria and when everything in the country stops for the big race. This is when more than 100,000 people head for Flemington in a carnival atmosphere, the cream of society dressed in their latest outfits to impress, the more outrageous out to shock, the grandstands a packed colourful blur cheering home the winner of this two-mile handicap (worth Aus$1.3 million to the winner in 1991 – the Blue Riband Epsom Derby was worth the equivalent of Aus$850,000)

This was Susan's chance to revel in the occasion. After lunch in their private box, she would head straight for the society-packed members' lawn, sip champagne and socialise in her inimitably extrovert style. If they had a runner in the Cup it was all the better. She had simply adored it when they had won the race with Beldale Ball four years earlier. Oh, the fuss, the attention!

Susan had fallen in love, too, with the harbourside Toison d'Or. She had put a lot of work into the house, much thought and energy going into the alterations and the decor, with emphasis on the layout and the colours, which now made full use of the gloriously clear quality of the Sydney daylight. She was so proud of her achievements with the house that, earlier in the year, when they were both over for the Sydney Easter meeting, Susan had opened her home to the public for charity, charging people $25 a head, and in three hours raised over $11,000 for the Royal Blind Society.

Now, for the next two months, there was only sunshine ahead: Australia for six weeks or so, then on with Robert to California for the Breeders' Cup meeting, the world's richest one-day race meeting with over $5 million in prize money. They might possibly take in Kentucky for a few days to catch up with developments at the stud farms, then, with some luck, they should get to their Barbados estate in time for Christmas.

Alas, while Susan was spring cleaning in sunny Sydney she could no longer 'fear no more the lightning flash' because the bolt that had struck her marriage only two years earlier now savagely returned to strike again, almost to the day and nearly in the same circumstances.

Towards the end of October, with Susan away, Sangster

attended an evening wedding reception at the Isle of Man's Palace Hotel, a large modernised Victorian establishment at the end of a once-popular promenade in the jaded resort of Douglas, a six-minute drive from Sangster's home. It was here that he met up again with the attractive slim young blonde Sue Lilley, whom he had known for several months. As they danced closely together – then danced some more – hinting at a certain amount of amorousness between them, Sue's husband, financier Peter Lilley, stepped into the equation and a few heated words were exchanged.

Now the Isle of Man might be the home of more than sixty millionaires who like the island because of its slow pace of life and its comparative safety, but high jinks of any description will soon spread faster than a bush fire, especially when the island's most famous resident is involved. It did not take long before there were rumours that Sue and Peter Lilley, the heir to the exclusive Lilley and Skinner shoe chain, were on the point of break-up.

Within days those rumours proved well founded when Sangster installed Sue in a suite at London's Dorchester Hotel while he flew to Sydney for a confrontation with Susan. If Susan was feeling more than a pang of *déjà vu* it was no wonder. Sangster's good old pal, Charles Benson, was staying at Toison d'Or too, right in the thick of it all just as he had been two years earlier during the Jerry Hall affair.

After a tearful confrontation during which Sangster suggested a separation, Sangster packed his bags and left the house, flying on to Melbourne and booking into an hotel on his own. Susan was naturally devastated by her husband's pronouncement but, although there was nothing much more she could do, other than reluctantly to agree to Sangster moving out, she decided she did not want news of a separation to leak out on her home territory.

She felt she just could not go through the Jerry Hall routine with the Australian press again, especially not during Melbourne Cup week. The pressure would be unbearable. What made matters more uncomfortable for her was that Sangster's youngest son Adam, then a teenager, was also staying with her, as well as Benson who remained at Toison d'Or after Sangster left in an effort to provide some sort of moral support.

Susan therefore put on a brave face and flew to Melbourne, staying alone in their usual suite at the Hilton. Despite the tumoil inside her, that gut-twisting hurt and sorrow which made it difficult for her to eat, let alone enjoy the lavish hospitality that was there in abundance, she had resolved to try to act normally. But friends soon noticed that there was something wrong with the usual fun-loving Susan. She was quiet and subdued – the champagne bubbles had gone flat.

In her heart of hearts, Susan believed that her husband would not leave her. Even when Sangster cut short his stay and flew off to Los Angeles, she reasoned to herself that this was just another fling. At forty-eight, maybe her husband's mid-life crisis had not yet petered out. Whatever he did, she believed he would be back. And she would wait for him.

Sangster had been making regular calls from Australia to Sue at her London hotel. She, too, was in a state of confusion. She was not totally happy about having left her four-year-old daughter Melissa at home with her nanny, even though she had spoken to the child on the telephone. But then came the call from Sangster with specific instructions: Book yourself on the next flight to LA.

Although Sangster's plans over the next few days involved a large business element, their execution with the new blonde at his side was hardly original. It was the same game plan as he would have implemented with Jerry Hall before their association fizzled out: he flies from Australia to meet the new woman in his life in Los Angeles, they fly down to Kentucky, where he shows her off at the November breeding sale, then they fly off into the sunset to Barbados. This time, however, it was Sue Lilley on his arm, a twenty-eight-year-old former would-be model, a pleasant Manx girl, who had been married twice already.

The press hullabaloo was predictable. Romeo Robert had done it again. And there could be no complaints, generally, about the treatment he received from the world's press apart from one or two malicious stories suggesting that Sue somehow did not care about her daughter's welfare while she was away, though of course she did. It was a difficult time for her too; the speed of everything, the flights halfway round the world, the uncertainty, the excitement. It was not the sort of thing that happened to a girl every day of the week.

After seven days sunning themselves at the Sangsters' Barbados home – Sangster's eldest son Guy went along too – the tanned couple flew to Ireland and into the glare of publicity at the horse sales at Kill in County Kildare, where they attended a pre-sale party. Then they flew off to another sale at Newmarket, where, between sips of champagne, Sangster introduced his friends to the new blonde on his arm.

Now public relations have never been Sangster's strong point, nor diplomacy in the face of his oft-tangled love life. He believed, no doubt, in his open, amiable way, that he was acting with great sincerity when he spoke publicly about still having a great amount of affection for his wife – 'knowing what she must be going through' – and that the last thing he and Sue wanted to do was to cause any unnecessary suffering to their families. This had a familiar ring to it, as his first wife Christine would have been all too well aware. But, considering only three weeks had passed since he had walked out on his wife, this public parading of his new love led some observers to feel that his remarks looked a little hollow.

Some of his acquaintances pointed out that he would have been better advised to have gone somewhere private with Sue, somewhere less obvious than the horse sales at which he was so well known, and then lain low for a while – if not to hide from the media pack, then out of respect for the feelings of his wife and Sue's husband.

But Sangster was having none of that. He had wanted to come out of the closet – and fast.

It was no wonder that Susan, once more, made that plaintive dash from Australia to esconce herself in the Nunnery and begin considering her position. It was a situation that proved intolerable for her when, within days, Sangster and Sue arrived back on the island and, together, promptly moved into the Palace Hotel, two miles away.

After a terse meeting with her husband the following day at The Nunnery, Susan immediately issued a statement to the press in which she said that she was deeply upset and had been put in an impossible position. She had therefore decided to seek either a divorce or a judicial separation. Now the recriminations would begin.

Sangster, naturally, considered himself a gentleman. So did Peter Lilley. There would be no fisticuffs, no shouting and ranting. For Lilley, who had been married before, the *coup de grâce* had proved a total shock. But he accepted it in the most civilised of manners, almost philosophically. Susan, however, was not simply going to pack her bags and return to her family and friends in Australia. She was too upset to do anything just now. She felt it was as if her husband had just gone 'snip' to seven years of marriage, and was now pretending that she hardly existed.

While accepting the situation as best she could, she later made plans to spend Christmas with her daughters and stepson Adam at Toison d'Or, a break to get away from the cold, suffocating atmosphere around her on the island. But when the time came to fly out, the strain and the heartbreak of the past several weeks hit her so hard that she suffered a nervous collapse while in London and was forced to return to The Nunnery. What had affected her particularly was a communication from her husband's solicitors banning her from staying at the Sydney home (she later got a court order to obtain access).

Back at The Nunnery, her life shattered, she received the attention of a full-time night nurse, while her two eldest daughters, Caroline and Ann, arrived from Australia to look after her and help her recover from her ordeal. Sangster, meanwhile, stayed away from his property, the headquarters of his racing empire.

It was at times such as this that the money hardly seemed to matter. Susan said that the main thing in her life now, other than her daughters, was the simple daily routine of getting up in the morning and striving hard to 'hang on in there'. She revealed that she had been hurt beyond words, saying that Sangster had shown no regard or respect for her or for their marriage. There had been no agreed separation nor even a breathing space to sit down and discuss the matter, she said, even though Sangster himself had declared within two weeks of walking out that they were to have a three-month separation. Her friends were quick to point out, too, that she had shown integrity in not speaking out over the Jerry Hall affair – a factor which Susan later felt had actually strengthened their marriage when they got back together.

People intrigued by the affair that had now knocked Prince Andrew and Koo Stark from the society columns began to wonder about Sangster's new love, a girl twenty years his junior.

Sue, maiden name Dean, is one of two daughters of an established Manx family. Her father Michael and his brother John (a former chairman of the Isle of Man Bank) own a large timber company on a five-acre site in Douglas which, ironically, almost backs on to Sangster's estate. In fact, when Sangster purchased The Nunnery, Sue Dean had not long left the boarding school on the island to which her parents had sent her when she was ten years old. After her education, Sue harboured ambitions of becoming a model and, for a period, she left the Isle of Man to live in London, where she attended a modelling school.

She developed into an attractive and friendly girl in her later teens, slim with long, straight, silky blonde hair, cut in a fringe at the front. While she turned men's heads, she was good-looking rather than pretty, attractive rather than beautiful, in some ways with the same freshness of Christine when Sangster had married her. While she had a good sense of humour and could be good fun, she was never boisterous, more the quiet type.

For a time in the mid-1970s, she was a regular at the Douglas quayside pub, the British Hotel, which was then the 'in' meeting place for many of the island's young men and women. It came as a surprise to some of her contemporaries when she announced she was getting engaged to another islander, Kevin Nicholson, son of a wealthy businessman who had founded and controlled the Shoprite supermarket chain.

Nicholson was twenty-one years old, she was eighteen. Good-looking in a Latin way, with dark hair, swarthy features and a moustache, he spent big to impress people and had his legion of hangers-on. He would think nothing of hiring an aeroplane and waltzing off to London or Paris with several of them in tow. Some of Sue's friends wondered what she saw in him because he hardly seemed to have a proper job. Others thought she was too young herself and that she should go out into the world and obtain some experience of life.

After their marriage, they went to live in one of the island's better housing areas and Sue stopped being part of the local pub scene on a regular basis. But, when she did pay an occasional visit to the British Hotel to catch up with news and see old friends, they could not help noticing how subdued she was.

Ultimately, her friends were not surprised when she told them she was getting a divorce. To them it was a good decision. She was desperately unhappy and, as there were no children from the marriage, which had lasted barely eighteen months, the split seemed not only inevitable but eminently sensible. It is doubtful that Sue ever sees her first husband these days, unless she happens to be driving along Douglas seafront and sees a rather weird, pathetic figure wandering around unshaven, unkempt and with a ghetto-blaster constantly on his shoulder.

Putting the sad experience behind her, Sue was soon back frequenting her old haunts and enjoying her single status. For a short period she went to live with a girlfriend 'across the water' in Liverpool and once again thought of becoming a model, joining a modelling agency there and beginning work on her portfolio. Although she was pleased with her pictures file, she felt that, at five foot six inches in height, she was not quite tall enough to make a real success of a modelling career.

But she hardly gave herself the chance because she was soon married again. This time it was to one of the island's 'new ressies' (new residents), Peter Lilley, someone who was on a different social level to her old friends at the British Hotel. Lilley was wealthy too, wealthier than Nicholson, and seemed a better catch. The bespectacled Lilley, heir to a fortune, was quiet, serious, slightly intense. They went to live in an 'estate' of executive homes, outside Douglas, some of which were pushing the half-million-pounds mark. When the Lilleys decided to start a family, Sue became happily pregnant with her daughter Melissa.

Delighted with their lovely child, the Lilleys decided a little later to have another baby. But it was a pregnancy that was to end in tragedy. For, after carrying the child for eight and a half months, the delivery had to be made by caesarian section. Sadly, devastatingly, the new baby was born with no windpipe and no kidneys. It survived for only a short time.

The Sangsters' divorce came through on 24 June 1985, a month and a day after Robert's forty-ninth birthday. Susan, who was now forty-two, had petitioned for divorce on the grounds of the irretrievable breakdown of the marriage, citing in particular her husband's adultery with Sue Lilley. Almost four months earlier, Sangster had been named as co-respondent in Peter Lilley's divorce from Sue, a decree that became absolute in that July.

Susan's divorce settlement from Sangster was thought to be in the region of £3 million plus a London property, the cash to be paid over five years. Exact details remained confidential, however, because of a legal requirement that Susan should keep quiet about certain aspects of their personal life. Although Susan had given her address as Toison d'Or in the divorce hearing, the home she loved so much was not part of the settlement. Sangster was going to allow Susan to live there until he put the house up for auction.

Now he and Sue were free to marry. The couple had been

living together at The Nunnery since Susan had moved out, her departure being a condition of the divorce settlement. And so, in August at a ceremony in the familiar Douglas registry office, Sangster and Sue were hoping that it would be a case of third time lucky for both of them. Their honeymoon was a racing trip to Deauville.

Susan, who had in the interim made Sydney her base, now had to consider what to do with her life. She had toyed with the idea of entering politics, but, in the meantime, had begun hosting the Terry Willisee television programme.

Within a few days of the Sangsters' wedding, however, Susan got married too. Her third husband was New Zealand finance and property man Frank Renouf, who, at the age of sixty-seven, was twenty-four years her senior. He was reputed to be one of New Zealand's richest men.

When Sangster had announced that he was putting Toison d'Or up for auction, arrangements were made to advertise the property in a dozen countries, including the Middle East, to where promotional videos were sent. But the estate agents need not have bothered. For, with a reserve of Aus$8 million, it was soon sold; the buyer at $8.1 million was Frank Renouf – it was a surprise for his new wife.

As what had been a momentous twelve months in the life of Robert Sangster drew to a close, the talk in the world of horseracing was now not about his headline-making romance, but about how he would rise to the challenge of the men from the Middle East. Sheikh Mohammed had not only just become top British owner for the first time, he was the first owner to win more than £1 million in prize money – over two and a half times the amount that had given Sangster his fifth championship the previous year. And as if to signal that the Arabs were here to stay – and in depth – Mohammed's Dalham Stud in Newmarket also topped the list as leading breeder.

Sangster knew he could not compete on outright cash terms.

Mohammed had scooped three classics with his brilliant filly Oh So Sharp (1,000 Guineas, Oaks and St Leger), while his eldest brother, Maktoum, had taken the 2,000 Guineas with Shadeed. The other classic, the Derby, had gone to Lord Howard de Walden's Slip Anchor. It seemed that Sangster could not compete with the extent of Sheikh Mohammed's wealth in many ways. Mohammed had given Oh So Sharp's jockey, Steve Cauthen, a helicopter, while every one of trainer Henry Cecil's stable staff received a $2,000 cash present.

Sangster had to console himself with the Epsom runner-up Law Society's subsequent win in the Irish Derby – even though it did run in Niarchos' colours. And, at Royal Ascot, a rousing win by his home-bred horse Gildoran (by Rheingold out of his own mare Durtal) won his second Ascot Gold Cup in the hands of Brent Thomson, the former New Zealand champion whom Sangster had brought over from Australia to ride the Swettenham Stud horses trained by Barry Hills.

But there was still plenty to look forward to next season. The most exciting project of all was Manton, where the former champion National Hunt trainer Michael Dickinson had set about transforming the 2,300-acre estate into one of the most modern training centres in the world and the best in Britain.

Dickinson was a gifted young man of thirty-two, serious and ambitious, yet with a gritty North Country resolve not to get too carried away with events. It had taken him over five months to make up his mind to join the Sangster operation. And even then he was not too sure he was making the right move. This was the same realism that had caused him to wonder what all the fuss was about after he had saddled the first five horses home in jump racing's most prestigious race, the Cheltenham Gold Cup, in 1983.

Although he had eventually signed a five-year contract with Sangster, joining him in the autumn of 1984, the plan was to set about the awesome task of rebuilding Manton from the spring of the following year before sending out his first runners in the 1986 season. In the meantime, with notebook in hand,

Dickinson would travel the world at Sangster's expense, picking the brains of the best Flat trainers and stud owners in the business.

With this young genius on his side, Sangster was planning for the future, a five-year plan, maybe ten. After all, O'Brien would be sixty-nine years old by the time Dickinson sent out his first runners from Manton. Although O'Brien would still train the syndicate horses and Dickinson would handle Sangster's own Swettenham home-breds, the Irishman could not go on for ever. Sangster had to make provision for that day. Okay, so the bloodstock market might be on the wane and it would mean a period of retrenchment here and there. But it was the future that was important. There was optimism on the horizon, big plans on the drawing board.

Sangster the gambler, some thought, was like the punter who had just taken a bit of a battering but whose slowly returning confidence told him that tomorrow was another day. If his luck was in then he would soon be back on the winning trail.

The big question now, however, was: would he?

SEVENTEEN

It's My Party

The fireworks at Robert Sangster's £100,000 two-day birthday-party bash at The Nunnery in May 1986 to celebrate his fiftieth year, a display which lit up the sky with a message saying 'Happy Birthday Robert Sangster', said a lot about the philosophy of the man; he was determined to go on having a good time no matter what. The party had everything for the 500 invited guests and was reckoned to be one of the most extravagant of the year apart from the royal wedding of Prince Andrew and Sarah Ferguson. As the champagne flowed guests danced and watched the star attraction, singer Paul Anka and his orchestra. There was an appearance, too, by the Band of the Royal Marines whose rousing rendition of Land of Hope and Glory was accompanied by a fitting display of patriotism by the guests who had been given miniature Union Jacks on sticks to wave in the air.

The fact that the giant firework display took place well after midnight when most of his neighbours were asleep, and that one of them, a local MP, led the round of furious complaints by marching to The Nunnery gates with only a coat thrown over his pyjamas, seemed to endorse the view of some of Sangster's friends that he lacked flair and imagination in the PR stakes.

While a large number of the island's residents telephoned the police and local radio station to register their disgust and alarm at the noise of the fireworks at such a late hour, including two hospitals less than a mile away, people were left wondering why he had not taken advantage of the situation to enhance his credibility with the local populace rather than damage it. If the Sangsters had bothered to contact the local newspapers and given advance warning of the display, bringing forward the timing of it to a reasonable hour, thousands more people would not only have appreciated the gesture, but have enjoyed the show too.

As it stood, people thought it was a case of the local squire lording it over the peasants – and not giving a fig what they thought. It did not reflect well on him, either, when the story made the headlines in the popular national press. Was Sangster in a position to complain when those people, who knew nothing of his achievements within racing, thought of him as nothing more than a rich playboy who loved the high life? Were those people wrong to turn their eyes skywards at his regular protests that the press should not write about his private life?

But this was the man who had made his own life public in order to make money by promoting his business. Even when the new Sue came along, had he not been quite willing to show off his new woman and allow almost every colour magazine under the sun to visit The Nunnery and take pictures of their home, their bedrooms and Sue in her latest Chanel, Saint Laurent or Bruce Oldfield? What were ordinary people to think when they read about the couple's lavish lifestyle? And how many of the island's other fifty-nine millionaires lived like that?

The only headlines some of them ever made were in the local paper when the likes of former gramophone magnate Daniel McDonald endowed Cambridge University with £26 million. In contrast, the Sangsters had almost an open line to the local society columnist, a contact established by Susan, and then continued by Sue. The levels of sycophancy reached such heights (or depths) that the local paper was even reporting on what sort of coverage the national newspapers gave the couple, including how many pictures were used of Sue – and what dresses she was wearing in those pictures.

If Sangster wanted to continue to be as open and friendly with the media as he was, then some felt he should have employed a public relations person, just as he would an accountant or bloodstock consultant, to help advise him.

His image within racing was going to lose some credibility too this season when, after much heralding of trumpets at the opening of Manton, the whole escapade fell flat.

Michael Dickinson had turned his round-the-world tour of some of the leading trainers into a fact-finding mission. Wherever he went and whenever people spoke, he was constantly – some felt frantically – making notes. It was as if he did not want to miss one drop of the honeyed wisdom that flowed from such legends as Colin Hayes or Charlie Whittingham in California. People found Dickinson likeable, very knowledgeable, but over-intense, almost paranoid about noting every bit of information as if he was going to have to write a thesis on the training methods of these successful men when he returned to Manton. Said one: 'I don't know whether it was the exertion of taking all those notes, the jet-lag, or our boring company, but he's the only guy I know who can fall asleep over dinner.'

At Manton's unveiling it was unanimously agreed that Dickinson had completed a wonderful job in transforming the estate into a first-class establishment with the most wonderful facilities. Virtually everything was brand new, constructed with almost obsessional secrecy, and seemingly incorporating every latest technological idea: the boxes, the banked landscaping, the renovated famous gallops – which included two of the best all-weather training tracks seen anywhere – the laboratory, the offices, the lads' hostels and housing for more senior married staff. It even had its own 'pub' called the Trelawny Bar, as well as a cricket pitch, tennis court, swimming pool, sauna and solarium.

The security was like no one had ever seen before. There seemed to be uniformed guards everywhere, demanding sight of visitors' passes, constantly speaking into their walkie-talkies. Some visitors got the impression that everything was all a little too intense.

And the bottom line was that this brilliant showpiece had gone disastrously over budget. The final bill, before running costs, was in the region of £14 million, some £4 million or so over budget. Just who was responsible for this was hard to fathom.

Remembering the words of Michael Jarvis, one of David Robinson's former trainers, who was forced by his patron not only to watch every penny, but to think like a businessman too, some people believed it was Dickinson who had gone over the top. Yet others thought that Sangster, the experienced businessman, should have come down harder on the spending.

Still, with forty-two of Sangster's own horses, mostly late-maturing two-year-old Swettenham Stud home-breds, Dickinson could start slowly, break himself in, assess the gallops, the feed, all the factors which go into making a balanced training centre, then with a season under his belt, start on the real job of training those horses as three-year-olds.

Shortly after the end of the season, however, seven months after launching the Manton hopes in a blaze of glory, Dickinson was sacked. He had sent out four winners worth less than £14,000 – not even enough to pay a few month's feed bill. This trainer who had broken records in the National Hunt field, a man whom Sangster had described as a genius and who had been snatched from under the noses of prominent owner Charles St George and the Maktoums, was now paid off on the residue of his contract, which was to have run until October 1990. The shattered Dickinson was the first trainer Sangster had sacked among the dozens he had employed throughout the world in all his years racing.

Sangster was saddened, almost embarrassed, to have finally pulled the plug. He was a patient man when it came to the trials and tribulations of the turf, he had seen it all before, knew the knockbacks all too well. In a way, it was not so much the lack of success, because Sangster hardly expected a rip-roaring start with the type of youngsters Dickinson was training. But there was puzzlement over some of the training methods, about which Dickinson became increasingly sensitive and secret. And it was not so much because the horses lost as how they lost. Sometimes they seemed to be running backwards rather than forwards.

Dickinson had never been one to attend the races and socialise on ordinary race days when he thought he could get on with the work at the stables – he had been like that during his National Hunt career. It could be reasonably argued, though, that it would have been politic to attend Sangster's favourite Chester May meeting with the stable's first runner, Veryan Bay, even if the Steve Cauthen-ridden 13–8 favourite was eventually beaten sixteen lengths in a two-year-old sprint over five furlongs. Some thought the Howard Hughes act was going a bit far.

After the sacking, Sangster pointed out that Dickinson had sent the yard's most expensive two-year-old, Juilliard, a colt who had cost almost a million dollars, to the minor track of Chepstow at the back end of the season, where the trainer proclaimed him to be in the very useful Group Three class after he ran second. But, against the wishes of Sangster, who wanted the horse put away for next season, Dickinson insisted on running the colt two weeks later in a minor race at Leicester, where he ran third (beaten a short head and a neck).

Other critics of Dickinson said he had taken horses to gallop at Brighton racecourse – even after the Flat season had finished. Perhaps, as Sangster was later to remark, Dickinson was five years ahead of his time and people were not ready for his innovative methods. The main problem between trainer and owner, though, was their inability to communicate. Some commentators translated this as Dickinson's dourness, almost an aversion to the fun-loving Sangster's partying style and determination to enjoy life. Some put it in more simplistic terms, noting Dickinson's failure to crack open a bottle of champagne when the boss arrived to inspect the joint. Certainly problems arose from the opposing personalities of the two men: Dickinson's often overplayed seriousness, his 'early to bed, early to rise' teetotal mentality against Sangster's humour and love of life.

While acknowledging Dickinson's industriousness and enthusiasm, Sangster said that he just could not communicate with him. Dickinson was adamant about his own ideas and refused to budge an inch. The breakdown was irretrievable. The men did not see eye to eye any longer, a situation that became manifest several weeks before the split when Dickinson wanted to sue newspapers after they had reported signs of discontent at Manton, whereas Sangster, after all his experiences, was happy to shrug it off, let it pass.

Dickinson himself has never spoken out about his version of events. Even when he eventually moved over to America and began training in Maryland with a fair degree of success, the silence remained. But this was not some sort of sullenness as though he had sulked off with his tail between his legs. It was simply that, as part of the settlement of his contract, he had signed an agreement requiring silence.

That silence has been subsequently rewarded, however, for in 1991 Sangster decided to send Dickinson three horses to train.

Supporters of Dickinson point out that when Sangster subsequently appointed his Lambourn trainer Barry Hills to take over at Manton for the following season, when he trained 101 winners, the successful Hills had brought over many of his own patrons and horses which had swelled the winner total. Therefore, it was unfair to compare totals. Whatever the merits of the argument, Hills helped Sangster to finish the 1987 season with a real rattle to win seventy-three races in Britain worth £468,000 and finish third to Sheikh Mohammed on the table.

One of the horses Hills did not manage to win with, however, was Juilliard, one of the causes of the Sangster–Dickinson disagreement. The Nureyev colt ran five times, was visored once, and looked as though he might not have been entirely genuine. And Sangster's best horse at Manton that season was the sprinter Handsome Sailor, a horse who finished his career having won seven races, including two Group One sprints, and over £220,000 prize money. Dickinson is proud of buying that horse as a three-year-old for Sangster from the small yard of Lincolnshire trainer Ron Thompson.

Most people in British racing agreed that it was a great pity that the Dickinson association with Sangster and Manton did not work out. For here was an emerging Flat trainer who would possibly have taken over the Vincent O'Brien mantle as

Sangster's number one in the not too distant future to continue the sydicate's amazing success of the last ten years.

To some degree, it could be said that the split occurred at a time when Sangster was feeling the pressure of the bloodstock recession like everyone else. Perhaps in the eighteen months leading up to the opening of Manton, what had been planned as a fairly laid-back start had become a little more urgent due to the changing financial climate. Dickinson, in fact, was said to have been most concerned when, within a few months of the Manton redevelopment being completed, Sangster had arrived there one day with Sheikh Mohammed. There were some witnesses of the visit who questioned whether Mohammed was simply there as a visitor – or as a prospective buyer.

Some professionals in Australia who had met Dickinson believed that his research around the world had clouded his mind rather than cleared it. They felt that Sangster had made a mistake in giving Dickinson that year off to travel around the world on his note-taking epic. It was thought that this had led him to try and pack into his own training system too many aspects of the various progressive methods and ideas he had witnessed, rather than allow things to evolve over a period of time. Some experienced professionals believed Dickinson would have been better starting with basics and adding on as time progressed. After all, Colin Hayes took twenty-five years to develop Lindsay Park – and he has not finished yet. Something that lent credence to their views was the building of the Manton barns which housed the stable blocks. One visitor was bemused when Dickinson told him that he had not been able to make up his mind whether to have an American style barn or a European one – 'So we built both.'

At this time, too, Sangster's confidence was dealt a body-blow by the poor form of the syndicate's horses with O'Brien at Ballydoyle, a string which included the unraced Seattle Dancer, the previous year's $13.1 million world-record yearling. In the fight for British supremacy against the Arabs the Ballydoyle setback could not have come at a worse time. O'Brien's string was suffering from a mystery virus which had laid low many of his horses, prompting the Irishman to close down the whole operation for several months. By the middle of June, in fact, O'Brien had trained just five winners. At the end of the season the Irish tally was twenty-one. Numerically it was the same total as in 1985, but the prize money, at IR£134,219 was IR£282,000 down on the previous year.

Some cynics suggested that this was the beginning of the end for Sangster and O'Brien, and this was why Pat Eddery had decided not to take up his retainer for the following season, instead joining Khalid Abdullah as first jockey to ride the Prince's array of horses which were handled by several different trainers. Eddery was already riding many of the Abdullah horses in England during the 1986 season because of his enforced lay-off from Ireland. Notable was the partnership with the brilliant Dancing Brave. It ultimately transpired that he had been offered more money to ride for Abdullah, an offer the Sangster syndicate were not prepared to match. This led many people to say that if Sangster could not keep hold of the best jockey in Britain then, indeed, the slide had set in.

There was great personal sadness in Sangster's life at this time, too. Shortly before Christmas, his father Vernon, one of the most respected men on Merseyside, died at the grand old age of eighty-seven. Sangster had flown over to the family home the night before Vernon peacefully passed away and could see his father's heart was failing. 'He was the best friend I ever had and I told him that at his bedside,' Sangster said.

Vernon was the Mr Modesty of the region he loved, a man who had but two hobbies in life, his business and his golf. Although he had managed to continue with both until into his eighties and hardly ever shirked a meeting or function connected with either, the latter year or two had seen him become increasingly unsteady on his feet, so much so that a lift was installed in the West Kirby home where he had lived all those years within sight of his beloved golf club.

The Reverend John Richards, a friend of the family, gave the address at the funeral, which was attended by Sangster, Christine, and their three sons, Guy, Ben and Adam, as well as leaders of commerce and industry from throughout the North-west of England and many of Vernon's and Peggy's friends. In a moving address, this is what he said: 'Vernon Sangster was not only highly successful in his chosen career, but he had personal qualities which endeared him to everyone who knew him. He was a cheerful man with a lively sense of fun. Above all, he was generous and kind.

'His good deeds were expedited without fuss. He was, by nature, a self-effacing man who throughout his life avoided the glare of popularity and publicity. Vernon possessed one sterling quality which surpassed all others – he never changed. Right to the end he was the same modest gentleman as when he first came to Merseyside all those long years ago.'

By the end of the 1987 season Stavros Niarchos had pulled out of the syndicate along with Frenchman Jean-Pierre Binet. Even Danny Schwartz, the stalwart since The Minstrel's purchase in 1975, wanted to reduce his interest. The slide was threatening to become an avalanche.

After Eddery's departure, the syndicate had managed to tempt the stylish American, Cash Asmussen, France's champion jockey, to leave his French trainer and take Eddery's place for the start of the 1987 season. But there were no Nijinskys, The Minstrels or Allegeds at Ballydoyle this year. Asmussen rode sixty-two winners to finish second in the Irish jockeys' championship, yet had to take much criticism from disgruntled Irish punters who were vociferous about his riding of several beaten odds-on shots. O'Brien's runners in Ireland were invari-ably heavily supported in the betting ring and short-head defeats, no matter what the excuse, do not go down well. The Texan got great pleasure out of riding Sangster's top-class sprinter Bluebird, a son of Storm Bird, to victory in the King's Stand Stakes at Royal Ascot, which provided O'Brien with his

first Group One event in Britain in three years. But with the likes
of Seattle Dancer not proving top notch – a bitter disappointment to the syndicate, especially Niarchos – the inevitable
conclusion seemed to be that the Arabs had all but won the battle
to dominate British racing.

But why this seemingly crazy scramble to dominate the
domestic scene in Britain? It was simply that British racing was
still considered the best in the world. It might lag behind the
prize money of other countries by a long way, it might have had
to import the majority of its young stock from America, and, like
a two-year-old which runs green, it might have plenty of room
for improvement. For tradition, prestige and depth of integrity,
however, the founding country of the thoroughbred was the best
place to race. And, despite Sangster's love of racing in other
countries and his vast international network, it was in Britain
where the flag-waving Englishman enjoyed his racing most.

By the end of 1987, after the overheating of the bloodstock
market had left the industry deflated, people like Sangster had
been forced to sit down and take stock of their situation.
Bloodstock values throughout the world had been slashed,
stallion fees were having to be realistically reduced in commen-
surate terms so that forthcoming young stock could find buyers
at the sales. Soon they would be reduced again. Breeders just
could not go on paying the high prices of the earlier eighties; the
'production' costs, that is the cost of stallion nominations, were
far outweighing the prices that foals and yearlings were now
fetching. Reluctance at the sales was also leading to a certain
amount of over-production.

The drop in sales prices at Keeneland, some experts believed,
was also partly due to the fact that the Arabs had been retaining
their world-class fillies for their own studs – thereby keeping the
progeny for themselves – rather than selling them, with the
progeny ending up on the open market, which would have
prompted keen bidding. However, it was more likely that the

Arabs had simply blown away the competition, for they were still buying up to 70 per cent of the Keeneland Selected stock every year. Without Sangster and company there to provide sustained competition, the Maktoums in particular had virtually a free hand.

In Kentucky, some stallion fees were cut by 20 per cent. A year or two later they were down another 25 per cent on the new figure. In Australia and New Zealand, too, it was a similar story. In Britain, the price of stock sold at the Tattersall's Highflyer sale had fallen by nearly 20 per cent in the three years from 1984 to 1987, while at Keeneland the drop in the average price of a yearling was 32 per cent over the same period – the figures exacerbated in real terms by the rise in the cost of living over the same period.

The financial realities of the slump were reflected in the accounts of Vernons, of which Swettenham Stud was a subsidiary – and for several years the main contributor to the group profits. The accounts revealed that bank borrowing had increased from £11.4 million to £50.6 million between 1983 and 1985.

The extent to which bloodstock had been playing a vital role in the fortunes of Vernons as a group over the years was reflected in the Swettenham Stud profit contribution. In 1985, group profits were £9.7 million, yet the pools side made a loss of £371,000 on a turnover of over £35 million. In 1983, Swettenham Stud alone had made a profit of £9.27 million. This increased to £11.7 million the following year when, by comparison, the pools side made only £1.2 million profit.

But, profitable as Sangster's bloodstock business had been – and some of his interests with Coolmore were a separate entity – the bank borrowing had reached a height that began to unnerve his bankers given that the slump in bloodstock values had not gone unnoticed – even to the extent that it had now created a certain amount of publicity in specialist financial journals. Indeed, during the middle eighties, Sangster had, once more, sounded the idea of floating the company on the stock market, this time with merchant bankers N. M. Rothschild. But they advised that the pools business was just not 'sexy' enough. It was steady but stolid, ex-growth. A public flotation in the middle of a roaring stock market (and before the Black Monday crash in October 1987), needed add-ons, a wider diversification with greater future growth potential – perhaps 10 to 15 per cent a year – before it could attract investors' money.

One of the financial advisers at the time was of the opinion that, although Vernons had tried diversification over the years, going into such areas as motorcars, vehicle leasing and finance, these businesses were not strong enough to provide a total package for Vernons to be floated. Maybe it was now that Sangster's own words, that he had neglected Vernons for the past ten years, returned to haunt him. But, in all honesty, he would have to admit that horses gave him much more pleasure than football pools.

In the final analysis, and with bank loans of somewhere in the region of £40 million, Sangster thought there was only one option open to him towards the end of 1987.

He would have to sell the family silver. Vernons had to go.

EIGHTEEN

'Everything's for Sale . . .'

After ten years at the forefront of the hobby that Robert Sangster chose to make his business, a gamble that could have gone either way but which ended with his successfully capturing a large slice of the world bloodstock market and, in many ways, creating his own, the fact that he could not afford to compete with the Maktoums at the major bloodstock sales had become all too clear. It had proven a painful and costly lesson. The bid to beat the Arabs, if it was ever thought a reality, was as feasible as Sangster single-handedly attempting to plug one of the oilwells from which the Maktoums' riches flowed. The tide of money was simply not for turning.

Now, with bank borrowings of over £40 million, circumstances had forced Sangster to alter his whole strategy. His financial advisers were Merseysider Ken Paul, the joint chief executive of Vernons, and fellow director Michael Heeley, a Manchester-based former director of the British Linen Bank, the merchant banking arm of the Bank of Scotland. Their despondency during a period which Sangster himself called 'very nearly a bloodbath' led to Sue Sangster labelling the two men 'Doom' and 'Gloom'.

In 1987 Sangster had sold more than $21 million worth of bloodstock worldwide and had bought just $1 million of stock. Swettenham Stud in Cheshire was sold for around £1 million to a property man who wanted to build a hotel and golf course on the site, while Sangster had earlier sold a large stake of his broodmare equity in Australia and cut down on his interests in South Africa too.

The death of his father had now left him with options; stark choices had to be made. Did he really want to continue with Vernons, or, for that matter, did his sons? After all, they were now all young men with a say in matters. Guy, who was now twenty-five, was quieter than his brothers, taking more after his mother. Unlike his father, he had been trained in financial management: so too had Adam, who was in banking. These were young men with fresh ideas on old problems, assets to any family-run business.

Like his two elder brothers, Ben worked in London, in his case for a firm of shipping brokers run by the brother of a Newmarket trainer. All three had flats in the City, where Sangster visited them regularly, usually for lunch. These were times reminiscent of when Sangster himself was a young man, meeting his mates in the Liverpool Kardomah café for their men-only luncheon club. Now, the father and three sons would look forward to their get-togethers. Sometimes it would be a sober, serious affair, an ordered well-cooked lunch, a few drinks and a chat about their lives and the business. Other times they would simply get together for the crack, probably drink too much and act boisterously, but have a bloody good laugh. It was moments such as these that gave Sangster enormous satisfaction: that he was close to his sons, that they were level-headed young men of whom he was proud. He was most grateful that Christine had brought them up so well.

Guy, who was a director of Vernons, had been working for a London stockbroking company, but was now an acquisitions analyst with a company called Thomson T-Line. This was a one-time Scottish caravan-maker, a virtual 'shell' company when it was taken over two years earlier by partners Julian Askin and South African Henry Biermann. Through shrewd acquisitions, the two men had taken the company turnover from £1.75 million in 1985 to £12.1 million in the sixteen-month period ending April 1987. They had also turned around several years of losses to produce a £750,000 profit in a fully listed public limited company that had become a small industrial holding company with interests in electronics and engineering.

Towards the end of 1987, negotiations began between Thomson T-Line and Vernons with a view to the former buying the pools company and its subsidiaries. These included a direct-mail distribution company and a firm of specialist printers. Sangster's own Swettenham Stud company interests were, obviously, not part of the deal. When the news became public, there were some observers willing to believe that Sangster was selling the family firm in order to give him funds for one final push against the Arabs. This was not the case, however, because he had already given up that idea. He knew it was pointless trying to compete with them at the sharp end. He was making plans to become a seller now, not a buyer. In fact there was one remark he reiterated during this period which lucidly summed up his change of direction: 'In this life everything is for sale – except the wife.'

The initial confirmation from Sangster that the deal was being discussed was couched in terms of a £100 million price for Vernons. He was at pains to assure the Liverpool workforce that their jobs would be secure and that the deal was in their best interests. Sangster was to remain as chairman of Vernons and also take up a seat on the Thomson T-Line board through a 3 per cent stake in the company. Thomson's Askin and Biermann, who had been given an option to purchase Vernons, began taking a good look at the company. They came to the conclusion that cost controls should be tightened up and efforts made to regain the 8 per cent market share Vernons had lost over the preceding five years.

Askin was also anxious that Vernons should respond to the disciplines imposed on it if it was to become part of a publicly quoted group. 'Up until now, every penny of cash generated has been Hoovered up and spent on horses,' he said.

Some two months later the deal was agreed. Thomson T-Line paid £90 million for the company. City analysts reckoned that Sangster would be left with a third after paying off his loans, bank guarantees and bloodstock debts. Sangster has said that the figure was nearer to £50 million – free of capital gains tax because there is none in the Isle of Man. Rumours that he had gone broke were very much exaggerated unless those rumour-mongers believed that someone who is down to his last £40 million or so in cash (plus his large international equine holding) was heading towards skid row. Sangster has emphasised, too, that none of the Vernons cash has gone into the horse business. He and his sons were aiming to make the business self-financing.

When Sangster said that he was to become a seller not a buyer, he did not mean he was selling up and quitting the game – even though he might have considered this at the lowest point of all the aggravation he had had to endure. The game plan now was that he would concentrate more on his bloodstock breeding activities, keeping some stock to race, and hoping to sell rather more than he would buy in a market that had now been fully tempered by reality.

The rationalisation by Sangster of his equine empire brought all his horse interests under the umbrella of a new company called the Sangster Group, which has its offices in the Wirral, five miles or so from where Sangster grew up. So there was to be a new start, a fresh look at the world – with his three sons taking an ever-growing interest in the business. With the sale of Vernons completed and the family link still maintained, Sangster could march forward with a realistic policy of accepting the facts of life vis-à-vis the Maktoums' dominance of British racing.

But the Vernons saga was not yet over. For within nine months of the sale to Thomson T-Line, a predator with an eye on the enlarged group surfaced in the shape of Cyril Stein of Ladbroke, the man who had all but secured Vernons for the Ladbroke Group fourteen years earlier, yet who had never given up hope that, one day, the pools business would be his. In the interim, Stein had built his group into a thriving conglomerate with an annual turnover exceeding £3.6 billion and pre-tax profits of more than £302 million. He surprised most people by launching a hostile 80 pence a share offer for Thomson, thereby valuing the company at around £160 million.

But the Thomson board were prepared to fight to keep their

independence. They had been considering a merger with the engineering company Suter, but this had now been put on hold while the battle was fought. Two 'white knight' allies of Thomson T-Line appeared in the shape of Liverpool businessman Brian Wolfson's Wembley Group, owner of the famous London stadium, which was preparing to make a bid. This was supported by Sangster's friends at Hanson Trust, Lord Hanson and 'Gordie' White (now Lord White), who took a 5 per cent stake at Thomson. But Stein, with almost 30 per cent of Thomson T-Line in his back pocket, was like a terrier with a bone. He raised his offer to 90 pence a share, valuing Thomson at £186 million, and finally clinched the sale days later. Stein's brinkmanship had paid off just as it had on countless other occasions in the course of the tremendous growth of Ladbroke over the years. This was something that must have had Sangster perhaps wondering what might have been had his father agreed to Vernons' merger with the then-bookmaking firm those fourteen years earlier.

As Sangster was announcing his resignation from the Thomson board, thereby severing the sixty-year-old family link with Vernons, Stein was running the rule over the pools business and preparing to sell off Thomson T-Line's other assets. He wanted the pools business, nothing else. This he subsequently began to do, raising somewhere in the region of £60 million, which valued the Vernons pools side at approximately £115 million.

Sangster's sons were now becoming more actively involved in the Sangster Group. Although Guy still worked for a former Thomson T-Line company, which had been bought by one of the former partners, he was the only son to be made a director of the Sangster Group. But the influence of all three sons was going to play an important part in the decision-making of the future.

As 1989 began to draw to a close, the estate of Manton was high on the agenda of items to be discussed. The plans Sangster had initially proposed for Manton had now been set aside because of the financial climate. But the contract under which Barry Hills was leasing the 2,300 acres had only one more season to run. Hills himself had won seventy-three races worth £479,000 by the end of the season to finish sixth in the top trainers' table. Sangster's own position in the owners' list reflected the dominance of the Arabs. Sangster was not in the top dozen owners while Mohammed and Hamdan Al-Maktoum occupied first and second spots with £1.2 million prize money each. Khalid Abdullah was third and Maktoum Al-Maktoum fourth.

Hills' owners at Manton were paying something like £35 a day per horse in training, but when Sangster took into account the cost of simply owning Manton, his own forty-strong stable of home-breds were costing him more like £42 a day each. The more the whole project was examined, the greater the conclusion that Manton should be sold. The capital cost of the estate, now reckoned by Sangster to be worth in the region of £15 million, could be far better employed by being invested. Such a sum could bring in more than £2 million a year interest – enough to pay for the training and running costs of 100 horses.

Although Sangster was keen to retain Manton, reasoning that he could still fit it into his future plans, his sons outvoted him at a meeting of the family trust. Compared to the prudence of investing the capital from the sale of Manton, the whole project was beginning to look like the proverbial white elephant. After the rather painful decision had been taken, the announcement was made in October 1989 that the Manton House Estate was on the market with an asking price of £15 million. But it seemed as if fate was beginning to conspire against Sangster because the move was made in the middle of one of Britain's worst slumps in the property market.

Throughout the next twelve months came a succession of prospective purchasers. The Japanese were said to be interested at one stage, although nothing materialised. To some observers, what soon turned into the Manton saga became reminiscent of the long-running serial in the early eighties over the future of Aintree racecourse, the home of the Grand National, when the Jockey Club eventually brought the tedium to an end and bought the course through its Racecourse Holdings Trust subsidiary.

As the months ground on and the market for equestrian property worsened, evoking descriptions of 'grim' and 'bleak' from estate agents who were used to selling six-figure properties, Barry Hills tried to put various schemes together based on a plan to split Manton into several smaller training establishments. The idea was that several trainers would buy 'training plots' to create their own yards within the estate. It was a restless period for Hills – business meetings, planning meetings, a great amount of background work to ensure a successful completion. But his final offer of £12 million was not enough. Sangster stood rock steady. At the end of the 1990 season Hills was forced to move back to his old Lambourn stables, which had in turn been occupied by his trainer son, John. The upheaval for Hills, his wife Penny, and their staff, was reflected in the sadness of their faces when the crunch came.

Sangster then announced that, until he could find a buyer, he would install a new private trainer at Manton. And his youngest son, Ben, would be the assistant. This was Peter Chapple-Hyam, a former pupil assistant to Hills (he had actually led up Gildoran when Sangster's horse had won the Ascot Gold Cup in 1984). Chapple-Hyam, aged twenty-five, from Leamington Spa in Warwickshire, had married Sangster's stepdaughter Jane Peacock – Susan's daughter – who had also been working for Hills at Manton.

Jane, the Peacocks' youngest daughter, had horses in her blood. She was determined to make a career in the business and had worked at Lindsay Park and with Brian Mayfield-Smith in Sydney and also at the National Stud in Newmarket. It was her father Andrew who had been keen for her to continue a family connection with bloodstock that now goes back four generations. Peacock had therefore contacted Sangster and asked if there was a job for Jane within his organisation. 'Robert was very kind and readily agreed to finding a job for Jane. He's very good like that, very generous. And, contrary to what some people might think, he and I are very good friends,' the politician said.

Throughout this period of the Sangster rationalisation and contraction, there had appeared one small chink of light in the otherwise hopeless cause of pursuing the best bloodstock in the American sales. If the Sangster–O'Brien–Magnier triumvirate had lost some of their wealthy syndicate members, why not try and raise several million pounds, not with a select few clients – but with thousands? It could be a sort of up-market racing club following the same policy that had worked wonders for the syndicate so many times before.

And so, in October 1987, the public company Classic Thoroughbreds was launched on the Dublin Stock Exchange with a capital base of IR£10 million. O'Brien was set up as chairman of the company and would train all the horses. He had a stake of just over 12 per cent, which cost him IR£1 million. Sangster and Magnier each put in IR£600,000 for an 8.3 per cent stake along with Michael Smurfit, head of the paper and packaging Smurfit Group. Cork meat wholesaler John Horgan, a racehorse owner in his own right for many years, put in IR£250,000 for a 3.2 per cent stake.

These five had therefore put some IR£3 million into the new company. The man behind the scheme was Dermot Desmond of the Dublin-based National City stockbroking group. With his contacts in the business world, he was able to attract institutional investment to the tune of IR£5 million. These included Citibank, Shield Insurance, Allied Irish Investment Bank and Irish Life. The other IR£2 million was raised from the general public.

In anticipation of the new company's flotation, O'Brien had already paid his usual visit to Keeneland the previous July, where he paid out over $3 million for four yearlings. Two of these were sons of Northern Dancer: a full brother to the 1984 Derby winner Secreto, which was subsequently named Classic Secret, and another which was called Maritzadoon. Their purchase prices, at $1.4 million and $1.25 million, reflected the state of a much more realistic market where the top price paid was $3.7 million (by Sheikh Mohammed for Warrshan). In fact, Mohammed's Darley Stud was responsible for buying seven of the sixteen yearlings who fetched a million dollars or more. At the end of the year, O'Brien had bought a total of thirty-eight yearlings, comprising twenty-nine colts and nine fillies. He had spent IR£7.6 million of the new company's money.

Classic Thoroughbreds was launched with a blaze of publicity, especially in Ireland, where television programmes were made about the new venture. Some 2,500 people clamoured to join the company, paying something like IR£750 each for their stakes in an issue that was oversubscribed four times. When the shares opened on the Dublin Stock Exchange at a value of 30 pence each, the general perception was that here was a splendid opportunity for the public to share in the fortunes of the syndicate that had become a legend in the racing world.

But it seemed that the Sangster–O'Brien–Magnier luck was rapidly running out. If Sangster's oft-quoted phrase that 'life is all about timing' returned to haunt him, then it was no wonder. For within a week of the flotation came Black Monday, the worst stock market crash for decades.

Although this setback was seen as something of a temporary one, it might have been taken as an omen. Indeed, the fortunes of Classic Thoroughbreds throughout its existence have, perhaps, mirrored the racing fortunes of the Sangster triumvirate itself. It seemed to follow the simple punters' law regarding the great imponderable called luck, which is interminably linked with the rule that you should never chase your losses.

The first season's horses included the potentially useful Classic Fame and Classic Secret, although both failed in Britain to live up to expectations. Classic Fame was later quite successful in America. The $1.25 million purchase Maritzadoon never saw a racecourse. Shareholders, however, appeared to have a jewel in the son of El Gran Señor called Saratogan, who, in his second of two races as a juvenile, finished half a length behind the dead-heaters Scenic and Prince of Dance in the 1988 Dewhurst Stakes. This seemed a re-run of a well-worn path that the Sangster syndicate had trodden over the years. Saratogan, in whom Classic Thoroughbreds had a 50 per cent stake, would now be aimed at the 2,000 Guineas the following season.

Before this race, the optimism that is required in abundance by anyone who is connected with racing was rife. The shares of Classic Thoroughbreds went as high as 41 pence, placing an asset value on the company of around IR£23.5 million. It seemed that sunny days were just around the corner, for if Saratogan was successful his value as a potential stallion would be in the millions. Alas, like some of the O'Brien horses before him, Saratogan promised much but delivered little. The colt was heavily backed but could finish only ninth in the first colts' Classic at Newmarket. Fitted with blinkers for the Irish equivalent, he finished sixth, then ran disappointingly in the Phoenix International in Ireland. Classic Fame ran in the Derby but finished seventh.

By Royal Ascot in June, when Classic Secret had also proved a failure, and their sprinting hope Puissance had sustained an injury, the shares had slumped to 16 pence. To some shareholders, the excuse that O'Brien's stable had suffered another virus seemed like the old, old story, and there were heated words at the shareholders' meeting.

It was not long before the half-yearly figures for 1989 revealed that the company had lost IR£5.7 million. The company won twenty races in Ireland that year, but with the pitifully low prize money on offer in all but the top races in Ireland, the total was only IR£92,000. The main reason for the loss was the write-down value of the stock which contributed IR£5.2 million of the loss. It was also revealed that the company had sold seventeen of its thirty-three three-year-olds.

In response to complaints that the company's horses did not

appear to be running often enough, Sangster and his fellow
directors decided to send several horses to two other Irish
trainers. The fact that these included horses which were to go
jumping (therefore having little residual value because most NH
horses are gelded) added to investors' fears for the future of the
company. That move, and the final year's total loss of IR£6.8
million, sent the shares plummeting again – this time to an all-
time low of just 9 pence.

In another tilt at the major sales following a cash call to
investors, who had coughed up another IR£5 million, O'Brien
had bought Keeneland's 1988 top-priced lot, paying $3.5
million for a Nijinsky yearling out of Tom Gentry's now-famous
broodmare Crimson Saint, and this was named Royal Academy.
And at the Tattersalls Newmarket sales, he had paid a British
record £2.4 million for a yearling that was named Classic Silver.
In the case of Classic Silver, once again that unknown correlation between cost and ability reared its ugly head. The horse
never set foot on a racetrack in earnest.

By November 1990, after much disillusionment, the shares
had halved again to 4.5 pence. Investors were now holding just a
seventh of their initial outlay. There was still a beacon to be lit on
the hillside, however, because there were hopes that the old team
of Lester Piggott and O'Brien could pull off a spectacular win at
the Breeders' Cup meeting in New York. Sure enough, as if
turning the clock back years, Piggott, who had only that season
returned to the saddle because it is the thing he likes doing best,
rode Royal Academy to win the Breeders' Cup Mile on an
emotional occasion. The shares leaped up to 10 pence on the
Monday after the weekend event before more sober counselling
prevailed. Classic Thoroughbreds owned only 40 per cent of
Royal Academy – the rest was owned by Sangster, O'Brien and
Magnier. When the euphoria died down, the shares slipped back
to 7.5 pence. For the first half of 1991 they remained in the
doldrums, stuck at around 5 pence.

Hopes of a Classic success, at last, rested on the colt,
Sportsworld, whom the company owned outright. He was one

of the six runners in the 1991 Irish Derby. But Sportsworld's fourth place behind the Epsom Derby victor, Generous, dampened enthusiasm for the shares even more. And when it was announced a little later that Classic Thoroughbreds had lost another IR£2.6 million, the shares slumped yet again, this time to 3p. It came as no great surprise, therefore, that in the August of 1991, the company announced it was to cease operations. If shareholders were lucky they might expect a fifth of their initial investment. The 'noble experiment' had failed, Michael Smurfit total shareholders. O'Brien announced he was reducing his string to just 30 horses. The end of an era was nigh.

In its four years of existence Classic Thoroughbreds was therefore seen as an umitigating disaster. The highly speculative nature of the investment had been fully noted in the prospectus when it advised that the purchase of shares 'should only be considered by those persons who could sustain a loss'. Some financial experts have pointed to the high risk which had to be balanced against the potential high rewards. But the launch came at a time when there was little upside in the bloodstock market, which was itself depressed. And it was a high-cost operation. Vincent O'Brien's services do not come cheap.

As the decade drew to a close, if Sangster ever felt in a reflective mood he could have surveyed the trials and tribulations of an emotional and eventful past ten years. He had been toppled from his top spot by the Arabs, had fought and lost a battle to outbid them. No longer was he willing or able to compete with their power. Manton had been something of an expensive disaster, while Classic Thoroughbreds had proved an embarrassment.

But there were other frontiers, places where the Arabs hardly ventured. He was still big in Australia, the land of sunshine, huge prize money and opportunity. His racing empire would be further developed Down Under.

NINETEEN

Every One a Winner

It was July 1988. Robert Sangster settled himself into his first-class seat on Cathay Pacific flight CX-101, the overnight from Hong Kong to Melbourne. After giving the Thai stewardess his jacket to hang in the aft wardrobe, he accepted a pre-flight drink at his window placing. This was a ten-hour journey he had made countless times, a visit to survey his Australian racing and breeding empire.

Throughout his stay he would see his racing manager, David Coles, who works from Adelaide, and his Melbourne-based racing accountant and business manager, Bob Atkins. There would be meetings, too, with some of his dozen or so trainers: the Cup King Bart Cummings, Tommy Smith, Colin Hayes, Brian Mayfield-Smith, John Hawkes.

In a ten-year spell in Australia, Sangster had become perhaps the most influential owner in the whole of the southern hemisphere. Of course, the glare of publicity had been intensified because of his marriage to Susan Peacock, but he was well-known in business circles too, having founded his Soccerpools operation, before joining with Rupert Murdoch and Kerry Packer to run the popular money-spinning Lotto (until that was eventually taken over by the Government). By 1985, soon after his divorce from Susan, his racing and breeding portfolio included shares in more than 100 Stake-winning mares in Australia and New Zealand. He was particularly interested in trying to achieve what he called 'twisting the globe a little', in that he was aiming to introduce the famous Northern Dancer blood into some of his southern breeding stock, a plan that he expected would take several years to come to fruition. He also aimed to see one day some of the southern-hemisphere blood racing in Europe, possibly America too. It was an exciting concept, as exciting to him as the whole racing and breeding scene in Australia itself.

Racing in his usual green, blue sleeves and green-spotted white cap, all Sangster's horses run in the name of his Swettenham Stud. Over the years they have won practically every major race in the country. In the period when the whole of the southern hemisphere was witnessing the exploits of one of its greatest horses in Kingston Town (thirty wins and unplaced only four times in forty-one starts, winning $1.6 million), Sangster was putting his own name on the map.

Beldale Ball's 1980 Melbourne Cup success in front of a Flemington crowd of 101,000 people not only provided him with his greatest thrill, but brought home to him the spirit of racing in Australia. Sangster, in fact, amazed himself at his unrestrained excitement at winning the great race, for years earlier he had ruffled a few feathers when he said that the Cup was overrated, not much more than a glorified handicap. Sangster soon learned that the Cup was part of the Australian psyche itself: the battling spirit, the nerve to go for it, the chance for the underdog to win. The Melbourne Cup has evolved through a purely Oz tradition – it is a week-long cocktail party that revolves around a 'one hundred dollar horse'.

But in a country where owners are not given quite the same prominence by the racing media as they are in Britain, Sangster made them sit up and take notice through a succession of big-race coups. In the year of the mighty Manikato, his Colin Hayes-trained Galleon, ridden by Brent Thomson, put an end to the run of the big chestnut sprinter in the 1982 Futurity at Caulfield. Thomson, like Manikato's rider Gary Willetts, was a former New Zealand champion, and was subsequently taken over to Britain by Sangster to ride his horses with Barry Hills.

Willetts, a respected senior rider on the Victorian circuit, has this to say of Sangster's influence on the racing scene Down Under: 'Without doubt, Robert Sangster has done a tremendous amount for our racing and breeding industry, helping to lift its profile. He always seems relaxed out here and is well liked – even if he did ruin what would have been a five-time record with Manikato in the Futurity!' Willetts, incidentally, never leaves Melbourne's Moonee Valley racetrack without stopping for a brief moment at the well-tended graveside of his old pal Manikato, who won eight of his nine starts there.

Sangster's Our Paddy Boy, whose record purchase for $250,000 in 1980 caused quite a stir, won the Sydney Cup the following year, as did the former Michael Stoute-trained Marooned five years later, the Mill Reef colt having been bought specifically as a cup horse by Sangster after he had run at Royal Ascot. In New Zealand, too, Sangster was stamping his mark, as when he startled everyone by spending over $2 million for twelve lots at the Trentham Sale. Of course, these figures were small fry when compared to Britain and America, but this is what made Australia and New Zealand such attractive investments to the Sangster operation. The level of prize money was phenomenal compared to the average price of a yearling. Here, he could race to win real money. As Bob Atkins will tell anyone who cares to listen: Sangster has never had a losing year in Australia – he always makes his racing division pay.

Australian racing has a great advantage over Britain's, simply because it is supported by the Government. Recognising that New Zealand was stealing Oz thunder, particularly in the breeding industry, the Australian Government in 1985 introduced wide-ranging tax concessions to an industry that turns over more than $20 billion a year and employs 250,000 people, thereby making it the country's third-largest industry. The concessions included the ability to write down the value of stallions by 50 per cent a year on a diminishing balance, to do likewise by a third for broodmares, and for breeders to offset these write-downs and any other losses against their income from any other source. These days British owners like Charles St George, Lord Howard de Walden and Lord Chelsea have horses in Australia; so has the American billionaire John Kluge, who races on his own account but also has a few in partnership with Sangster.

Kluge, who is said to have a personal fortune reckoned to be in the region of US$5 billion (it would have been $2 billion higher but for a 1990 divorce settlement to his third wife), was introduced to Australian racing through Sangstser and Rupert Murdoch. It was Murdoch who bought Kluge's Metromedia Incorporated, a group of television stations for US$2 billion in 1985. Kluge, whose Australian horses are managed by Ron Hutchinson and whose racing general manager is Michael Bramwell, the former manager of Britain's National Stud in Newmarket, was the man who bailed out Tommy Smith's Tulloch Lodge public company in 1989 by injecting $8 million into the company. This allowed Smith to settle a similar outstanding bill for forty-five yearlings he had purchased for the three-year-old company after it ran into problems following the collapse of its main underwriter, the Spedley Securities group. The deal was negotiated by Sangster's long-time friend, Billy McDonald.

Tulloch Lodge's problems followed those experienced by Bart Cummings, who ran into difficulties with a syndicate he helped run which was undersubscribed, forcing him to announce that he was going to have to find buyers for yearlings worth $23 million. It seemed that, as with Sangster's and O'Brien's Classic Thoroughbreds, big names and big money do not always guarantee success in the public company stakes.

The Australians like Sangster. He is one of the personalities of their society, treated with reverence, given the star treatment on television. They like his dry sense of humour and, being a somewhat chauvinistic country, there is an admiration for someone who can 'pull the sheilas'. The man himself enjoys the country, its sunshine and its relaxed way of life. He is seen to act just the same with a strapper (lad) in the stable yard as he does with the Governer-General. Although Sangster is proud to be

English, the Australians do not consider him to be the typical upper-class pom. Maybe that is because he spent so much of his time on Merseyside, with his father a great Northerner, and because there is an acknowledged warmth in the people of the North of England lacking in their southern counterparts. Or maybe it is a case of horses for courses, that having a pie and a pint in an open-neck shirt in a pub in Kilmore is a different environmental track from the business suit and the regulation brown trilby that is part of the 'club' uniform on the racetracks of Britain.

The gruff veteran writer Jack Elliott has sparred with Sangster on many occasions. Friends for fifteen years, Elliott chuckles at how he gave Sangster a tough time on one of the British visitor's first appearances on Elliott's long-running *World of Sport* television programme.

Said Elliott: 'Before the programme, Robert asked me if we couldn't liven things up a bit, make it a bit more controversial. So I thought, Right, you bugger, I will. I kicked off as usual: "G'day, Robert, and welcome to the show." Then I waded in: "Now tell me, did you sack Lester Piggott or did he sack you?" Well he nearly fell off his chair because he wasn't expecting it. The programme went on in this vein for quite some time and after we had come off the air, he said to me: "Jesus, Jack, I feel as if I've just gone ten rounds with Mohammed Ali!" But in the end he gave as good as he got and it provided some lively entertainment.'

Elliott, a legend himself in Australian racing (and a man whose bark is worse than his bite), was one of the first to meet Sangster when he made that first visit back in 1974. 'We met up at the Southern Cross Hotel in Melbourne and the next day I was doing a tour of Victoria's studs for *World of Sport*. Robert expressed great interest in what I was doing so I invited him along. I think it was then that he saw the untapped future in Australia, something he has gone a long way to promote.'

Sangster had to make an important journey to Australia in 1990 to outline his plans to his 'next generation' trainers, David Hayes (who had now taken over from his father in Adelaide), Brian Mayfield-Smith in Sydney and John Hawkes in Melbourne. He wanted to tell them that the plan would soon be for his middle son, Adam, to leave his banking job with James Capel in Hong Kong and come out there to live, working alongside David Coles and assisting him to oversee the operation. This was part of the Sangster scheme to reconcentrate his efforts in the southern hemisphere, re-establish some of the strength he had had to relinquish during the financial squeeze of the mid-eighties when he had thought it best to offload some of his extensive breeding interests.

This he did in 1986 in Australia's largest bloodstock deal. Sangster sold a 70 per cent share of his operation for $17.5 million to one of the country's first public companies, Australian Racing and Breeding Stables Ltd, otherwise known (quite ironically for Sangster) as ARABS. Sangster's Australian portfolio at this time was therefore valued at $25 million, although it had been valued at $30 million a year or two earlier.

The deal was transacted in true tycoon style on the telephone, but only after negotiations which lasted nine hours. In a 'conference' link-up by telephone and telex from The Nunnery, Sangster and his lawyer negotiated with the ARABS Sydney-based chairman John Messara and the company's lawyer and director Philip Esplin, while in Melbourne Bob Atkins sat in his office on the twenty-fifth floor of the Collins Street offices of his accounting firm, Peat Marwick, tying up loose ends of the deal. At the end of the marathon when the verbal handshakes had been concluded, Sangster had disposed of shares and nominations in thirty-one stallions based in Australia and New Zealand. These included stallions such as the double-duty Coolmore horse Godswalk, Arch Sculptor, Without Fear, Luskin Star and, most noticeably, fifteen lifetime nominations to the champion sire, Sir Tristram (for whom an American syndicate had made an unsuccessful US$27 million bid in 1983). There was a total of eighty-nine broodmares in the package, forty-six foals and an undertaking from Sangster that ARABS would have access to the Swettenham Stud racing stock once those horses had retired.

The move was seen by Sangster as a strengthening of his ties with Australia rather than the reverse. The cash generated by the sale would allow him to purchase between seventy-five and a hundred yearlings at the following year's sales and he would still race independently under the Swettenham banner. The ARABS enterprise would now be the largest bloodstock company in the southern hemisphere – so Sangster regarded the deal as a beneficial partnership. ARABS itself owned shares in several stallions, and while the company was keen to expand on its main business of bloodstock breeding, Sangster's plan now was to expand on his racing activities.

John Messara and Sangster had crossed each other's paths several times since Messara had stepped in to become the major shareholder in ARABS, a company which had been started in 1970 by racing administrator George Ryder. A couple of years earlier Sangster had joined with the company and its then chairman Bob Lapointe, a Canadian responsible for introducing Pizza Hut and Kentucky Fried Chicken to Australia, in purchasing the Sydney stables of Nebo Lodge at Rosehill. They bought it for $2.3 million, then spent another $1 milion developing one of the best training complexes in Sydney, installing Brian Mayfield-Smith there.

The tall, dark and handsome Messara, son of a wealthy Egyptian family who lived in the seaport of Alexandria, where they ran an import–export company, is similar in some ways to John Magnier. They are both sharp, very shrewd, and play long on the future. Messara was sent to Australia ahead of his parents and attended a Sydney boarding school at the age of ten, later gaining an accountancy degree from the University of New South Wales. He was now on the road to a career in commerce. In 1973, at the age of twenty-six, he bought a seat on the Sydney Stock Exchange and progressed to develop his own stockbroking company. His family had been owners of racehorses for two generations and Messara, though keen on racing, was particularly interested in the breeding business. He acquired several broodmares, the first of which was Scomeld, the 1978 VRC (Victoria Racing Club) Oaks winner at Flemington. He bought into the Middlebrook Stud and began syndicating stallions, the first being Rancher, the 1982 Blue Diamond winner and undefeated two-year-old who was syndicated for $1.5 million. He felt that his fast-growing operation was becoming too big for Middlebrook so he bought out Lapointe's 41 per cent stake in ARABS (allowing Lapointe to buy ARABS' share in Nebo Lodge). At the same time, Messara sold Middlebrook and his own bloodstock interests to ARABS, then later added the impressive Blandford Park and Newhaven Park studs to the portfolio.

Sangster's tie-up with Messara's company was a not dissimilar move to the partnership he had made all those years before with Magnier. Said Messara: 'When we bought that seventy per cent it suited both sides. We were keen to expand our bloodstock holdings and the deal gave us a quantum leap in that direction, while Robert was interested in becoming a seller at the time.'

To some extent, Sangster's decision to cut back on his Australian breeding stock and switch the emphasis of his breeding activities to the northern hemisphere was taken because of a recurrence of an old niggling problem that refused to go away. It was the one he had experienced at Britain's Newmarket Sales in the early days when he tried selling yearlings instead of foals and found there was a market resistance – as if he was only selling his yearling cast-offs. Being a racer, buyer, and commercial breeder can sometimes prove an awkward combination. Although Sangster ran all three arms of his bloodstock empire on a separate basis, there was still sales resistance to some of his stock even though it was being offered for sale in Australia as part of a purely commercial operation. This meant he was having to race more of his home-bred horses than was commercially viable or desirable. Now, though, he could go out into the market – the Sydney Easter Sale, the Magic Million on the Gold Coast – and buy his own racing stock. The purchases would be made within a business context and with a specific budget in mind.

In past years Sangster had tried to overcome whatever market resistance there was by demonstrating his *bona fides* in a novel manner. For several years he had organised his own sale in South Australia, offering yearling lots in pairs and giving successful bidders the option to keep whichever of the two they wanted. He even offered to buy back up to a quarter of each retained purchase as part of the deal.

It has taken Sangster's operation a good few years to get near to fathoming out the southern-hemisphere market and its bloodstock. In the early years, and perhaps with the same (temporary) dash of jingoism that caused him to be critical of the Melbourne Cup, he considered many of the Australian blood-lines to be weak. While there was no doubt that he and O'Brien and Magnier had hit the American vein almost at first strike with regard to the US blood and its European application, it was not easy here. He at first thought that, if he brought out 'better bred' racing fillies and colts, a gradual upgrading of the home stock would ensue. He now feels, however, that the Australian and New Zealand-bred mares possess an inherent toughness, a quality of soundness that has evolved over decades to cope with the predominantly firm ground prevalent on most racetracks, especially in the days before the technology of efficient sprinkler systems. Faults in conformation are therefore much more quickly detected in the southern hemisphere than in Europe, where the racing takes place, generally, on an easier surface.

Both Sangster and Messara have shown their like-minded philosophy by putting forward radical proposals in an effort to 'internationalise' the Australian industry and help shake off some of its inherent parochiality, which both men feel has held back the country from becoming a major world player. Sangster has long held the view that Australian bloodstock would benefit from having one exclusive national sale, run on the lines of

Keeneland with a select catalogue of 300 to 350 yearlings on offer. Messara, too, believes this would tempt overseas buyers which would in turn bolster an economy feeling the effects of recession more than most countries. Both men would also like to see the southern-hemisphere breeding season come into line with its northern counterpart – a revolutionary move that would certainly open up Australia and New Zealand to the rest of the world.

As it is, the southern-hemisphere horses are six months younger than their American, Japanese and European equivalents. This is obviously a serious drawback for anyone contemplating buying southern-hemisphere stock to race in the north – unthinkable in the case of horses who would be running as two-and three-year-olds because they would be six months less developed. Sangster has had the support of several eminent veterinarians in his argument. The reasoning is that it is easier to get mares in foal in Australia during the northern covering season of mid-February to mid-July. But there have been suggestions made in Britain that its own covering season should be put back two months to start in mid-April when the spring climate is more conductive to mares getting in foal. New Zealand-bred National Hunt horses have long been popular in Britain, but these late-maturing horses are still regarded as 'babies' at four and five years old – when top-class Flat horses have been and gone. The chances of a southern-hemisphere alignment, however, appear slim no matter what the commercial benefits. Tradition, to say nothing of the racing calendar, indeed Australasia's own conservatism, will prove a mighty weight to shift.

The ARABS group, which later changed its name to Arrowfield ('everything we produce you can buy'), has maintained close links with Sangster and Coolmore. The Irish stud, in fact, bought a 20.7 per cent stake in Arrowfield in 1989 when Coolmore's Australian subsidiary, Calogo Bloodstock AG, paid just over $12 million for a parcel of 4.8 million shares. The shares had been acquired by Messara in a deal from the estate of the late New Zealand breeder Sir Woolf Fisher, when he traded Arrowfield's stake in Fisher's famous Ra Ora Stud in Auckland, birthplace of the legendary sire of broodmares, Sovereign Edition. The move enabled John Magnier to join Sangster, O'Brien and Messara on the Arrowfield board.

Within a year, however, the Coolmore connections had entered into yet another deal with Messara. This time they cancelled their shareholding in Arrowfield, as well as cancelling 2.5 million share options, and paid the company just over $9 million cash to buy all of Arrowfield's stud land holdings, which included 2,547 hectares of farm and spelling (resting) property in the Hunter Valley outside Sydney. The Coolmore company now leases the land (valued at $17 million in the deal) to Arrowfield.

Messara is impatient with tradition if he thinks he has a better way. 'It might be traditional for breeders to own land but Arrowfield, being a public company, is about cash flow and revenues, too. Obviously we need the use of the land but not the capital asset. Our main concern is in the ownership and income produced by stallions. This is the activity we think is suitable for a public company.'

The deal therefore gave Coolmore a tremendous opportunity to enter the land market in Australia, something they had been aiming to do for some time. They would still own stallions jointly with Arrowfield, fifty–fifty partnerships in horses such as the double-duty Danehill. This was a partnership reviewable after three years when the success or otherwise of the particular stallions could be assessed. And Arrowfield would have access to many of the other Coolmore stallions who were sent to Australia such as Last Tycoon and Bluebird. Said Messara: 'Coolmore have a great network of people and contacts throughout the world, something they have built on over the years. The likes of Danehill should prove a great asset to Australian breeding. We simply have to import this sort of blood to improve our stock.'

Danehill, a son of the Northern Dancer colt Danzig, was sold by Khalid Abdullah for £4 million after his three-year-old career in 1989. The colt rounded off a five-win record by taking the Group One Ladbroke (formerly Vernons) Sprint Cup at Haydock Park, having proved best at sprint distances. Two other colts by Danzig in the same year had even higher price tags. These both belonged to Sheikh Mohammed: Polish Precedent (£7.2 million) and Shaadi (£4.5 million).

Danehill's first-season covering fee in 1990 was set at $37,500 in Australia, and IR25,000 guineas at Coolmore. Said Messara: 'I think this type of arrangement gives the breeders in both countries a good deal. It is far cheaper than the stallion standing in only one country and therefore the whole sport is lifted.'

But there have been setbacks and not every stallion turns out to be a winner. The purchase of Tolomeo at $4.5 million (syndicated by Messara into forty-five shares at $100,000) made the son of Lypheor the country's most expensive imported stallion when he arrived for the 1984 breeding season after a successful career in Britain (he had also won the 1983 Arlington Million in Chicago). But after a couple of crops, Tolomeo was sold on to Japan for $1 million. Messara's view was that trainers and owners might have been getting at the stallion's stock a little too early. 'If there is a drawback to Australian racing it is that they are very quick to damn a horse here. The pressure on producing early two-year-olds is tremendous. In other words we found that Tolomeo was not what most breeders would think of as a commercial stallion. But the market here is beginning to gradually wake up thanks to the likes of Sangster. We perhaps did not have the capacity until the last two or three years to handle the influx of northern-hemisphere stallions. Thankfully, that is now beginning to change.'

Messara has paid several visits to see Sangster and the Coolmore partners, either at The Nunnery or in Ireland, and echoes many people in Australia who are glad of the Sangster input: 'He has put in plenty over the years and has a soft spot for Australia and its people. Racing people want him to win here. They appreciate his good sportsmanship and his support of many causes.'

These days, Sangster's Australian racing empire is concentrated in three centres: David Hayes at Lindsay Park (Adelaide), Brian Mayfield-Smith at Rosehill (Sydney) and John Hawkes at Epsom (Melbourne).

With Sangster's backing at Nebo Lodge in a triumvirate that included Lapointe and the renowned Millie Fox, Mayfield-Smith ended the thirty-three year reign of Tommy Smith as Sydney's champion trainer in the 1985–6 season, a position he held for the next two years. It was this period that brought his biggest break when he trained Sangster's Marauding to win the Golden Slipper Stakes in 1987 (having previously handled Sangster's Marooned).

Sangster and Lapointe decided to sell the Nebo Lodge site for redevelopment in 1991. But, in new quarters, the determined, forty-six-year-old Mayfield-Smith has demonstrated the hardworking, ambitious flair that has seen him rise from a Cairns apprentice electrician, who switched to a life with cattle and then horses in the Queensland outback, to one of the country's leading trainers.

The former Adelaide jockey John Hawkes is something of a contrast to Mayfield-Smith and his outwardly serious demeanour. Openly humorous and lively, with a spring in his step, the teetotal, keep-fit fanatic Hawkes trains his horses in a brightly coloured tracksuit – and greets his owners at the track in a conservative business suit. Sangster chose him to spearhead his Melbourne operation from an ultra-modern $1 million yard called Carbine Lodge, at Epsom in south Melbourne, in 1988. With fifty horses in full training, Hawkes trains for a syndicate which includes Sangster and Lapointe (their Nebo Lodge company bought Carbine Lodge) as well as other big owners such as Bob and Jack Ingham, the 'chicken king' brothers, and the ANZ Bank Bloodstock Syndicate headed by Moonee Valley chairman, Norman Carlyon.

Hawkes was fifteen when he rode his first winner and turned to training when he was only twenty-one, rapidly making a name for himself in South Australia, where for many seasons he was the perennial runner-up to Colin Hayes in the trainers' championship. Weight problems in the saddle forced the early start to his new career, yet despite coming relatively new to the Melbourne scene, Hawkes has a great deal of experience behind him for a man in his early forties.

Among his early successes was the brave filly Toltrice who in 1972 won fourteen races including the VATC 1,000 Guineas-VRC Oaks. Galena Boy's 1975 VRC Derby, and King Helmet's VATC Futurity a year later, emphasised this young man's determination to stick around a while. Other big wins came with Mighty Manitou (AJC Sires' Produce Stakes), Harpagus (VATC Oakleigh Plate) and that terrific last-gasp outside run of English Wonder to clinch the SA Derby.

TWENTY

Rainbow's End

In Robert Sangster's yellow-walled study in the east wing of The Nunnery is a picture of the racemare Audrey Joan. She was the one horse among the thousands he has owned which was never for sale, one of the very few over which his heart simply had to rule his head. Swettenham's foundation mare was dear to him, a reminder of his starting point on the long haul some quarter of a century ago. The old girl has gone now, but her bloodlines are still part of the Sangster empire in Australia. Her best produce was a little grey filly by Sangster's own stallion Godswalk, who turned out to be a real battler like her mother. Named Pure Of Heart, she became a darling of the Australian turf, winning several Group events, and is now a broodmare herself.

There are other photographs in their silver gilt frames around the living rooms of the Isle of Man home, children being the manifestation of his new life: Sam, four, one-year-old Max Edmund, and his stepdaughter Melissa. He is now a grandfather, too. His eldest son Guy and his wife Fiona have a son. Sue has done her best to see that his life, through their children, has taken on new dimensions. Now, he is able to give more time to all of them, which is in contrast to when he was a young man himself. Then, his children with Christine were just, well, there. By his own admission they were around, but he had little time or inclination to appreciate them as little people, to play with them on the carpet, tell them stories, take them out in their pushchairs to feed the ducks, like many fathers do. Now, though, he knows the shape and feel of a plastic Ninja Turtle.

Sue has even managed to persuade him to cut down on some of the extravagant entertaining. She recognises that her husband is naturally generous, although several of the freeloading friends have now had to take a back seat.

But Sangster's world is still predominantly male-orientated (the first Susan once accused him of only wanting women as trinket-like 'diddly ducks'). It is doubtful, too, that Sue would ever make a new man of him even if she wanted to. His handicap is entrenched in that respect: boys' boarding school at the age of eight, boys' public school to the age of eighteen, the Army, the rugby club, the golf club, the generation gap – simply too many factors to expect a transformation. It is probably because of the men's-club atmosphere in which his world has revolved that some women who have met him felt he was ill at ease with them despite his reputation as a romeo. While some women have obviously found him charming and attractive, others have found him bland with little repartee.

He has tried several public variations on a theme, however, to change any negative impressions he might have given. Curiously, he once agreed to take part in the Harry Secombe Sunday-night 'God slot' television programme called *Highway*, in which guests talk about their lives and their Christian beliefs. Now there are monthly services in the chapel within The Nunnery's grounds, but the Sangsters are not among the thirty or so regular worshippers. For a fleeting moment, this apparently new-found religious fervour prompted some of Sangster's friends to wonder if he had perhaps given up his love of gambling, or had maybe gone as far as to quit the champagne. It was patently obvious several months later that he had not, however, when he was stopped in his car by police on the island after they had spotted his white Mercedes veering about on the road to his home from the airport. A two-year Isle of Man driving ban ensued when he pleaded guilty to having consumed almost a whole bottle of wine.

And he has gone as far as publicly trying his hand at the culinary arts, something at which both he and Sue had previously admitted defeat. He appeared on a television programme in which chef Kevin Woodford, a former partner with the Sangsters in the Isle of Man Woodford's restaurant, set out to show Sangster how to cook a meal for himself. While recognising that he had never had to do such a thing in his life before, viewers of the attempt were bemused to see Sangster ready to prepare his meal in the kitchen at The Nunnery smartly dressed in an immaculate dark blazer over a casual polo-necked sweater. A pinafore, Sangster must have felt, would have been taking things just a little too far. But the blazer at least added spice to Sangster's own version of kitchen-wear.

Being in his lofty position in life, Sangster has probably upset some people, although any resentment, he feels, is usually because of jealousy. But he has felt let down by some people whom he thought were friends. Sangster maintained that it was one former friend who started rumours about his being in grave financial difficulties at the time he sold Vernons. In Australia these rumours reached ridiculous proportions. He was disturbed, too, by the uproarious affair at his old haunt on the Isle of Man, the Palace Lido, when a charity ball Sue and he had organised was most embarrassingly interrupted.

Because of her own sad experience, Sue has been a tireless worker for Birthright, the research arm of the Royal Society of Obstetricians and Gynaecologists, a charity patronised by Princess Diana which carries out research into helping produce healthier babies and mothers. A weekend of fund-raising activities had been arranged, including a golf tournament at Castletown Links, followed by a Saturday-night grand ball at the Lido, which has one of the biggest ballrooms in Europe. Sangster's friend from his old Marbella days, Sean Connery, was among the 350 high-society guests who had paid £100 a head to attend the glittering function. Also present were Michael Parkinson, singer Chris de Burgh and several other show-business personalities.

But, only minutes after they had all sat down to a nine-course banquet prepared by Kevin Woodford, there was a dramatic entrance by police, who were accompanying the island's principal debt-collecting bailiff, Malcolm Kelly. In full sight of the assembled guests, they marched across the ballroom from the main doorway. Kelly was armed with writs for gambling debts of over £168,000 from the very Casino complex in which the ball was being held. Indeed the Palace Hotel and Casino group owner Jonathan Clague was sitting on the top table. As guests' mouths dropped in astonishment over their hors d'oeuvres, the bailiff marched over to a table and slapped a writ for alleged Casino gambling debts of £12,000 on Sangster's friend and bloodstock agent Billy McDonald.

Amidst a stunned silence, the party gatecrashers then made their way across the middle of the dancefloor to the furthest table at the far end of the room to serve a similar writ for debts of £156,000 on another guest, Irish horse transport company boss Michael O'Sullivan. At this point, Sue Sangster, furious at what she saw as an audacious intrusion, leaped from her seat and tried to intervene. But bailiff Kelly was having no interference in the execution of his duty. 'Unhand me, madam, or I'll have you arrested,' he warned her.

After the police and Kelly had left the ballroom, Sangster was almost speechless with rage. The audacity of it, the embarrassment. He quickly collared Jonathan Clague (son of the former racehorse owner, Sir Douglas Clague), and the pair went outside into the Lido car park. A heated argument ensued for several minutes, after which Sangster, trembling and choking back tears, announced that he would never again in his life set foot in an establishment owned by the Palace group.

The affair was a most upsetting interval in an evening which, when a semblance of normality returned, went on to raise over £220,000 for Birthright. The Sangsters tried to put on a brave face for the rest of the evening and managed a smile when jokes about the embarrassing incident were made by Charles Benson in his usual role as auctioneer at the charity auction after dinner. In fact McDonald had donated a bottle of a rare vintage claret to the auction and this subsequently fetched £3,600. Benson, however, suggested that his friend might want to keep it to drink himself – 'in that small room where they'll put you wearing that suit with the little arrows on it'. The auction was also boosted when Sue's second husband, Peter Lilley, paid £800 for a pair of riding boots for their daughter Melissa. The Birthright ball was only one of many charity functions in which Sangster has been involved over the years and his good deed have raised upwards of £500,000 for various organisations, from the British Olympic Appeal to the Save the Children Fund.

Several days after the fiasco, Sangster lambasted the Casino for allowing so much credit to his gambling friends. With particular reference to O'Sullivan he said: 'I was annoyed that credit of over £150,000 was given to this man. It is hard to imagine a Rockefeller or Rothschild being allowed this credit in any other country.

'Perhaps it has something to do with the free drink dispensed at the Palace, which is illegal in English casinos,' he complained. However, some people took Sangster's comments with a pinch of salt as there are many casinos around the world including the Isle of Man where alcoholic drinks are legal – just as they are on any British racecourse.

Almost two years after the incident that had rocked the island's society, the Palace group were still chasing their alleged debts, which in O'Sullivan's case had been outstanding since 1986. McDonald, who confesses to being stupid over his past gambling, was facing a claim for £30,000, which was allegedly the amount of three dishonoured cheques, less almost £18,000 returned to the casino in gaming chips.

There have been many incidents, in fact, where the name of Robert Sangster has featured prominently in the media. Society columns eagerly reported on the day when he attended the London wedding of his young Manton trainer, Peter Chapple-Hyam to Jane Peacock in 1990, though it was his ex-wife Susan who stole the show because she was in the company of two of her former husbands – Sangster and Andrew Peacock. Susan, by now was in the unusual position of being husbandless, having divorced Sir Frank Renouf after three years of marriage, a union that, towards the end, had resulted in a highly public wrangling match in Australia which had centred around their famous Sydney home. The former Toison d'Or had been renamed Paradis Sur Mer, but paradise was hardly in it towards the end of their marriage. Susan probably had a few words to say, too, at the wedding of her daughter, about the bulldozers which had moved in to the former delight of her life. For, two months earlier, Paradis Sur Mer had become Paradise Sur Rubble – the whole house had been demolished by its new owner to make way for two or three new houses at $10 million apiece.

The Maktoum brothers spent something in the region of £10 million on bloodstock in Britain alone in 1989, a figure with which Sangster could not hope to compete. They spent millions more at the Keeneland Select and the September sales, too. And at the end of the season, Sheikh Mohammed, predictably, retained Britain's top spot among the owners while Sangster remained unsighted. His £142,000 of British prize money was not much more than a tenth of that of his rival. Hamdan Al-Maktoum was runner-up to his younger brother, with just £70 separating the pair. But Hamdan had, at last, won the Derby with Nashwan, a brilliant chestnut son of Blushing Groom, who also carried all before him in the 2,000 Guineas, the King George VI and Queen Elizabeth Diamond Stakes and the Eclipse Stakes – all Group One races.

The following season saw the brothers exchange places at the top, increasing their winning prize money totals to £1,536,815 and £1,498,195 respectively. Hamdan, of course, had one of the best fillies seen on the British turf for decades in Salsabil. She won the 1,000 Guineas, the Oaks, she beat the colts in the Irish Derby, and she landed her fourth Group One race in the Prix Vermeille at Longchamp. But Salsabil went the way of many a horse in the Prix de l'Arc de Triomphe as if proving that athletes can only sustain optimum form for a certain period of time. Her top class form from early May fizzled out in the Paris sunshine in October. She finished 10th of the 21 runners, recording her only defeat as a three-year-old before being retired to the paddocks.

Sangster had a very respectable year in Britain this season, finishing fifth with twenty-four winning horses (forty-one races won) compared to Hamdan's seventy-six (127 races won), and Mohammed's 122 (176 races won). The disparity in the number of winning horses in the two leaders' camps, when compared with Sangster's, revealed the measure now of the Arabs' quantative might in Britain. But the bare results did not tell half the tale. The people who thought Robert Sangster was a name of the past, part of an historic golden era, were having to revise their opinions.

Little of Sangster's international success is ever published in Britain, or if it is, the news is spasmodic, never all-embracing. It is interesting, therefore, to record from statistics kindly supplied from Mark Glyer, Sangster's racing manager, that in 1989, for instance, Sangster reaped 176 wins worldwide. In 1990 the figure was just three short of 200. So it can be seen that, on the international context in which Sangster operates, the success is far greater than the bare British results suggest. The number of Sangster's worldwide 'black type' winners of Group or Stakes races is impressive, too. In the period from 1986 to halfway through the 1991 season, a period of Arab domination in Britain, Sangster recorded 226 Stakes winners throughout the world.

The results of Sangster the Shrewd in another area, his first love of breeding, were beginning to make an impact as the pattern of the new decade began to emerge. He might not be able to match the buying power of the Maktoums, (a fight in which he had painfully, though sensibly, thrown in the towel), but in this glorious uncertainty of horseracing, he had discovered there is more than one way of winning. Suddenly, some of the stallions in which he had major shares were begining to make quite an impact on the world breeding scene. And once more, the blood of Northern Dancer was his ace in the pack.

The great Northern Dancer was put down in November 1990 after suffering a severe attack of colic. He was twenty-nine years old. Three months earlier his stud-mate and 1977 dual-Derby-winning son, The Minstrel, Sangster's first major break, had been put down at the age of sixteen in Kentucky after contracting the chronic lameness disease, laminitis.

Northern Dancer's passing marked the sad finale of one of the most phenomenal international breeding stories in the history of the thoroughbred. So influential have the bloodlines of this stocky little bay horse become that, on his death, it was reckoned that within just two or three years, over half of the world's thoroughbred population would have Northern Dancer blood in their pedigrees. The statistics of his twenty-two-year career until his retirement three years before his death reflect the stallion's unique contribution: he sired a record 143 Group or Stakes winners from his 634 foals, 295 of whom fetched the incredible sum of almost $184 million at public auction. Importantly, he was also the sire of successful sires. His own son Nijinsky reflects that potency. At the time of his sire's death, Nijinsky was responsible for 131 Group or Stakes winners in twenty years at stud. By the time of Nijinsky's own death, in April 1992, the English Triple Crown winner had surpassed Northern Dancer's total.

In an appropriate memorial to the great stallion, the mild-mannered, pipe-smoking Charles Taylor, son of Northern Dancer's breeder, Eddie Taylor, and president of Windfields Farm in Maryland, where the horse was buried, told John Karter of the *Sunday Times*: 'We've all been a bit tearful here. It might sound ridiculous to attribute human qualities to a horse, but Northern Dancer had them. He was a feisty, gutsy, complex character who always knew he was number one. He hated it when mares were brought in to be mated with other stallions on the farm. He would go berserk because he thought they should all be for him.

'When it was his turn, you could hear him hollering a hundred yards away. He would dance out on two legs in a state of high excitement, then get straight on and mount the mare. Afterwards, he would simply snort as if to say: "Where's the next one?" Sadly he was not the same towards the end of his stud days. He would carry out his duties just as proficiently, but he seemed embarrassed to do so. He knew his powers were waning.'

Sangster, O'Brien and Magnier had put their money, their skill, their very souls into the belief in Northern Dancer. It had paid off on the racetrack and now, after the death of the great stallion, they stood to benefit yet again.

The Coolmore empire controls several sons or grandsons of Northern Dancer: Alzao, Be My Guest, Caerleon, Last Tycoon, Lomond, Royal Academy, Sadler's Wells and Try My Best. Lomond, who was champion first-season sire in 1987 and has a pedigree that is more attractive to the US market, now stands at their Ashford Stud in Kentucky with the likes of El Gran Señor, Storm Bird, Seattle Dancer and Woodman, sire of the top-class French horse, Hector Protector.

The criticism of Coolmore's modus operandi, which has been referred to previously, is that it has sacrificed quality for quantity. Chief critic, Tony Morris, claims that Coolmore has based its operation on the lines of the great stallion stations of Kentucky, but that it does not possess the advantages of the US operations. These include the vast pool of quality broodmares available in America, the required international market for the progeny, and the sound home-based racing industry which has sufficient prize money to underpin the high cost of production. Some stallions, it is claimed, have therefore not had the select band of broodmares required to enhance their reputation, the accent being placed rather on financial turnover with the resultant overpricing of stallion fees and oversubscription (with poorer-quality mares being serviced).

In the stallion Sadler's Wells, however, Sangster, O'Brien and Magnier appear to hold a key to the future. Even their most vociferous critics are forced to admit that Sadler's Wells was, in 1991, the best sire in Europe. He is probably destined to become the stallion of the nineties, possibly taking over the mantle of Northern Dancer himself. What is particularly pleasing to Sangster is that they bred Sadler's Wells themselves, and raced him successfully (and ran him more in keeping with the tradition of the sport than many of the syndicate's other top horses).

Sadler's Wells raced nine times, in fact, as a three-year-old in 1984, showing top-class form from a mile to twelve furlongs, and winning four of them (three at Group One level): the Irish 2,000 Guineas, the Eclipse Stakes and the Phoenix Champion Stakes.

He is out of Sangster's Fairy Bridge, a filly Sangster named after the small road-bridge half a mile from The Nunnery where local tradition has it that the fairies which live in the dell must be bid a good morning or evening – or bad luck will prevail! Sangster must have made a friend of the fairies, for he knows Fairy Bridge's family well and planned the mating himself. The twice-raced filly's own dam, Special (who is also the dam of Nureyev), is a half-sister to Sangster's muzzled colt of 1977, Marinsky.

But perhaps his good friend Billy McDonald forgot his lines when passing over the bridge on his many visits to The Nunnery from the airport. Poor McDonald's luck ran out in a big way when he 'did his brains' on Marinsky in the top sprint race, Newmarket's July Cup, in which Marinsky was disqualified for bumping Gentilhombre, despite winning by one and a half lengths. Otherwise McDonald would probably still hold a valuable interest in Fairy Bridge today. The desperately unlucky Irishman subsequently had to sell his interest in Fairy Bridge and in Alleged to Sangster for cash to bail himself out of trouble with the old enemy, the bookmakers.

The first three crops of Sadler's Wells have included these top-class performers: Salsabil, In The Wings, Old Vic, Prince Of Dance, Scenic, French Glory, Braashee, Runyan and Sadler's Hall. Another son, Blue Stag, was runner-up for Sangster in the 1990 Derby. His book of mares covered in the 1991 season was considered to be exceptional – a world-class array of Group One winning performers whose progeny will have the whole of racing waiting expectantly before they begin to race in 1994.

Caerleon, whose quality of mares has been steadily

improving, hit the jackpot in 1991 when his son, Generous, winner of the previous season's Dewhurst Stakes, continued the Dewhurst–Classic link by winning the Derby (the runner-up, Marju, was sired by Last Tycoon). The colt also won the Irish Derby and the King George VI and Queen Elizabeth Diamond Stakes. The owner of Generous was Ahmed Salman, the nephew of Khalid Abdullah.

Sangster had ten of his own high-class mares booked to Sadler's Wells in the 1991 breeding season. These included the likes of his 1980 Prix de l'Arc de Triomphe winner, Detroit, the former top class sprinter, Amaranda, Lady Capulet, Rein Mathilde, Clandestina and Savannah Song. He had eight mares covered by Caerleon, too; among these was the evergreen, Shellshock, also Rhein Bridge, Night of Wind and Tremulous. And in America, at the Ashford Stud, Woodman had covered sixteen Sangster mares, a select band which included the three-time Group winner, Acushla, also Fairy Dancer, Pirouette and Star Pastures.

If Sangster was feeling a little pleased with himself as the 1991 season unfolded then it was no wonder. He had ridden the storm from the Gulf, stopped battling against the new waves and had learned to float, relaxed, with the tide. He was now in a position to look forward to the future with a much greater degree of confidence. His new trainer at Manton, Peter Chapple-Hyam, was steadily notching up the winners and showing much promise. In Ireland, his trainer Tommy Stack, the man who rode Red Rum to his third Grand National victory, seemed, at last, to be getting the breaks. Barry Hills was knocking the winners in and awaiting the Classic success that will surely be his before long. And Vincent O'Brien had teamed up again with Lester Piggott after Cash Asmussen's replacement, John Reid, had decided to return to freelancing in Britain.

O'Brien was now seventy-four. His son David had become disenchanted with the game after training several top-class horses on his own account, but then, one season, found himself with a moderate bunch. The lifetime shares he had in one or two of those stallions, however, would bring him an annual income well into six figures. It was his younger brother Charles who was heir-apparent to the Ballydoyle Stables.

Magnier, a wealthy man now, was bullish about the prospects for Coolmore. Recessions were cyclical. With the boost from Sadler's Wells and Caerleon he had confidence in the future. Everyone involved with Coolmore, in fact, felt the frisson that goes hand in hand with the optimism of the game.

Sangster himself was at peace with the world. Now, for the first time in many years, his personal life had an inner contentment, a quality of life that no amount of money could buy. Sheikh Mohammed was even a sporting rival. They all enjoyed the crack even if it did get pretty serious at times. And, after all, Mohammed, despite his incredible outlay, had not yet won the Derby. None of his Epsom runners had finished better than eighth position. Nor had he won that other prize he coveted, the Prix de l'Arc de Triomphe.

Sangster, though, had won the Derby twice, had even been runner-up in the world's greatest event three times. He had won the Arc three times too. Mohammed and his brothers still had an awful lot of catching up to do. And who could say that Sangster would not win another Derby or the Arc?

In Australia, too, his empire was bearing fruit; over 100 racing stock now and, in the five years since the sell-off to Arrowfield, a new breeding force of 100 broodmares. Just one of his colts, Canonise, had won him over Aus$1.6 million in 1991. His overall world prize money was many times that.

Some may ask if the Robert Sangster phenomenon was because of the man or because of the market. It was probably a combination of both – his desire to rule the world of horseracing at a time when the market was ripe for that to happen. That he had the nerve for the initial gamble, indeed the stamina and enthusiasm to continue at times when the going got tough, is in itself quite remarkable. He can look back on those years, those glorious intoxicating years of pure gold, and say, quite rightly, that he was number one.

The punt had paid off.

Index

Index

241

A Selected List of Biographies Available from Mandarin

While every effort is made to keep prices low, it is sometimes necessary to increase prices at short notice. Mandarin Paperbacks reserves the right to show new retail prices on covers which may differ from those previously advertised in the text or elsewhere.

The prices shown below were correct at the time of going to press.

☐	7493 0647 5	**Dickens**	Peter Ackroyd	£7.99
☐	7493 0113 9	**Peggy Ashcroft**	Michael Billington	£4.99
☐	7493 0238 0	**Maxwell: The Outsider**	Tom Bower	£5.99
☐	7493 0357 3	**The Murder of John Lennon**	Fenton Bresler	£3.99
☐	7493 9177 4	**My Left Foot**	Christy Brown	£4.99
☐	7493 9826 4	**Churchill – A Life**	Martin Gilbert	£9.99
☐	7493 0152 X	**A Woman named Jackie**	C. David Heymann	£5.99
☐	7493 9005 0	**The Orton Diaries**	John Lahr	£6.99
☐	7493 0641 6	**Getting it Together**	John Harvey-Jones	£5.99
☐	7493 9082 4	**Timebends**	Arthur Miller	£7.99
☐	7493 0544 4	**Jimi Hendrix: Electric Gypsy**	Shapiro & Glebbeek	£12.99
☐	7493 0781 1	**Vivien: The Life of Vivien Leigh**	Alexander Walker	£4.99

All these books are available at your bookshop or newsagent, or can be ordered direct from the publisher. Just tick the titles you want and fill in the form below.

Mandarin Paperbacks, Cash Sales Department, PO Box 11, Falmouth, Cornwall TR10 9EN.

Please send cheque or postal order, no currency, for purchase price quoted and allow the following for postage and packing:

UK including BFPO	£1.00 for the first book, 50p for the second and 30p for each additional book ordered to a maximum charge of £3.00.
Overseas including Eire	£2 for the first book, £1.00 for the second and 50p for each additional book thereafter.

NAME (Block letters) ....

ADDRESS...

....

☐ I enclose my remittance for ....

☐ I wish to pay by Access/Visa Card Number ☐☐☐☐☐☐☐☐☐☐☐☐☐☐☐☐

Expiry Date ☐☐☐☐